For
Suzanne,
"Annuit Coeptis"

E Boylen
Mullevine

For the Sake of Humanity, Let Us Pray
That This Book Turns Out to Be What the
Political Left Will Label It:
"Conspiracy Theory"

THE

LORDS OF

SEDUCTION

Has An Illuminati-Islamic Alliance Inserted
A Puppet Into The White House?

E. Gaylon McCollough, M.D.

Argus Enterprises International
North Carolina***New Jersey

The Lords of Seduction © *2010*
All Rights Reserved by E. Gaylon McCollough, M.D.

A-Argus Better Book Publishers, LLC

For information:
A-Argus Better Book Publishers, LLC
9001 Ridge Hill Drive
Kernersville, North Carolina 27284
www.a-argusbooks.com

ISBN: 978-0-9846439-3-6
ISBN: 0-9846439-3-1

Library of Congress Control Number: 2011931702

Book Cover designed by Jennifer K Arnold
and Isabelle Susan Powell

Printed in the United States of America

Author's Note

The Lords of Seduction has been nearly seventy years in the making. Having been bred and reared in a patriotic, middle-class, Judeo-Christian environment, my eyes and mind were opened to the laws of Man—and God. At a young age, I learned to recognize Evil when I saw it and to call it what it is ...

I want to thank my wife, partner and confrere of nearly 47 years, Susan Nomberg McCollough, for understanding why I had to write this book.

I would also like to thank both Jennifer Arnold and Charlene Baker for helping prepare the manuscript for publication and A-Argus Better Book Publishers for having the courage to publish it.

The concerns herein expressed are not that of a single individual. Rather they represent the collective voices of an unshakable nemesis to America's enemies—*the proud American patriot,* who—without being vilified or shouted down, seldom gets the chance to express his or her sentiments about the direction in which their United States is being led.

As a physician I was trained to diagnose diseases and conditions that have historically proven to be detrimental to the human mind and body, and to offer remedies when threats to health, safety and welfare of my fellow human beings are discovered. It is that same training and code of ethics that have led me to the conclusions reached in *The Lords of Seduction.*

My mission is to encourage Americans of all races, religions, creeds, and ideologies to do what many failed to do in the 2008 presidential election: look at Barack

Obama for what he *is—and represents—*rather than what he *pretends* to be. There is much we still do not know about the man who currently occupies the Oval Office—much that the American people deserve to know.

Even after reading *The Lords of Seduction,* you will still not know everything you should know, but you will know more than you did ... and that's a beginning.

I have made every effort to rely on hard evidence; however during the half century that I've spent in training and practicing medicine—over and over—I have also been shown that the secret to prevention and early detection lie in paying attention to early warning signs ... before the precautionary signs and symptoms become manifest as outright infirmities. It is in the spirit of prevention and early detection that I draw attention to a nation growing weaker by the day ... and a world engulfed by premeditated chaos.

Though I perform my "day job" (facial plastic surgery) with subtlety and finesse, I write more like I played football: straight ahead, fearless and all out, without concern for pejorative labels that America's enemies might hurl my way.

I believe in the good and the positive, but I have also learned to keep a watchful eye out for trouble. You see, I'm a former quarterback, converted to the offensive line. I'll always *think* like a quarterback, but I also realize that someone has to do the dirty work ... in the trenches. I've never minded getting my nose bloody—nor do I now—so long as my beloved America emerges from the crucibles of seduction, *re-founded* and mightier than ever.

Preface

The Lords of Seduction postulates what could be the greatest ruse of the 20th and 21st centuries—that President Barack Hussein Obama (a/k/a Barry Soetoro) is a "puppet" whose strings are manipulated by an Illuminati-Islamic Alliance (I-IA) and that he was selected because he was coached to loathe the U.S. and the Judeo-Christian God in whom it trusts. The evidence for this assertion is compelling: the 44th U.S. President is the latest in a long line of "pawns," controlled by mighty men who appear to have "bred and reared" him "since childhood"[1] for the position he *now* occupies on the world's stage ... and another role yet to follow.

The Keynesian-like experiment that Barack Obama was groomed to front is quickly becoming a win/lose tug of war—a win for America's enemies and a losing situation for the vast majority of the American people. Obama*Change* failed to restore the "hope" that was promised. Not surprisingly, the president's policies are intentionally destructive. These same despot sentiments and tactics have long been embraced by handlers who schooled Barack Obama to champion a social revolution that would ensure an Illuminati-Islamic take-over of the world.

Of concern to the American people is that President Obama's puppet-masters (a "supranational sovereignty of intellectual elites and world bankers[2]") are aligned with various factions of the Muslim Brotherhood and a newly-

---

[1] All words and phrases in quotes are taken directly from *The Protocols of the Learned Elders of Zion,* http://www.biblebelievers.org.au. Italicized words are author's emphasis
[2] David Rockefeller, *Comments to the Trilateral Commission, 1991*

organized "revolutionary faith" known as Black Liberation Theology. Each of these theosophies is committed to the radical teachings and politics consistent with those of 1960's activitist, Malcomb X. Left unchecked, America's Judeo-Christian foundation of governance will be replaced with one that embraces Marxist, Leninist and Sharia ideologies.

It was not until I dissected—line by line—an ancient cipher (*The Protocols of the Learned Elders of Zion*) that I came to understand the documents' timeliest revelations: **Why Barack Obama? Why now?** The answers to these questions will raise the ire of those who have been blindly seduced by the I-IA's Siren-in-Chief.

What history affirms to be a horoscopy of international despotism, *The Protocols,* was drafted by a cabal of conspirators who denounced God and created instead, a "revolutionary faith" based upon Luciferian theosophy.

Unashamedly, the self-designated "despots" chronicled how they intended to "control the press," "emasculate universities" and "choose presidents ... and judges," all for the purpose of ruling "the affairs of the whole world."[3] Generation by generation, their mission has been passed down to heirs of thirteen ruling families that collectively comprise an Invisible Empire (The Order of the Illuminati.) An ominous profile of these overlords jumps off the pages of *The Protocols.*"[4]

That's why—for the better part of six centuries—the original document (and each subsequent time-sensitive revision) had to be hidden from the masses. Otherwise, the

---

[3] *Protocols of the Learned Elders of Zion,* Ibid
[4] *Ibid*

peoples that the "supranational sovereignty"[5] intended to rule would see that they were being seduced into Orwellian-styled bondage.

This book is intended to be provocative and offers no apologies for revealing the obvious: that we, the American people, are unsuspecting subjects of one of the most ingenious cons in recent history. With the assistance of a complicit press and Hollywood's Left-leaning labor union (The Academy of Motion Picture Arts and Sciences,) the Illuminati's Sirens of "change" are doing precisely what they were bred, reared and recruited to do: lure Americans toward the beaches of apathy, swoon *the people* into an altered state of consciousness and replace America's long-standing and proud tradition of exceptionalism with a culture of decadence, dependence and servitude.

A glimpse into America's past will affirm that the U. S. flourished under the leadership of men and women who placed prudence before politics and patriotism before globalism. Then, the Hidden Hand of the Illuminati seized the strings of the U.S. Government and Judicial System ... and things "changed" for the worse.

The contrast between a 'bred and reared' socio-political 'pawn' and a battle-proven freedom fighter committed to the noble mission of self-determination and capitalism could not have been more clearly demonstrated than when (in a May, 2011 telecast) Israel's Prime Minister, Benjamin Netanyahu, sat beside President Barack Obama during an the Oval Office exchange of ideologies. The contrast was further expressed when (before a joint session of the U.S. Congress) the stately Prime Minister schooled U.S. lawmakers on the eminent

---

[5] David Rockefeller, Comments to the Trilateral Commission, 1991.

dangers of Sharia Law and those sworn to impose it upon the world ... by all means necessary.

Don't take my word that a Sharia-like culture is planned for all the peoples of the world. Wait until you have read *the rest of the story*—the ugly details of a planned social and cultural coup d'état, spelled out in detail in *The Protocols.*

Illuminati disciples will rush to label what I have offered as just "conspiracy theory," a pejorative term often stamped on a body of work that *conspirators* wish to discredit. For humanity's sake, let us pray that debunkers are right; and I am wrong.

Whatever truth emerges, of one thing you—the reader—can be sure. The minions who were chosen—or volunteered—to protect the puppet-masters of an Illuminati-Islamic Alliance will resort to all manner of false claims and personal attacks (The Rothschild Formula). They will attempt to deflect attention *away from* discovering the identities and mission of *the real* Barack Obama and the mighty men who have long pulled his strings, like professed social reformist, George Soros, a former Nazi enabler.

Because I know how the political Left reacts when its agenda is called out, allow me to make something perfectly clear. If any element of racism and bigotry arises out of *The Lords of Seduction* and the revelations herein disclosed about President Obama and/or his council of "specialists"[6] and "advisers,"[7] it is solely initiated and promoted by those upon whose toes—or agenda—my book steps. The only race that this treatise is intended to

---

[6] *Protocols of the Learned Elders of Zion,* Ibid
[7] Ibid

promote over any other is the God-embracing segment of *the human race*. And the only beings and/or organizations it is intended to demoralize and demote are those that would *"undermine all faith, to tear out of the mind the very principle of god-head and the spirit, and to put in its place arithmetical calculations and material needs."*[8]

An evil Hand surely guided the drafting of the infamous *Protocols of the Learned Elders of Zion*[9]. The document has long been the subject of controversy. Some scholars claim that it is a fraud and created to paint Jewish people in a bad light. Chapter 1 of this book will provide the necessary background information to reinforce the author's premise that devout Zionists (Christians *and* Jews) *were not* involved in drafting, revising, nor implementing *The Protocols*. Obama promoter and financier, George Soros, is another story, but will be addressed, herein.

The best evidence that *The Protocols* is a living document—and should be taken seriously—can be found in the words of one of the globalists' ranking members. During a meeting of the Trilateral Commission in 1991, the late U.S. banking and oil mogul, David Rockefeller re-stated the "Elders'" plan when he addressed the body:

> "We are grateful to the Washington Post, The New York Times, Time Magazine and other great publications whose directors have attended our meetings and (we have) respected their promises of discretion for almost forty years.

---

[8] *Protocols of the Learned Elders of Zion*, Ibid
[9] Ibid.

"It would have been impossible for us to develop *our plan for the world** if we had been subjected to the lights of publicity during those years. But, the world is now more sophisticated and prepared to march towards *a world government.** The *supranational sovereignty of an intellectual elite* and *world bankers** is surely preferable to national auto-determination practiced in past centuries."[10]

Rockefeller's revelation is riveting, making reference to the plan published centuries before in *The Protocols,* a complicit press, and a coming World Government that would be controlled by few insiders. When he made these remarks, the American Illuminist must have believed that they would never reach the "lights of publicity." Rockefeller's speech proved to be an ominous omen of things yet to come. And, the venue of the disclosure is as troubling as its content. He was speaking to an international organization comprised of powerful businessmen and women, academicians and politicians. Like all governing bodies, Rockefeller's "supranational sovereignty" operates according to its own official rules and a pyramid-structured hierarchy with a small number near— or at—the top, the profiles of which are exposed in *The Lords of Seduction.*

To better understand President Barack Obama's "puppet" role in the Illuminati's master plan, one has to familiarize oneself not only with *The Protocols,* but with a

---

[10] http://www.rense.com
* Emphasis added

modern-day amendment to the cipher. The *Cloward-Piven Strategy* was crafted to provide socialists with a proven way to collapse America's economy by overloading the welfare system and driving the country into bankruptcy, thereby making it easier for America's enemies to conduct a non-violent coup d'état.

The sinister ploy to sink America originated at New York's Columbia University under the direction of two of Barack Obama's professors. In a future chapter, we will explore how President Obama's "Stimulus Packages" and Healthcare Reform Act incorporate the principles of the Cloward-Piven Strategy.

Whenever it is possible, I will continue to use the conspirators' own words for verification of the hypothesis here-in presented. In the end you, the reader, will have to determine if the founders of a new, Godless "revolutionary faith" pose a threat to America ... and take the appropriate course of action.

It is this writer's hope that *The Lords of Seduction* will be viewed as an eye-opening call to action, and that patriots of all ages, races, and religions will put the things that divide us aside and pay closer attention to what powerful men and women do and less to what they say; for only a short window of opportunity remains to buoy a sinking Ship of State.

While some would have you believe that America's problems are too complex for the average citizen to understand and that—in the grand scheme—one person's actions don't matter, I couldn't disagree more. When you have completed *The Lords of Seduction* you will understand why I feel confident in making such a statement.

An enlightened electorate is a democracy's best defense against the Lords of Seduction.

E. G. Mc

CHAPTER 1

"Change" can be a bitter pill to swallow, especially when administered by professed enemies of Man ... and God." From all appearances, a secretive Luciferian Empire has joined forces with radical Islam to create an Illuminati-Islamic Alliance, out of which will emerge a global *un*godly government. How can I offer such a proposition? I have read the document that outlines the plan and witnessed examples of its implementation. And, I am driven to share my findings and the premeditated misery they herald.

When it comes to the dark arts of illusion and deception, the Lords of Seduction are wizards. From history we know that a few mighty men and women have controlled the ebb and flow of world events and that these overlords enter into alliances only to *use* a "partner" for cover, while a Hidden Hand manipulates armies of "puppets" from the shadows.

So, knowing that seduction is the stuff from which revolutions are made, individuals, organizations, or nations finding themselves caught up in "change" should *question everything* ... no matter how ridiculous the proposition might initially seem.

When historians look back at the United States of America, they will ask: why was "change" necessary? Why would the Americans voluntarily give up an envied way of life? What was so awry that her foundation had to be taken apart? They might ask: who was Barrack Hussein Obama? Among all the likely candidates, why did he become the face of "change" and why did *the people* continue to follow him when it became clear that he had deceived them?

To see what historians may see, we must first, examine the world that Barack Obama may have been "bred and reared" to rule ... or at least *front* for an Invisible Empire that pulls his strings. We will also attempt to answer the question: whose agenda is best served by the kind of "change" for which Barack Obama was groomed to bring about? Have we finally allowed ourselves to become—as Mark Twain concluded—the "damned human race?"[11] What must America do to overcome a failed social experiment in affirmative action, political correctness, redistribution of wealth, and reassignment of liberties? Can the U.S. be *re-founded* as: "one nation, under God, indivisible, with liberty and justice for all?"

Answers to a tangled riddle can be found in the afore-referenced document known as: *The Protocols of the Learned Elders of Zion.* When you read how your destiny—and mine—has been planned by a group of self-designated, atheistic despots, you are not going to like the answers you get. And, if you are of Judeo-Christian heritage you should be stirred by how the godless overlords behind *The Protocols* made it appear that *you* (Zionists) are the "despots" to whom the document refers.

---

[11] *Letters from the Earth: Uncensored Writings by Mark Twain,* Bernard DeVoto, Harper Perennial, New York, N.Y., 1962.

Though there are many more troubling, one of the messages woven through *The Protocols* is: "Change" has a face. It has consequences and comes with a price. "Change" is a double-edged sword—a socio-political instrument that may be used to 'protect and defend' all of God's creations or to inflict agony, death and destruction in its path. History affirms that the *Lords of Seduction* are skilled masters at inflicting agony, death and destruction on their march toward absolute sovereignty—freeing themselves from the laws of God and Man ... *but, only if the people allow it.*

Though written centuries ago, Homer's *The Odyssey* provides insight as to how the *Lords of Seduction* can be rendered powerless. The solution lies in a mythical conversation between the oracle, Circe, and the hero, Odysseus:

> "You will come first of all to the Sirens, who are enchanters of all mankind by the melody of their singing ... They sit in their meadow, but the beach before it is piled with boneheaps of men now rotted away ... You must drive straight on past, but melt down sweet wax of honey and with it stop your companions' ears, so none can listen ... but if you, yourself, are wanting to hear them (the Sirens songs) then have (your companions) tie you hand and foot ... If you implore (your companions) to set you free, then they must tie you fast with even more lashings."

In many ways, America's odyssey through what Alexander Tyler described as "The Cycle of Democracies" parallels that of Odysseus. According to the ancient fable—though the Sirens beckoned—Odysseus and his men escaped a trap. Having been rejected by those they intended to seduce, the Sirens flung themselves into the waters and perished. Homer was trying to teach anyone who would heed his warning a lesson for the ages.

Is it possible for the U.S. to escape the trap of seduction that is currently being orchestrated by the Sirens of an unholy alliance comprised of the Invisible Empire and radical Islam, or what I will hereinafter refer to as: "*The Illuminati-Islamic Alliance (I-IA)?*" IF enough like-minded Americans are willing to face up to the fact that our way of life is under siege and direct our attention to re-founding America in the image of all that is sacred, the answer to the foregoing question is: YES!

Are the continuous refrains of "change" emanating from the mouth of Barack Obama enough to cause Americans to swap a free and independent republic for a One-World Government—an Orwellian global culture—created by an "international sovereignty of intellectual elites and world bankers"[12] ... the Invisible Empire, Hidden Hand, Shadow Government, Bilderbergers, Moriah Conquering Wind, Elders, Illuminati or whatever name various segments of the *Lords of Seduction* might be called?

Over the past three decades, I've made it a point to study the origins and evolutions of the human race—and the cultures that mankind creates—from every conceivable angle. In *Let Us Make Man* (the prequel to the Annunaki

---

[12] David Rockefeller, speaking at the Bilderberger Meeting in Baden, Germany, 1991

series) I reviewed the book of Genesis from theological, mythological, and scientific points of view, linking the three disciplines together in a single ideology that I called "Divinely-Engineered Creative-Evolution." It was there (in Genesis 6:4) that I discovered the best explanation of the origin of the Illuminati's adopted ancestors (*The Annunaki,*) hybrid beings that appear to be the product of an unsanctioned inter-species liaison, when "the sons of God came into the daughters of men, and they bore children to them, the same became mighty men ..."[13] If they are convinced that they (the 13 ruling families) descended from the wayward "sons of God," it could explain why they feel allegiance to the supreme leader of the rebellion—Lucifer.

In *The Oath* (book II of the Annunaki series,) I took readers into the inner sanctums of American politics and exposed a plethora of socio-political secrets that the masses are not intended to know—secrets that "mighty men ..." in the U.S. Government intended to keep for themselves.

In *The Annunaki Enigma: Armageddon 2012* (book III of the Annunaki series) my co-author (Dr. Symm Hawes McCord) and I took readers to the front lines of Armageddon where (because of Annunaki involvement) prophesies older than those revealed in *The Revelation to St. John, the Divine* materialized at Israel's borders.

Although the second and third of the four books are works of fiction, their underlying themes are based on factual events occurring in the Bible and in the reality of what has since transpired, much of which is revealed in *The Lords of Seduction.* And the research involved with producing the four books pushed me further down the road to realizing the true nature and danger of a document

---

[13] *Holy Bible:* King James Version, Collins, U.K., 1611, p. 12

I uncovered, entitled, *The Protocols of the Learned Elders of Zion.*

The Lords of Seduction could well be the fifth in the Annunaki series of books, in that it deals with the ongoing influence of the "sons of God" and the "daughters of men" on the world's stage. Believe me, I wish this book were fiction. However, as eerie, bizarre, and frightening as it may appear, *The Lords of Seduction*—unlike the other four books—deals with stark, naked reality; reality that threatens the human race, as we know it.

I use the term, "Armageddon" to describe the end of one cycle of the Great Experiment and the beginning of another. Insight into the beginnings and endings can be found in the Holy Scriptures as well as in mythology. The Phoenix Myth provides a clue into the multi-dimensional process known in this realm as: *reincarnation.* But, is it really necessary that a nation crash and burn in order to be re-created from the ashes of its own destruction? Is it possible to recognize the mounting signs of a crash *before* they occur and "change" course of a destiny that is being created for us—not by God, but by God's professed enemies—an unholy alliance of mortal beings who have been convinced that they descended from the enlightened "mighty men ..." addressed in Genesis 6:4 and in the Koran (Surah 11:40)?

If one group of individuals has been deceived into believing that they are "mighty men" spawned from the mixed genes of celestial *and* mortal beings and *another* believes that their God (Allah) gave the Earth to them and directed them to kill off followers of any religion other than their own, it is easy to see how either group, or both, could believe themselves to be superior to the rest of us mortals ... and to behave accordingly.

Though I can only speculate that founders of the I-IA interpret Genesis and the Koran in such a manner—given Lucifer's seductive powers—it would be easy to convince a mixed gang of power-thirsty overlords that when God gave "dominion over the earth" to the early inhabitants of this planet, the passage was directed at their adopted hybrid ancestors—the Annunaki. It would also be quite easy to persuade those who believe themselves to be *super-mortal* sovereigns that the Great Flood destroyed all but Noah's family and the unaccounted-for hybrid intellectual "giants, the mighty men of renown,"[14] *The Illuminati.*

And, when Islam's prophet, Mohammad, wrote in the Koran that the angel of God revealed how the world was meant to be changed, it would be equally as easy to persuade Mohammad's followers that—in the eyes of the Almighty—they are the one true religion and meant to dominate or destroy those of any other religious persuasion.

If—as the Scriptures pronounce—Lucifer seduced Adam and Eve, it is conceivable that he and his disciples could seduce anyone willing to trade their souls for power, or who were indoctrinated to hear only the truth according to Sirens who intend to use them for personal gain.

Imagine—for a moment—that you are the patriarch (or matriarch) of one of the remaining thirteen Annunaki families and that you are charged with the task of indoctrinating your successor. You are preparing to tell the member of your own family, who has been selected to replace you on the Illuminati's Inner Circle, about why your family is superior to the others, because you were taught from early childhood that your family stemmed from beings specifically addressed in the Scriptures—super-

---

[14] Genesis 6:4

mortals—who have been given "dominion over the earth." What do you think such a patriarch/matriarch would say?

First, he/she would have to explain how the world was intended to be ruled by your family—and a dozen others. Then, the next-in-line would be given access to the secret plan that was used to consolidate power among the ruling families. And, finally, you (the young heir/heiress) would need to be groomed for such an onerous responsibility by a team of trusted teachers and guides until such time as you were ready to take your seat at the Inner Circle's table. Surely, the team of teachers would require you to read and digest documents that pertained to the history of the dominating organization and/or its bylaws and mission statement. You would also have to be enlightened about those you were expected to seduce and, ultimately, dominate.

So, in order to better understand these messages contained in this book, consider yourself an heir/heiress to the world's most powerful coalition. As you read the pages that follow, consider yourself being groomed for a critical leadership position in a select body of individuals whose decisions will direct the course of history ... because you *are* that kind of heir/heiress! The future is yours to create. If you are a citizen of the United States of America, you have a reserved seat at the table—a ballot-marketing table in the place where you cast your vote *every* Election Day. As a member of the American electorate, you have *a voice* in crafting the policies of this nation and seeing that they are carried out as you (and your fellow Americans so designate). Until the Illuminati-Islamic Alliance takes it from us, the electorate still possesses the power of the ballot box. *We, the people,* control the United States government ... or at least we think we do. I say this because the possibility exists that we have already relinquished the ability to choose our leaders to a Shadow Government, and don't yet know it. Are we, then, simply being seduced by a "supranational sovereignty" into believing that America's lawmakers and judges are *elected*, rather than *appointed* by the Hidden Hand (as *The Protocols* pronounce)? Are our votes counted and tallied *as they were actually cast?* Are individuals and organizations already in place to see that elections turn out the way that serves the Illuminati's purpose? Don't discount the possibility. The stakes are high; and the Illuminati are accustomed to playing with a stacked deck.

Here's what is at stake. At the beginning of 2011, the U.S. appears to be the only remaining obstacle between the practice of "national self-determination" and One-World Government ruled by the thirteen ruling families of world bankers and intellectual elitists. Right before our eyes, *self rule* is gradually slipping away. The "supranational sovereignty" is having its way with America's (and the rest of the world's) economy, food, and energy supplies. An equally cogent concern is the possibility that the "supranational sovereignty" is in bed with radical Islam.

Earlier in this book, I introduced the possibility that radical Islam and the Invisible Empire—known as the Hidden Hand of the Illuminati—might be working hand-in-hand to bury America and the U.S.' Middle-East ally, Israel. Now that a man, who was raised a Muslim, occupies the most powerful office in the world, the Illuminati-Islamic Alliance is one step closer to achieving its goal. In a future chapter, I will put additional pieces of a tangled web together so that the bigger picture can be visualized.

It is no secret that Islamists have long been committed to the destruction of Christians and Jews. I have also suggested the origin of the Islamic-Jewish conflict. The Muslim's Holy War (jihad) all began when a father chose between two sons that were born of two different women. The banished son, Ishmael, became the father of Arab nations, which comprise the vast majority of Muslims worldwide. The chosen one, Isaac, became heir to the House of Abraham. Later, The Scriptures tell us that—following an encounter with an angel—Isaac's son, Jacob, was renamed "Israel." This name change is the basis of Jacob's twelve sons becoming known as the "Children of Israel" (Israelites). These twelve sons would then become patriarchs of the twelve tribes of Israel, out of which the religion known as Judaism would eventually emerge.

So, the modern-day conflict between Muslims and Zionists (Jews *and* Christians), whom Muslims refer to as "infidels," arises out of the fact that the ancient tribes of Israel inherited the birthright and lands that—according to the laws and traditions of the time—belonged to Ishmael and his offspring.

It is also possible that the "intellectual elites" among the Illuminati, contrived a masterful scheme to fan the fires of conflict that began in biblical times, using Islam as an able-bodied emissary to do its bidding on the world stage. The risk of such a plan is that the Illuminati might not be able to reel in the radicals among the nation of Islam should Islamists be able to deliver on their promise to destroy the existing governments of the free world on their way to global conquest ... in the name of Islam's God, Allah.

Perhaps, the Inner Circle of the Illuminati know how devoted Muslims are to their clerics and expect to be able to seduce Islamic leaders at a future date ... or invoke the Rothschild Formula to destroy them as well. An alliance (I-IA) between world bankers, intellectual elites and the

Arab nations that control the retrieval and exportation of oil is really not that hard to figure. One only needs to remember the age-old axiom, "The enemy of my enemy is my friend," to understand how an Islamic-Illuminati Alliance (I-IA) would serve the purposes of both bodies ... even if no "official" agreement between the two enemies of Judeo-Christian ways of life existed.

Whether independently or in concert, Islamic clerics and the Illuminati's "supranational sovereignty" have each realized that the way to seduce the Judeo-Christian world is to play up the teachings of their religions. Especially those that teach "Do unto others as you would have them do unto you," and "Turn the other cheek." If the I-IA could make the Judeo-Christian world believe that Islam is a religion of peace (a deceptive tactic that is clearly spelled out in the *Protocols of the Learned Elders of Zion),* the I-IA could seductively place a noose around the necks of trusting free world leaders and prepare for a day of execution.

An article, entitled, "Muslim Mafia" by P. David Gaubatz and Paul Sperry may contain the key to lifting the veil of secrecy currently shielding the existence of an un-holy alliance between radical Islam and the Order of the Illuminati. The *Protocols of the Learned Elders of Zion* may well provide the evidence needed to expose the greatest sham ever perpetrated on humanity. In the following chapters we will begin to dissect *The Protocols* line by line and expose the intent and methods of the self-proclaimed "despots" that created the document and are implementing its plan to perfection. But, before we delve into the plan, we need to look at one of the I-IA's members, the "Muslim Mafia."

Two investigators, by the names Gaubatz and Sperry, reported: "It is very alarming that we actually have the enemy's playbook for their so-called 'Grand Jihad' against North America, yet we refuse to seriously confront the threat to our sovereignty and our way of life."

What *this* author finds even more unsettling is that liberal politicians in virtually every branch of government appear to be running interference for the enemy, attacking anyone who points out the professed intent of the Muslim Mafia. Those on the Left refuse to see the obvious: radical Muslims have joined with a Shadow Government to bring a plan fleshed out in *The Protocols* to fruition.

Radical Muslims have said that they believe it is their religious duty to rid the world of "infidels" (Christians and Jews). The evidence is strong that Muslims and the Illuminati have found a way to direct the finger of blame (for the world's troubles and their mutual desires to collapse democracies) toward Jews and their Christian brethren. By adopting a sinister plan that contains the term "Zion" in its title, the I-IA could profit from diversionary chaos without being "subjected to the lights of publicity," as stated in David Rockefeller's speech to the Trilateral Commission. The unsuspecting reader would blame Jews for the despot plot that *The Protocols* espouse, providing cover for the real perpetrators.

Freedom-loving Americans and our allies must wake up before it is too late and also realize that we are being seduced by power-thirsty and committed enemies—radical Islam, the Order of the Illuminati, and whoever—or whatever—pulls their strings. By their own admission, all arrogantly pride themselves in the art of deception.

According to Gaubatz and Sperry, the Muslim mantra is:

*"I swear by Allah that war is deception.
We are fighting our enemy (infidels) with a
kind heart. Deceive, camouflage, and
pretend that you're leaving while you're
walking that way. Deceive your enemy."*

To be blunt, those who comprise the Illuminati-Islamic Alliance (I-IA) are accomplished and unashamed Sirens and skillful liars. As their combined manifestos (*The Koran* and *The Protocols*) purport, mastery of deception is key to the success of their mutually-envisioned global conspiracy—to support terrorism and replace the democratically-instilled principle of "national auto-determination" with Sharia Law, which appears to be totalitarianism cloaked in a burqa.

To further the author's theory that the leaders of radical Islam are masters of seduction, let us examine several examples of high profile Muslim leaders who say one thing ... and do another.

A White House guest of both President Clinton and Bush, Sami al-Arian assured his hosts he was both peace-loving and patriotic. "I am a very moderate Muslim person," he said. "I also condemn violence in all its forms."

All the while, al-Arian was secretly running a U.S. beachhead for Palestinian terrorist. In a speech at a Cleveland mosque, he once thundered: "Let's damn America, let's damn Israel, let's damn their allies until death."

And, regardless of what he now says *publically,* in *Audacity of Hope,* President Barack Hussein Obama, wrote: **"I will stand with the Muslims should the political winds shift in an ugly direction."** Knowing that President

Obama was raised a Muslim, can he be trusted as the Commander-in-Chief of what radical Muslims call "A nation of infidels" (The United States of America)? In a future chapter, I will show how President Obama perfectly fits the section of *The Protocols* entitled, "We (global overlords) Choose Presidents."

Abdurrahman Alamoudi, the supposed pillar of the Muslim community also went from the White House to the Big House (prison), but not before developing the Pentagon's Muslim chaplain corps and acting as a goodwill ambassador for the State Department. Publically, he too strongly denounced terror. "We are against all forms of terrorism," he claimed. "Our religion is against terrorism." Privately, however, he raised major funds for the terrorist group al-Qaida and was caught on tape grumbling that Osama bin Laden hadn't killed enough Americans in the U.S. embassy bombing.

Ali Al-Timimi, a noted *imam* and native Washingtonian, also put on a moderate face in public while secretly plotting against the U.S. The internationally known scholar had U.S. government clearance—and even worked for former White House Chief of Staff, Andrew Card, when he was at the Transportation Department. Al-Timimi was even invited to speak on Islam to the U. S. military.

Publicly, the *imam* denounced Islamic violence. "My position against terrorism and Muslim-inspired violence against innocent people is well known by Muslims," he said. But privately, a darker picture emerged. Five days after the September 11, 2001 terrorist attacks, he called the attacks "legitimate" and rallied young Muslim men at his District of Columbia-area mosque to carry out more "holy war" and "violent jihad" against Americans.

Al-Timimi even cheered the *Columbia* space shuttle disaster, calling it a "good omen" for Muslims because it was a blow to their (Islam's) "greatest enemy," affirming the conclusions presented in this book—that Islam views the United States of America not as a land of unlimited opportunity, but a land in which opportunity must be limited and brought under the heavy hand of Sharia Law. He also said the U.S. "should be destroyed." This high-profile so-called "moderate" Muslim is now behind bars for soliciting terror and treason. But, there are many more from where he came—martyrs willing to die, killing Christians and Jews anywhere we live.

According to their religious beliefs, Muslims have *a duty* to help form Islamic governments, instill Sharia Law worldwide and should be prepared to take up arms to carry that out. Investigators say this "revolution ideology" is taught to Muslim teens by Malaysia's *tarbiya* department.

Tarbiya is the process of indoctrinating young or new Muslims. The sitting president of the United States of America was a Muslim teen when he lived in Indonesia. Not one reporter from the mainstream media has ever asked him what he was taught about *tarbiya* in those days.

One passage in Malaysia's *tarbiya* guide states that Western materialism and secularism are evil and that Muslims should "pursue this evil force to its own lands" and "invade its Western heartland," until all the infidels shout "*Allah Akbar!*—Allah is great."

A reference from the Holy Bible provides insight into the significance of Barry Soetoro's childhood teachings and how they might influence decisions he is making as an adult ... currently on behalf of the American people. A providential passage, from the Scriptures, gives notice to people everywhere: "Rear up a child in the way he should ᵘ and when he is old, he will not depart from it." If Soetoro's/Obama's Muslim teachers believed that—for the rest of his life—"the way he should go" was to follow the teachings of the Koran and Sharia Law, it is difficult to see how Barry Soetoro/a/k/a Barack Obama could totally abandon the lessons his Muslim clerics and adoptive father taught him in those early days. The questions that should be asked to President Obama include:

- "When you were a young man growing up in a Muslim home in Indonesia, were you taught that Allah wished for Muslims to rid the world of Christians and Jews? And, if you were taught these things, at what point did you abandon them ... if you have?"
- "Did your childhood *tarbiya* teachings cause you to apologize to the world for what you called 'America's errors of the past'?"
- "Did what you were taught about the U.S.—as a young boy and in college— impact your opinions of America's Constitution and capitalism?"
- "Now that you are Commander-in-Chief of the greatest fighting force in the history, has your opinion of America's role in the world changed?"
- "When you were taught that Western materialism and secularism were evil, did such teachings become the basis of your animosity toward Americans earning more than $250,000 per year

and the free enterprise system that allows upward ascendency on the scale of prosperity?"
- "Of all your teachers, who—among them—impacted your social, political, and religious views most?"

Americans deserve to know the answers to these questions. And, President Obama has an obligation to the American people to answer these questions frankly and honestly. Hopefully, some independent-thinking reporter will ask them, one day.

Muslim teachings encourage the (Islamic) faithful to "wage war," investigators say, so that the United States is "wiped out" and only the law of Allah—*Sharia Law*—operates in the land. Muslim Brotherhood propagandists like Imam Zaid Shakir preach to the Muslim community in America about waging a *cultural* jihad (holy war) now, and a *violent* jihad later—once the proper "infrastructure" is in place. This is an important warning for liberals and those who have been seduced by Islam. Claiming to be a "religion of peace" is perfect cover while preparing for a violent jihad. *"First infiltrate and convert, then wage jihad,"* the Imam reiterates. "Use deception and propaganda—putting on a friendly face—until the time is right. Then drive the sword into the backs of the enemy. We have to start doing the real tough, nitty-gritty, unglamorous, boring work of developing our organizational and institutional strength in this country," Shakir added. "If we put a nationwide infrastructure in place and marshaled our resources, we'd take over this country in a very short time." Is Barack Obama the culmination of such a strategy?

Knowing that this is part of an Islamic plan, one has to wonder why those who swore oaths to "protect and defend the U.S. against all enemies, foreign and domestic" aren't aggressively pursuing this self-professed enemy (radical Islam), rather than providing cover for them. Is it a matter of allegiance? President Obama's upbringing and the words he wrote in his book about "siding with the Muslims" when the "political winds begin to blow in an ugly direction" is troubling and should be on the mind of every patriot, regardless of party affiliation.

At the time of this writing, New York Congressman Peter King has initiated congressional hearings to see how deeply the swords of radical Islam already penetrate American society. As expected, the political Left has come out against King's hearings, calling them "unfair," but a nation needs to know when, how, and by whom its national security is being threatened, especially if a *professed enemy* resides among us. This writer would like to think that Congressman King is upholding the oath to which he swore when he took office and that all who took the same oath—and oppose him—are either naïve or in the tank for the Muslim Mafia and their partners in the I-IA.

To turn a deaf ear to the side of political wars that are influenced by the same forces out to destroy the U.S. and the American way of life is nothing short of insanity ... unless of course the powers that be are a party to the plot.

Diversion is a tactic of war—holy wars included. While these words are being written, labor unions are rioting in Wisconsin against a bill that addresses out-of-control spending by a state whose coffers have been emptied by the same costly policies that the unions want to continue. Union bosses call the Wisconsin bill a threat to unions. Wisconsin's woes are a symptom of what is happening all around America, beginning in the nation's capitol. Those feeding at the federal and state troughs have been convinced by their bosses that there is an endless supply of money—*other people's money*. All that is needed is to extract it from the job creators and wise investors—those making more than $250,000 per year. Where are these and other demonstration promoters when it comes to raising the bar against a professed threat to state and national security—bankruptcy? I am reminded of a term that I once read in a book, whose name escapes me. The word is "crazymaking," a proper description of those who refuse to see the threat of deficit spending and are led into the arena of self-serving conflict. The lesson for today's financial woes does not come from some new internet sight. It originates from an age-old fairy tale—a children's story about greedy villagers who killed the goose that laid golden eggs. But, that seems to be the "union mentality." It is why many corporate "geese" are flying away to more hospitable states ... or countries, reducing by the day the number of jobs available to American workers.

American workers should learn from history—from examples that have stood the test of time. Union bosses may be "puppets" to the mighty men of the I-IA and may not have the best interest of the workers at heart. And, it is the responsibility of the members to see that the people they elect to represent them act with prudence and foresight ... while they still can. Should the Muslim Mafia and the Illuminati be successful in their plan to seize the world, collective bargaining will no longer be an issue, anyway.

Listen to what an Islamic strategist has to say about softening America's opinion of Muslims, Sharia Law, and the I-IA's plan to make it the law that all Americans could *be forced* to observe: "If the American people accept Islam, the implications for the world are obvious. This is the most powerful and influential nation on earth, without any argument," Shakir said. "So if the people here (in the U.S) become Muslim, then the implications of that for the world are quite obvious." Shakir gleefully remarked that this is only made possible thanks mostly to America's *blind religious tolerance** (and willingness to accept the intentional inequities of political correctness.)

If the preceding statement can be believed, America's enemies have every reason to want to paint Congressman King in a negative light, along with any other American who brings their conspiracy into the open. With Congressman King's hearings, the winds of political change are beginning to stir. We'll see where President Obama lines up. Hopefully, some patriotic reporter will ask him that during his campaign for reelection. By supporting Barack Obama and the union bosses that are beholding to him, the average union member does not know how he or she is playing into the hands of radical Islam, creating diversions while the Brotherhood tightens the noose.

Gaubatz and Sperry also noted: "While the Muslim Brotherhood is outlawed in other countries, the U.S. has not yet designated the group a terrorist entity or foreign threat, even though The Brotherhood has stated clearly that (as is also promoted in *The Protocols*) it supports "violence of any kind, including that demonstrated by union workers against employers, violent jihad, and is dedicated to replacing the U.S. with an Islamic theocracy."

The authors of *Muslim Mafia* went on to point out: "After 9/11, federal investigators noticed that most of their leads traced back to the (Islamic) Brotherhood. In fact,

---

* Emphasis added

almost every terrorism case, active or inactive, ties into the Brotherhood nexus, whether directly or indirectly.

America's greatest challenge in this ongoing national security threat is its reluctance to admit that our law enforcement agencies are some fifty years behind the intelligence gathering techniques of Islamic terrorist groups and their agents such as CAIR, (the Council of American-Islamic Relations and ISNA, (the Islamic Society of North America) and that there could well be Muslims—or Muslim sympathizers—holding offices and positions of extreme power in the U.S. government and unions, today.

It is highly probable that men and women who truly want to "defend and protect" the U.S. may not have considered the unholy alliance between the Illuminati and radical Islam—or what I have labeled the Illuminati-Islamic Alliance (I-IA). How could I make such a connection?

As a writer, I view my role as a catalyst, to make you—the reader--take a new look at old problems ... to see the influence of an unholy alliance (the Illuminati-Islamic Alliance) in destructive trends that are taking place throughout America. I hope to demonstrate—with true-to-life examples how the Hidden Hand and the "Muslim Mafia" uses people like you and me (without our knowledge) to carry out a plan memorialized centuries ago within the *Protocols of the Learned Elders of Zion* ... an ingenuous plot—and masterfully engineered coup d'état.

Stay with me as we continue to examine mankind's mysterious—and often misguided—love affair with "change." We'll examine the identity and under-handed agenda of thirteen powerful families who have taken it upon themselves to re-create the world and the strategic plan they developed to accomplish such a mission.

We'll take off the societal blinders and see how moral engineering, "political correctness" and "affirmative action" are creations of one of America's greatest enemy—the Illuminati—and has been used to its advantage, not that of Americans who think it was established for their benefit. We'll explore the two kinds of "change"—those which *enhance* life as well as those that threaten life as we know it in the nation we know as The United States of America. We'll see which of these categories the "change" championed by the Illuminati-Islamic Alliance's most recent Siren, Barack Hussein Obama, fits. Perhaps, he is what he appears to be—one of the Illuminati's "administrators ... not trained in government ... a pawn" who was, himself "bred and reared from childhood" to front for the coming Illuminati-Islamic Alliance? The clues for such a possibility are right there ... in *The Protocols.*

> "The *administrators,** whom we shall choose from among the public ... *will not be persons trained in the arts of government,** and will therefore easily become *pawns** in our game in the hands of men of learning and genius who will be their advisers, specialists *bred and reared from early childhood** to rule the affairs of the whole world."

Barack Obama's (a/k/a Barry Soetoro's) multi-cultural links make him the perfect candidate to front for an Illuminati-Islamic Alliance. It was Barack Obama, who Libya's Muslim tyrant, Moammar Gadhafi addressed as, "our son."

---

* Emphasis added

Excerpts of a 2011 letter that Moammar Gadhafi sent to President Barack Obama began with the salutation: "*To our son, the honorable Barack Hussein Obama* ..."[15] The letter went on to say "even if there were a war between Libya and America, you would remain my son and I would still love you. I do not want to change the image I have of you ..."

It is also important, here to note that Louis Farrakhan (recipient of the Rev. Jeremiah Wright Lifetime Achievement Award) has made pilgrimages to Libya to establish and maintain relations with Gadhafi and that Rev. Jeremiah Wright was described by Barack Obama as his "spiritual adviser." Could the links be more than coincidence? In this one—and in upcoming chapters—I will expand the intriguing circle of players and "pawns" that surround Barack Obama and why Americans should be concerned about the people with whom he has been—and remains—associated.

Gadhafi's letter speaks volumes about how the Muslim world and its leaders view their beloved "son" and how the United States of America should watch carefully as its Commander-in-Chief appears to run interference for the Illuminati-Islamic Alliance. As you will come to see, it's all right there—in *The Protocols.*

To question President Obama's past seems to tantamount to inviting an attack by the mainstream media and some political pundits. But because there are still many unanswered questions about President Obama's past, his eligibility to serve as president of the United States of America will continue to be fodder for any truth-seeker.

---

* Emphasis added
[15] The Huffington Post, March 20, 2011, "Excerpts of Letters from Gadhafi to World Leaders."

In their Canada Free Press article two licensed investigators, Doug Hagmann & Joseph Hagmann demonstrated why many people question if President Obama is who he claims to be:

> "Promising to be the 'most transparent' president in history, Barack Hussein Obama II is the most deliberately opaque president who has withheld many more records than his birth certificate. Not only has he withheld his records, he has *fought* to keep them hidden from public view, amassing legal fees that some claim to exceed a million dollars of his own money, and perhaps twice that amount if pro-bono and other legal work is counted.
>
> "The issue is much greater than the birth certificate or where Obama was physically born, as he could have been born in the Lincoln bedroom during the John F. Kennedy administration and still be ineligible to hold the office of president under Article II, Section I, Clause 5 of the United States Constitution. *Our founders determined that future presidents must be born to **two parents** who are both U.S. citizens*****. Clearly then, the place of Obama's birth is merely one concern, while the citizen aspect of his parents remains another.
>
> "But the scam goes much deeper. Reviewing only the admissions of Barack Obama, we are told that Obama was born to U.S. citizen Stanley Ann Dunham, legally

---

* Emphasis added

adopted by a foreign national named Lolo Soetoro, had taken the name Barry Soetoro, and was given Indonesian citizenship. He was raised as a Muslim in Indonesia, and attended a school there that accepted all faiths. At one point, Barry Soetoro moved to Hawaii to reside with his grandparents after Lolo Soetoro and Stanley Ann Dunham divorced. Obama completed high school as Barry Soetoro. Much is missing from his early years, including a legal name change from Barry Soetoro to Barack Hussein Obama II."

According to a Washington, D.C. AP report, posted on YahooAnswers.com:

"Americans for Freedom of Information" released copies of President Obama's college transcripts from Occidental College (a liberal arts college located in Los Angeles, California). Released today, the transcript indicates that Obama, under the name Barry Soetoro, received financial aid as a *foreign student* from Indonesia as an undergraduate at the school. The transcript was released by Occidental College in compliance with a court order in a suit brought by the group in the Superior Court of California. The transcript shows that Obama (Soetoro) applied for financial aid and was awarded a *fellowship for foreign students** from the Fulbright Foundation

---

* Emphasis added

Scholarship program. To qualify, for the scholarship, a student must claim foreign citizenship."

And, the Hagmann and Hagmann report further concludes:

"Absent of any document to show the legal process of a name change within the U.S., it is likely that the man sitting in the Oval Office is, in fact, Barry Soetoro.

"The above would also serve to explain the discrepancies with his social security number and region of issuance, a matter we (Hagmann and Hagmann) are very familiar with in our capacity as licensed investigators. The reasons we have (most frequently) seen published concerning the allegations of the association of multiple social security numbers with Barry Soetoro and Barack Hussein Obama has always bothered us, but not necessarily for the reasons often published. After careful and extensive analysis, it appears that many of the numbers and name variations associated with Obama are what we would describe as 'database chaff.' It is not uncommon for database repositories to erroneously associate different numbers, addresses and sometimes names to an individual. The reasons for this are many—and beyond the scope of this article. But it happens."

Further investigation has revealed the identity of the man who's Social Security Number (SSN) has been illegally stolen and used by Barack Obama.

"The man's name is Jean Paul Ludwig. He was born in France in 1890, immigrated to the United States in 1924. Mr. Ludwig was assigned SSN 042-68-4425 in or about March 1977. Ludwig lived most of his adult life in Connecticut. His SSN begins with the digits 042, which are among several reserved for Connecticut residents. Obama never lived or worked in Connecticut, so there is no reason for his SSN to start with the digits 042.

Now comes the best part. Ludwig spent the final months of his life *in Hawaii*, where he ultimately died. Conveniently, Obama's grandmother, Madelyn Payne Dunham, worked part-time in the Probate Office in the Honolulu Hawaii Courthouse, and therefore had access to the Social Security Numbers of deceased individuals.

Here is where the plot thickens. The Social Security Administration was never informed of Ludwig's death, and because he never received Social Security benefits, there were no benefits to stop and no questions were raised. The suspicion, of course, is that Dunham, knowing her grandson was not a U.S. citizen—either because he was born in Kenya (sired by a Kenyan father, nullifying the requirement that *both* parents be U.S. citizens) or he became a citizen of Indonesia upon his adoption by Lolo Soetoro—merely scoured the probate records until she found someone who died who was not receiving Social Security benefits, and 'selected' that SSN for Obama.

Although many Americans do not understand the meaning of the term 'natural born citizen', there are few who do not understand that if you are using someone else's Social Security Number it is a clear indication of fraud."

Perhaps, the elder Mrs. Dunham was aware that her grandson had been "bred"—and was being "reared"—for some greater purpose. If the fraudulent use of a Social Security Number proves to be valid, Barack Obama's qualifications to serve as president of the United States will be absolutely nullified, affirming the absolutely greatest of all seductions. But, there is more:

"It has become apparent that at some point, the individual who was known as Barry Soetoro began using the name Barack Hussein Obama II. Based on our investigative findings, it was at about this same time period that the Connecticut issuance of the social security number appeared and became 'attached' to the name Barack Hussein Obama. It can then be reasonably reconciled that Barry Soetoro became Barack Hussein Obama while he was a young man in New York following his mysterious trip to Pakistan on a passport that was likely not issued by the U.S. (raising additional questions about his citizenship).

"To understand how a virtually unknown (and untested) politician from Illinois could rise to occupy the most powerful position in the free world in less than a decade after he became a state senator, one must take a few steps backward to understand the complete picture, and that Obama was *selected* * long before he was *elected* * to become president (of the U.S). Problems with his background were numerous, however, including but not limited to his parental lineage and place of birth. These problems became apparent through a private vetting process by his handlers, or those who are known as the 'power elite' in the latter half of the last century (The Illuminati). His handlers were and are globalists of the highest order, extending from George Soros to those above him on the proverbial pyramid capstone of globalists.

"The globalists (Illuminati) had direct and indirect ties to the Dunham family and in particular, Obama's mother. Consider, for example, that Peter F. Geithner (father of Obama's Treasury Secretary Timothy Geithner), worked for the Ford Foundation

---

* Emphasis added

and oversaw the work of Obama's mother, Ann Dunham, while she was developing 'micro-finance programs' in Indonesia. In brief, Obama's mother set up a large loan system in Indonesia akin to the savings and loan structure of the 1970s and 1980s. To gain a better understanding of her activities in finance, despite her background in anthropology, recall the BCCI scandal of the late 1970s. The Luxembourg-based Bank of Credit and Commerce International [BBCI] was involved in a massive illegal enterprise that defrauded depositors, laundered drug money, smuggled weapons and assisted such notorious outlaws as international terrorist Abu Nidal, (regarded as one of the most ruthless among anti-Israel terrorists). In fact, some of the same "players" who existed then continue to exist in Obama's circles ..."[16]

The BCCI - Obama - Geithner - Nidal connection extends even deeper into global politics. According to Los Angeles Times writers, Sara Fritz and Pritz and Joel Havemann, in their August 4, 1991 article, "BCCI founder, Agha Hasan Abedi promoted his banks to the Muslim world as an alternative to what Abedi called 'the Jewish-dominated banks of New York'."[17] His friendship with many respected political leaders, such as former President (and Trilateralist) Jimmy Carter and former British Prime Minister Lord Callaghan--as well as the

---

[16] Canada Free Press, *The Unraveling of Barack Hussein Obama II, a/k/a Barry Soetoro,* - Doug Hagmann & Joseph Hagmann Friday, April 8, 2011
[17] *The Independent,* Agha Hasan Abedi, Nicholas Kochan, August 9, 1995,

bank's ability to employ the services of many prestigious, high-priced law firms—gave the bank the political muscle to squelch criminal investigations whenever they began.

At a time when America's national security and financial stability is at stake, President Obama's past and the people with whom he and his family associated calls for further investigation. If Barack Obama/Barry Soetoro is ever to be viewed as the "transparent" Commander-in-Chief he promised to be, he should willingly come forward with the necessary evidence to prove that he meets the Constitution's criteria to serve in the office to which he has been elected ... or the American people should vote him out of that office. The American people deserve to know that their president is not a "puppet," cleverly—and in deference to the rules of qualification—maneuvered into office by America's enemies. *We the people* must be convinced that our president is a patriotic American who will stand—*not with the Muslims*—but with those he was elected to lead should the "political winds begin to blow in an ugly direction".

In the next chapter, we'll take a look at the "super-power" of self-designated despots who, *first*, cloaked themselves in the sacred aprons of Zionism, then Freemasonry and the robes of Catholicism while bearing the 'Talisman of Lucifer' underneath. We'll look more closely at the Illuminati's newest ally—Islam. We'll also expose how members of what *The Protocols* call a "revolutionary faith" have successfully seduced members of well-intended organizations and religions ... and—with their "puppet" in the Oval Office—are positioned to do more. To demonstrate their far-reaching implications, we'll examine lessons from history that teach how to preserve the United States of America—the one remaining wall of justice standing between a world ruled by a tyrannical "supranational sovereignty and governments *of the people, by the people, and for the people.*"

Regardless of your political or theological ideology, I urge you to stay with me to the end. While *The Protocols* speak for themselves, I will do my best to remain optimistic that we can save humanity from the grip of an unholy alliance intent on executing the greatest of all seductions, with a favored "son" at the helm.

When we are done, it is my hope that your mind—as has been mine—will be stretched. I'd like to believe that you will never again see the world *as you have been indoctrinated* to see it. You will see the Obama style of "change" for what it truly is: the permanent replacement of faith-based, fiscally sound Americanism with the iron hand of negatively-based, secular socialism—and with it—the death of what remains of human rights. More importantly, you will listen more closely to what politicians and media spokespersons say and be more cautious in casting your vote in future elections.

CHAPTER 2

Who are the Illuminati? And, if they are who they seem to be, why should the American voter care?

Is what globalist, David Rockefeller referred to in his 1991 address to the Trilateral Commission the same phantom group of Godless despots that novelist, Dan Brown, demonized in *The Di Vinci Code, Angels and Demons,* and *The Lost Symbol?* Or, are they simply a loosely-structured group of "intellectual elites and world bankers" that—individually and collectively—possesses the resources to affect world markets, influence the leaders of nations and multi-national corporations, and do whatever they believe to be in their own best interest? I don't know if any member of the Inner Circle's "out-group" will ever truly know the answers to these questions.

After years of research, Wes Penre became convinced that The Illuminati are part of a small group of despots who intend to commandeer the U.S. In *The Secret Order of the Illuminati: A Brief History of the Shadow Government,* Penre concluded:

> "The men who control the Illuminati are members of thirteen wealthy families. Who they are has always been a well hidden

secret, and the leadership has gone from man to man over generations ... Not many people knew who these families are exactly, but quite recently this has become known, due to people from the Illuminati who have left the Order and revealed this most remarkable information. So here are the names of the 13 families—the world's Secret Government ... Astor, Bundy, Collins, DuPont, Freeman, Kennedy, Li (Chinese), Onassis, Rockefeller, Rothschild, Russell, Van Duyn, Merovingian (the European Royal Families)."

Another investigator, Texe Marrs (author of *Circle of Intrigue*) concluded the "Inner Circle" of the Illuminati represents *geographic territories.* This governing body ("supranational sovereignty") is comprised (in part) of members from the U.S.A., Canada, France, Austria, Great Britain, Spain, and South Africa.

Stewart A. Swerdlow, author of (*Blue Blood, True Blood: Conflict and* Creation) found that the next tier down in the hierarchy of the Illuminati is known as the *Committee of 300.* On his website, "The Illuminati Hierarchy," Swerdlow writes: "These families include such notable names as Agnelli, Balliol, Beale, Bell, Bouvier, Bush, Cameron, Campbell, Carnegie, Carrington, Coolidge, Delano, Douglas, Ford, Gardner, Graham, Hamilton, Harriman, Heinz, Kuhn, Lindsay, Loeb, Mellon, Montgomery, Morgan, Norman, Oppenheimer, Rhodes, Roosevelt, Russell, Savoy, Schiff, Seton, Spencer, Stewart/Stuart, Taft, and Wilson. And, there are many others."

Swerdlow goes even further, raising questions about worldwide institutions. "The Committee of 300 *uses* many well-known institutions to accomplish its goals, including the Council on Foreign Relations, Bilderburgers, Trilateral Commission, Club of Rome, Royal Institute for International Affairs, Mafia, CIA, NSA, Mossad, Secret Service, International Monetary Fund, Federal Reserve, Internal Revenue Service, and Interpol, to name a few ... these are private organizations or corporations set up as public service devices ... all for the purpose of serving the Inner Circle."

Though the mighty men who conduct the affairs of these organizations generally rule from the shadows, in May of 2011, Binyamin Appelbaum and Sheryl Gay Stolberg published a New York Times article directing the lights of publicity toward the International Monetary Fund. Excerpts from the article are revealing and affirm its role in "ruling the affairs of the whole world," as *The Protocols* promise.

> "It is an international island in the midst of the American capital, a sharp-elbowed place ruled by alpha male economists ... This is life at the International Monetary Fund, the lender of last resort for governments that need money and, under the leadership of Dominique Strauss-Kahn, an emerging force in the regulation of the global economy.
>
> But with Mr. Strauss-Kahn's arrest earlier this week and indictment on Thursday on charges that he tried to rape a New York hotel housekeeper, a spotlight has been cast on the culture of the institution ... The laws of the

United States do not apply inside its (the
I.M.F.'s) walls ... The I.M.F., created in 1945,
has 2,400 employees evaluating the economic
health of nations ... When nations borrow
money from the fund, they *typically must agree
to adopt economic reforms*[*], and employees are
sent to watch their progress.

It is hard to say why Strauss-Kahn (nicknamed by his
fellow Frenchmen [and women] "The Great Seducer") was
in the U.S. when the alleged events that led to his arrest
took place. There are a number of possibilities but clearly,
another "puppet" that had apparently been "bred and
reared from childhood" by the Inner Circle made a fatal
mistake. The error he made could have *preceded* the
alleged sexual assault charges. The IMF director had
recently been overtly critical of certain world bankers,
accusing them of *causing* the global economic crisis. It is
also very possible that the Rothschild Formula was
invoked, thereby bring about the IMF head's resignation
and effectively destroying the presidential hopes of the
leading candidate to challenge for the next president of
France.

Strauss-Kahn met another one of *The Protocols'*
criteria for presidency. The professed socialist and former
member of the Union of Communist Students had in his
past "some dark, undiscovered stain" that had previously
been smoothed over by the powers that be within the
influential Illuminati.

While conducting research for my novel, *The Oath*
(A-Argus Better Book Publishers) I came across a plethora
of disturbing revelations about The Illuminati. Among

---

[*] Emphasis added

them was the document that prompted me to write this book: *The Protocols of the Learned Elders of Zion.* In *The Oath,* I decided to let characters in the novel report on my findings.

In his upcoming State of the Union Address—the one he never got the chance to deliver—*The Oath's* main character, President Mason Edmonds, intended to reveal the findings of *Operation Annuit Coeptis,* a top-secret operation that he commissioned to investigate how the Illuminati had worked its way into positions of power throughout the United States. Somehow, the president's intentions found their way to the Inner Circle of the Illuminati; and *The Rothschild Formula* was set in motion. President Edmonds was assassinated. However, the speech he had prepared was delivered, verbatim, by an (equally-as-patriotic) successor. This is what Congress and an anxious television audience heard:

> "In 1776 while American colonies were breaking away from an oppressive European monarchy, a secret confederacy was being established in Bavaria by a German-born law professor, named Adam Weishaupt. He and his hand-picked group of powerful European families were in the throes of creating an ambitious plan designed to take over the world.
>
> "In 1861, with the shot fired on Fort Sumter, the United States was successfully split, geographically and ideologically ... much more so than existed prior to the incident off the shores of Charleston, South Carolina. Tens of thousands of men died

in a conflict that was billed as "The War Between the States," when, in reality, it was a war between ideologies, whether people should be the master of their own minds and actions or whether they are to mind their masters. The war was conceived and orchestrated by outsiders, based far from our shores ... in Europe.

"In order to achieve their objectives, the Draconian gods of an emerging *Invisible Empire* successfully pitted Americans against Americans, financing both sides of the War. By doing so, they could ensure that *they* emerged victoriously.

It was a premeditated holocaust in which The Illuminati watched from the sidelines as brother massacred brother, believing that they were fighting to either save the Union or the Confederacy.

"When the carnage ended, bondage simply took on a different face. Pre-war slave masters were replaced by new ones, wearing the cloak of a seemingly-omni-potent government—not just in southern states, but throughout the nation.

"Thirteen powerful European part-iarchs who made up The Illuminati's Inner Circle had done what they set out to do, gain an even stronger foothold in the new world.

"When The Civil War ended—and with it the death of states' rights—The Illuminati had a forever divided nation in their grasp, never to release the grip. President Lincoln saw what was happening and set out to right a *greater* wrong. Because the *Rothschild Formula* was invoked, he never got that chance.

"Convinced that the world is theirs to rule, the 'supranational sovereignty' determine where, and what kinds of, chaos best serve their purpose. They seem to know who will win *before* conflict breaks out or votes are cast." Through their environmental minions, they create disasters that lead to more regulation. They set forest fires. They create so called accidents at nuclear power plants and commit acts of terror inciting oil spills. Each havoc-reeking environmental disaster is orchestrated so that they can gain greater control of the populace through government regulation.

"From historical documents, it appears that not only were the French Revolution and U.S. Civil War engineered by The Illuminati, but World Wars I and II, the failed League of Nations, its successor (The United Nations), Global Warming, and the global economic crisis of 2009. In each case (following their constitution—*The Protocols of the Learned Elders of Zion*) the *Illuminati* engineered the sacrifice of fellow human beings, fortunes, national wonders, and, sometimes, nations to restructure a world to their liking.

"One-World advocates also expand their spheres of influence by employing a *gentler* style of warfare—a tried and true weapon of mass destruction known as *progressive liberalism,* or '*gradual* social reform'.

"Until I received *OAC's* final report, I had never read books written by Karl Marx and Vladimir Lenin. However, I knew that they were the fathers of progressive liberalism and its reform objective: Communism. I had to familiarize myself with the thought processes of two of capitalism's most notorious enemies. What I learned is that the tactic of conquest known as *progressive liberalism* and its cousin, *socialism,* are both based on *evolution* rather than *revolution.* Revolution is reserved for the rapid overthrow of government, usually by force.

"During its investigation *OAC* discovered that the *Protocols* that guide The Illuminatists' actions describe clever ways to kill *the human spirit*—worldwide—and, in turn, abolish human rights, thereby subjugating the masses to a small group of self-anointed overlords.

"When pieces of the puzzle are aligned, a recognizable image begins to emerge—a single World Government created *of The Illuminati, by The Illuminati,* and *for The Illuminati,* with a single purpose in mind—world domination. (This was written prior to the revelation that radical Islam had entered into an alliance with the Illuminati)

"How could a few brazen men and women acquire such arrogance and gain such power? The answer is simple: money—to be exact, *debt.* They control the purse strings of much of the world. They finance wars and the conflicts that *they* create. In the world of The Illuminati, the lender is the master of the debtor. To owe is to be owned. To be owned is to be enslaved. So, bondage by any other name is still bondage, regardless of the social disguise in which it is dressed or flag that flies above its seat of government.

"One of the tactics used successfully by The Illuminati against capitalism is named after two left wing professors at New York's Columbia University, ostensibly, President Obama's alma mater. I say ostensibly because the President has refused to release his transcript from this University and students who attended the same classes Mr. Obama claims to have attended, swear that they never saw him on campus. More on this later.

"*The Cloward-Piven Strategy* (that emanated from Columbia University) explains how it is possible to bring about the fall of capitalism—by intentionally creating *debt* and its accomplice, *premeditated poverty.*

"First, governments with one-world intentions assume the role of *caretaker*, providing entitlements to targeted portions of the population. Then, people at both ends of the social spectrum are encouraged to accumulate more debt than they can ever hope to repay. When hope seems lost, Big Brother comes to the rescue, redistributing money from the public coffers. With each hand out and each bail out, additional caveats of subordination are required of the receivers, until there is no more wealth to redistribute. The economy collapses. (Does this scenario have an Obama-like ring)? And, a dictator—in this case The Illuminati—moves in to pick up the pieces.

"Over the years, all manner of *emissaries* have assimilated into America's culture to do The Illuminati's bidding. Others have been recruited from within and organized into political action groups and civil liberties unions. As was done in Hitler's Germany, the youth were targeted and turned against the very form of government that gave them the right to voice their opposition.

(Ninety-percent of the German people watched while ten percent—the Nazi's—changed Germany).

"Regardless of age or place of origin, the organizers' instructions were to *change* the U.S. from a capitalistic system to one based on socialistic principles—more specifically the *Illuminati Principles*. As *The* Protocols dictate, they began infiltrating America's educational systems rewriting history, making heroes of fellow Illuminati emissaries, changing textbooks and curricula, indoctrin-ating our children into viewing their parents, government and the world from an *anti*-capitalist point of view.

"They created animosity among religions and among races. Cleverly, they encouraged *Americans* to split loyalties by inserting a hyphen between the term 'American' and the name of some country in which distant ancestors might have lived. They fostered class warfare, further dividing Americans along income lines and social standing. America's successful entrepreneurs were fair game. Hard-working men and women were ridiculed and taxed, while the super-rich Illuminati watched from the sidelines, padding their already inflated bank accounts and portfolios.

"America's—and God's—archenemy has successfully used every conceivable faction of the age-old war tactic: 'divide and conquer.' And, because Americans were not properly forewarned by a complicit press, The Illuminati's plan was—and is— working to perfection.

"Backed by the gods of the New World Order, Illuminati disciples gained positions of leadership and influence in

America's primary seats of power—
Washington, D.C., New York, Chicago,
and Hollywood. The reason: centralized
seats of power are easier for an aggressor to
surround and seize. From these centers of
influence Illuminists were able to change
both how Americans viewed them-selves as
well as the manner in which the world sees
us.

"By using high profile entertainers as
mouthpieces, The Illuminati set out to
deceive *the people* into believing that
capitalism and conservatism—not Marxism
or totalitarianism—were the greatest threats
to a utopian-like world.

"From a variety of platforms,
Illuminati disciples challenged venerable
institutions, fostered dissention, altered
laws, instilled 'political correctness,'
applauded immorality, rewarded incompetence, denounced God, and—with the
mainstream media's assistance—swayed
public opinion from 'father knows best' to
a '*government knows all*' way of thinking.

"America's near death experience has
been in the making for a very, very long
time. In the 1940s, under President
Franklin Delano Roosevelt, and to create
the kind of debt they needed to impose on
Americans, Illuminatists saw to it that the
unmatched U.S. gold reserves were
depleted. Then, they defrauded the
American people into believing that a Social

Security Trust Fund would ensure prosperity in retirement years, though they raided the Fund each year to finance other social programs, each designed to win the allegiance of the non-working class at the expense of working people.

"It was no coincidence that in the 1960s, progressives began to make the U.S. dependent on foreign oil and gas, while the drug-soaked 'Hip Generation' demonstrated for *making love* instead of a war intended to stop the spread of Communism. Illuminati disciples in the White House and Congress installed far-reaching social programs intended to drain the treasuries of individuals and institutions alike.

"As the U.S. was being pressured into *abandoning* nuclear energy, in breakneck fashion, other countries around the world built nuclear plants. It was 'unfair," we were told, for the U.S. to be the nuclear superpower of the world. It has always been the *Invisible Empire's* goal to orchestrate the destruction of every arbitrary power that could threaten their own.

"Throughout all America, Illuminati-supported political action groups were demonstrating in the streets, at airports, and to lawmakers, and were successful in preventing the U.S. from becoming an energy independent nation. Today, as planned, we are heavily reliant on oil from nations that don't particularly like us. And, nations with whom we've had major disagreements in the past—China and Japan to be exact—now own our debt. As lenders, they are in a position to influence U.S. policy.

"Although the U.S. *built* the only trans-oceanic connection within the America's with taxpayer money, the Panama Canal was given in the 1970's to Panama during the Carter Administration. The Canal is now controlled by China. Historians will look back and ask, 'What were the American's thinking?'

"The craziness goes even farther back. The Great Depression of the 1930s achieved one of The Illuminati's goals. It drove many independent banks all across the U.S. out of business. As intended, the people and their government were then forced to borrow money from banks that The Illuminati controlled, many of which existed in countries that were not traditional allies of the U.S.

"Another result of the Great Depression of the 1930s as well as with the Great Oil Embargo of the 1970s was an evolutionary shifting of influence, power, and wealth—the vast majority *away* from the people, toward global business, bigger government, and then to a 'new*er* world order' ... one created and manipulated by The Order of The Illuminati.

"Now, let's fast forward to 2008. It is also not a coincidence that at the direction of an insistent Democrat-controlled Congress, many lenders threw away the keys to sub-prime lending locks and that shortly thereafter, credit was suddenly tightened. Fannie Mae and Freddie Mac were left holding a sea of uncollectable debt. Banks stopped lending money, worldwide. While Wall Street and many banks were turned upside down, a few 'sacred cows' made billions and parked their fortunes offshore in secret bank accounts.

"As The Illuminati had planned, the economy tanked, not just in the U.S. but globally. That's how recessions are created *by The Illuminati*, allowing the 'world bankers and intellectual elites' to accumulate valuable assets at fire-sale prices ... and all at the expense of American taxpayers.

"What you, my fellow Americans, need to know is that there is not now—nor has there ever been—a shortage of oil, nor money.

The Illuminati, acting in concert with the, then, all-too-cooperative administrations in Washington, the oil companies, and OPEC (a Muslim dominated Brotherhood) periodically decide to cut off the pipelines, preventing oil from entering U.S. ports and lending institutions from lending.

Originally, this was done to drive *independent* oil companies and locally owned gas stations out of business. Then, the ploy spilled over into the financial sector. The result was that companies controlled by The Illuminati eliminated competition. And, a large part of America's wealth was redistributed to Muslim Kings and Dictators, who deposited their new-found wealth in banks owned or controlled by the Illuminati. Although monopolies were clearly dealing cards from the bottom of the deck, the Federal Trade Commission and the mainstream media remained silent.

"The same is the case with nuclear energy. Since pressures were brought to bear by environmental groups—who have always been Illuminati puppets—oil exploration in the U.S. has been hampered. Who benefits from the international oil conspiracy or domestic oil spills of the man-made kind? Who benefits from a ban on building nuclear power plants? Who benefits from federal mandates restricting domestic drilling of oil and natural gas ... or mining America's clean-burning coal? Certainly, it *is not* the American people who benefit from such decisions. It was *and is* the large oil and gas magnates, their Muslim-dominated OPEC allies and international bankers, who continue to transfer wealth *out of America*. These are the gods of new world order, the architects of a One-World Government. And, it is *they* who always seem to profit. While they do, the mainstream media bow to these gods and remain silent."

"As we enter the second decade of the 21st century, we are facing *another* Illuminati-contrived crisis. In the fall of 2009, what remained of the levies around responsible government was over-run. Madness and imprudence flooded Washington. In break-neck fashion, Congress and the president set about nationalizing everything in sight. Americans were led to believe that the government could spend its way into prosperity and needed to do it as quickly as possible. Intellectual elites who had never run as much as a lemonade stand were put in charge of solving the country's multi-*trillion* dollar financial woes. Some of those responsible *for creating* the financial crisis were charged with resolving it. That's the way the Illuminati work. At the pleasure of the White House, professed communists were appointed to serve in oversight positions. And, as the shackles of bondage tightened, the *mainstream* media remained silent.

"Banks, the automobile industry, carbon emissions, and healthcare were brought under the control of the federal government that, in turn, answered to a worldwide sovereignty of intellectual elites and bankers. Presidentially appointed "czars," not Congress, were put in place to see that retribution and wealth redistribution policies were carried out. Spending spiraled out of control and the national debt rose to unprecedented levels.

As intended, a hole was dug for future generations of Americans, out of which they are never expected to climb. The shackles of bondage tighten; the *mainstream* media honors its oath of 'discretion' to the Illuminati and remains silent.

"And although it was discovered that Illuminati-supported scientists had cooked the data on Global Warming, governments at home and abroad initiated legislation and moved toward treaties to further regulate free enterprise by limiting 'carbon emissions.' The champion of this globalization movement is none other than a former Vice President of these United States, a Nobel Prize recipient who stands to make billions from the 'Cap and Trade' industry.

"As part of globalization efforts, monies collected from 'cap and trade' tariffs were promised to third world countries, ostensibly to assist them in complying with the new United Nations emission standards. The wheels of World Government are turning at an unprecedented speed. Not surprisingly, the billions collected from industrialized countries (like the U.S) are slated to be deposited in none other than ... The World Bank or International

Monetary Fund, both of which are controlled by The Illuminati. And, as the shackles of bondage are tightened, the mainstream media continues to be silent.

"The so-called *Swine Flu Pandemic* of 2009 is yet another example in which premeditated chaos was used to test the waters of government-controlled healthcare. There is absolutely no data that the flu season of 2009-2010 was any worse than previous years, or that the vaccine forced on many people the world over, made one shred of difference. In many cases, complications from mass vaccination exceeded any good intended. The only people who benefitted from the Swine Flu scare were companies that produced and/or distributed the vaccine, companies controlled by The Illuminati. And, the mainstream media reverently remained silent.

"*Change* had been promised to the people of the world and *change* we got—more change than any of us outside the Inner Circle expected. Truly, a *New World Order* has been in charge—The Order of The Illuminati.

"A Draconian global government by The Illuminati, and for The Illuminati.

"As were the characters in the children's story—*The Emperor's New Clothes*—honor-able members of Congress in this chamber and the American people, were duped. The only 'hope' Americans experienced was that my predecessor, the White House and this Congress would come to their senses.

"Every public opinion poll indicated that you, *the people*, wanted your government to secure its borders, stop giving citizen's rights to non-citizens, and refrain from spending money it didn't have. The people want its government to stop mortgaging their children's and grand-children's futures and put the long-term interest of America *first*. And, while America bleeds, the complicit *mainstream* media remains silent.

"In keeping with a tradition of selective reporting, major networks and newspapers failed to point out that the kind of 'transparency' and 'change' the previous administration promised during the Presi-dential campaign of 2008 was, simply, non-existent. In contrast to the Watergate scandal of the 1970s, investigative reporters in the mainstream press seem more focused on finding fault with Tea Party participants than reporting on the reasons why Tea Party participants have come out of their homes and places of business to make their voices heard.

"Clearly, the United States has been under siege ... and for a very long time. And, you—*the people*—knew not. Although you had the right to know, the mainstream media chose not to reveal the truth.

"With New World Order gods gaining ground and assuming more positions of influence and power over the past century, the U.S. has been falling behind in The Culture Wars.

"America is beginning to resemble an embryonic *Oceania*, George Orwell's futuristic totalitarian society. Throughout the land, Illuminati owned politicians, lawmakers, judges, and financiers confiscate freedoms from 'the people' and relegate them to the Federal Government. Treaties and legislation are being drafted to circumvent the Second Amendment of the Constitution and take guns away from law abiding citizens. History shows that this was done in Nazi Germany, prior to World War II and the Holocaust that cost more than ten million innocent people their lives.

"Gun control is not about public safety. To the contrary, it is an Illuminati ploy designed to ensure that the people can't organize a militia and fight back against the mounting control of a totalitarian form of government.

"The America we see around us today is indeed a changed nation from the one that the Constitutional framers founded. Today's America is a product of both genetics and environment. We are a nation of *legal* immigrants, who came here to build a life based upon religious principles. Today, in contrast, religion is under attack by *The Changers*. We are also becoming immune to the very existence of the evil forces that seem committed to controlling *everything* in our environment.

"To paint the United States in the worst possible light in the eyes of the rest of the world, the entertainment industry glorifies the worst of American culture, turning out programs and movies depicting violence, drugs, and explicit carnal interaction. And, the *mainstream* media remains silent, except—that is—for when they routinely attack conservative citizens who peacefully and truthfully bring anti-American propaganda and actions to the forefront. It is how the *Rothschild Formula* works—discredit and destroy those who do not agree with *The Invisible Empire's* agenda.

"What I have presented to you tonight are *the facts* as *Operation Annuit Coeptis* found them to exist in the first decade of the 21st century. *OAC* took a good long look at 'change' and what they saw was terrifying. It concluded that—though it was later in coming than originally predicted—George Orwell's book, *1984,* was beginning to look more like fact than fiction.

"World bankers, intelligent elites, the mainstream media, and politicians are all "Big Brothers" controlled by a single overbearing patriarch: *The Invisible Order of the Illuminati.* This power-driven band of falsely-enlightened men and women live by a different set of rules than they expect the rest of us to live by.

"Because of *OAC's* findings, I became convinced that America is at a crossroads. I stand before you tonight realizing that I am risking everything to let you, *the people and the people's representatives,* know the truth about the shaky and disturbing State of our Union, the individuals and forces responsible for its decline and the challenges that lie before us.

"What happens next cannot be forecast with any degree of certainty. America's destiny now lies in *your hands*—an informed electorate. However, if the past is any indication of the future, I predict that the mainstream media *will not* remain silent after this address. I expect them to paint me as an 'out of touch and misguided conspiracy theorist.' And, those of you who agree with me and *OAC's* findings will be, as well. One way to bring complicit media around is to turn away from their channels, beginning immediately after I have finished my remarks. Stop buying or reading their publications, and log off their websites. They survive by ratings and the advertising revenues that high ratings command. Drive the all-powerful ratings of those who refuse to report the truth down and cut off their life blood—advertising dollars. That's a peaceful way to bring them to their knees. Conversely, support those who are unafraid to share the truth with you. Those of us who believe in self-determination can take America back without ever pulling a trigger; without reaching for a club; without launching a missile. We do so by turning out on Election Day—every single Election Day— and replacing the sponsors of imprudence with those who exercise prudence.

"My fellow Americans, my wish is that what I have revealed to you this evening is no more than a series of unrelated coincidences and that the picture I have presented to you proves to be no more than a theory; but to call what I have shared with you a 'theory' would be telling you yet another lie. And, you have been fed lies for far too long.

"The self-anointed gods of the Invisible Global Empire known to us as *The Illuminati* and a complicit press do not believe that you are smart enough or committed enough to put the pieces of the puzzle together. They think that you have grown soft, no longer care, or are afraid to offend anyone, even though they may be stealing your freedom and/or confiscating your hard-earned resources. Frankly, I think they have misjudged you. And, I hope that you will rise up, throw off the shackles of bondage, and stand with me. Together, we will show the Shadow Government that

it has under-estimated the American spirit
that burns within our hearts."[18]

Though the fictitious President Edmonds's speech was
also published as fiction, much of it is based on research
conducted by this writer and other investigators, who spent
endless hours digging deeply into the connection between
powerful families who control much of the world's wealth
and—therefore—a significant part of the power that drives it
in whatever direction they choose.

Can I validate that all my conclusions are one hundred
percent accurate? No, I can't; however, as a physician I
have learned to look at the signs, symptoms, and origin of
disorders that affect the human body. In that vein, from all
the information I can gather, the signs and symptoms of
global disorder point to the Hidden Hand of the
Illuminati—the group that one of their own, David
Rockefeller, identified as an "international sovereignty of
intellectual elites and world bankers."

Once I have presented other evidence to back up my
conclusions, I will address the all-important question: How
do patriotic Americans take our nation back? Perhaps, the
answer lies in the fact that The Hidden Hand functions
under a *veil of secrecy and seduction*. Again, a children's
story reveals answers. When the true identity of the
Wizard of Oz was exposed, the power he held over people
was lost. He was just an ordinary man behind an imposing
front with loud speakers.

This is what we must, now, do: confront the "Wizards
of Evil." Expose them for what they are and relentlessly
remind every American of the Invisible Empire's stated
intent: *to own the world and each of us in it.* First,

---

[18] *The Oath,* E. Gaylon McCollough, MD, A-Argus Better Book Publishing, 2010

however, we must look deeper into the identity of this secret organization; then we will reveal the identities of its allies ... and puppets.

CHAPTER 3

With each passing year, I pay more attention to what people *do* and less to what they *say*. I have also learned to appreciate the sayings of individuals who lived the advice they gave to others, especially if the words were spoken by men and women baptized in the fires of experience. I am reminded of a quotation that applies here: "everyone is ignorant in some things." Ignoring this truism is a group of "supranational sovereigns" and the other half of the Illuminati-Islamic Alliance who believe that they know better than the rest of us how we should live our own lives and who—or what—we should worship.

Fact is: mortal sovereigns have no clue of how the people they rule actually live on a day to day basis. That's why "intellectual elites and world bankers" are ignorant as to how to create a voluntary sense of loyalty and lift patriotic, working, law-abiding Americans up. That's why the Lords of Seduction have to resort to the despot methods outlined in *The Protocols: "force and make-believe,"* and why Sharia Law is required to direct the thoughts and actions of the radical arm of the Muslim faithful. The intellectual elite and world bankers were given no divine right to govern others. Their expertise is in creating and promoting ignorance; confiscating what is—by

God's will—the peoples'; buying favors with other people's money and orchestrating class warfare within a society.

Shakespeare was the first to record: "The past is prologue." From studying history, I have learned that ignorance and oppression have always led to revolution, while knowledge and unshackling the human spirit have brought about renaissance. The Illuminati also knows this to be true. That's why they have to *ensure ignorance* among the people that they use in their quest to rule the world.

Truth is the great emancipator. Knowledge *of the truth* empowers people to make prudent decisions and plan for the future—to dream great dreams, pursue great causes and to see more, do more, and be more. This is precisely why the Illuminati know that they have to control the media. By doing so, they can better dictate what the people know ... and believe to be possible. Or more accurately stated, what the people *think* they know. By controlling the media, the "Wizards of Evil" can indoctrinate children and sway public opinion for generations to come until lies become the new "truth," ...

So, how do we combat these "Wizards," the Lords of Seduction? The answer is to follow the advice given to Odysseus by Circe—turn deaf ears to the Sirens' songs or, at least, be bound and refrain from falling into their trap. View "the news" with skepticism, knowing that what is being reported is only *part of* the truth—and that the part that is being reported may be slanted to sway public opinion to the truth, as defined by the I-IA. Learn to read between the lines and listen between the words; for it is there that clues lie. An example of how Islam has already influenced America's laws is demonstrated in a slight-of-hand addition to Obama*Care*.

Clearly, the hand of Islam was involved in crafting Obama*Care. On* page 107 of the 2000+ page bill is a word, not known by most Americans. The word is *Dhimmitude*, a word that President Obama used recently in one of his addresses. Dhimmitude is the Muslim system of controlling non-Muslim populations that are conquered through jihad. Specifically, it is the taxing of non-Muslims in exchange for tolerating their presence and as a coercive means of converting conquered remnants to Islam.

So that Muslims in the U.S. may "tolerate" the rest of us, the President and Congressional Democrats found it necessary to compensate them in America's newly proposed healthcare plan? What were Congress and the president thinking? Surely Dhimmitude didn't appear in the bill by accident. One of the reasons that Nancy Pelosi wanted Congress to read the bill *after* it was signed into law may have been to hide the inclusion of Dhimmitude and other politically-desirable waivers to the Democrat base.

Obama*Care* allows the establishment of Dhimmitude and Sharia Muslim diktat in the United States. Muslims are specifically exempted from the government mandate to purchase insurance, and also from the penalty tax for being *un*insured. As part of the president's "exemption package" Muslims receive special treatment. Though Muslims voluntarily immigrated to the U.S., their religion considers insurance to be "gambling," "risk-taking," and "usury" and is thus banned. So, knowing that insurance was a way of life in America, Muslims must have come here to *change* our culture rather than to assimilate. This fact could also explain why President Obama continues to insist that "America is not a Christian nation." Nor—in his mind—is she a Jewish nation. So what kind of nation is she? Why are the only new laws being implemented to protect religious beliefs those that favor Islam? It would be an interesting question for some reporter to ask the president in a future news conference or on the campaign trail.

In the healthcare bill passed by President Obama and a Democrat-controlled congress, Muslims are specifically granted exemption based on religious beliefs that consider all kinds of insurance a form of gambling.

In contrast, *non*-Muslim Americans are subject to IRS liens placed against assets, including real estate, cattle, and even account receivables, and will face hard *prison time* if we refuse to buy insurance ... or pay the penalty tax. Meanwhile, Louis Farrakhan and his Nation of Islam will have no such penalty and will have one hundred percent of his health needs paid for by Obama's *de facto* government insurance, if it is allowed to stand. Non-Muslims will be paying a tax to compensate Muslims for tolerating us in our own land. This is Dhimmitude. And, President Obama signed off on it!

For the Illuminati-Islamic Alliance (I-IA) Dhimmitude serves two purposes: It enriches the Muslim masters and serves to drive converts to Islam. In this case, the incentive to convert to Islam will be taken up by those in the inner-cities as well as some members of the godless Generation X, Y, and Z types who—as a result of the Hidden Hand's puppeteering tactics—have no moral anchor. If it means free health insurance and no taxes, more Americans may be tempted to convert to Islam, thereby raising the Democrat Party's voting base and becoming a to-be-dealt-with voting bloc.

Clearly a new day has dawned in America ... and—to the detriment of the American patriot—in the White House. It is the responsibility of patriots to gather the available information about the quiet conversion of the

United States into a nation far removed from the intent of the founding fathers. Use the most reliable sources available and come to your own conclusions; share your thoughts with others; and remind all you know that *there are no coincidences.* As sad as it may sound, Americans have to proceed as though *everything* is part of a master plan to bring all of us under the rule of a Sharia styled One-World Government ... because all indicators are pointing in that direction.

Is what I have proposed to this point in this manuscript a conspiracy theory? Keep in mind that a theory is based on supposition ... and "some evidence." It no longer becomes a theory when facts and events prove it right ... or wrong. And actions speak louder than rhetoric—even that read from Teleprompters.

When a group of men—who have the resources to do so—say that they are going to establish a "supranational sovereignty" and abolish governments currently based upon "auto-determination," the people had better take note. When members of one religion say that they intend to convert the world to that religion and replace the Law of the Land with the laws of its religion, people who promote the separation of Church and State had better take note. And if it appears that the stated intentions of the two forces that have made such pronouncements begin to unfold—unopposed by a nation's leaders—it time for *the people* to act.

* * * * * * * * * *

If tyranny is learned behavior, who are its teachers ... and who were the teachers' teachers? The answer may be found wherever Evil resides—where the will to enslave people outweighs the will to embolden them. And, from the looks of things, the schools of global despotism are turning out graduates at breakneck speed ... while Lucifer smiles.

The Lords of Seduction follow the lines of temptation outlined by Catie Smith in her publication, *The Devil's Temptation.* According to Ms. Smith, evil forces "heighten the senses to such a degree they overpower the mind. They use temptations and pay-offs. When the sensual temptation is great, it orders the pre-conditioned mind to stop reasoning. Sirens speak to you, using no audible sound." Ms. Smith continued:

> "Through (transcendental realms) they call us by name, saying, 'Come to me. Come with me into the inner sanctums of earthly powers.' The mind says, 'You know this isn't good for you.' The seduction continues. 'Go ahead, indulge. It is wonderful. You want it. You're worth it. You deserve it.' Then when we tell the mind to be quiet, we are listening only to *the call* of seduction."[19]

Ms. Smith's article goes on to explain: "When a battle between the senses and the mind take place, emotions will erupt." The Lords of Seduction are keenly aware of the arts of temptation and mind control. They know how to manipulate the human mind; and in doing so, move the masses in whichever direction the Illuminati-Islamic Alliance chooses, including the eruption of emotions.

Smith goes on to say:

---

[19] *The Devil's Temptation,* HubPages, Catie Smith

"The truth is: the mind doesn't always control us. The senses get titillated and convince the mind to be quiet. To meet his needs, Lucifer disguises himself in something that is good."

Ms. Smith adds:

"None of us would consciously say 'yes' to anything we knew the devil founded. That is why we scream and run when the monster is revealed in scary movies, or haunted houses. The idea is to run as far as we can, as fast as we can from the demonically evil creatures. It is instinctive. Therefore, he (Lucifer) has to get around this by pretending to be something that isn't going to harm you, but it going to help or enhance you (like the promise of 'change').

"It looks like it is going to be a good thing, until you say 'yes' and take it unto yourself. Once you accept it, it reveals its' ugly nature and destroys you ... the addiction takes over, and bam! You are slammed shut in a trap."

Ms. Smith's thoughts were aimed at another threat to restoring a healthy economy—obesity. Two-thirds of all Americans are overweight; and the fastest growing segment of the U.S. obese society is *children.* Obesity stems from cravings, many of which are planted into our minds through the intentionally seductive advertising of unhealthy foods. The intentional indoctrination of children and adults to crave things (entitlements) that—in the long term—

are not good *for us* is both an art and science—a science that has been mastered by those out to master our every thought and action.

Other researchers agree that the way to rule people is to rule their thoughts and attitudes. In his book, *The Art of Seduction*[20] Robert Greene provides an unsuspecting nation with the tactics of modern-day political and social seducer's. As you read the list, consider how the Hidden Hand could achieve the goals set out in *The Protocols.* Some have already been introduced in previous chapters, but deserve repeating ... in context:

- *Choose the Right Victim* (a trusting people who believe in the good and the positive—the American people).
- *Create a False Sense of Security—Approach Indirectly* (the indoctrination of America's youth to question the wisdom of patriotic parents and the policies of the U.S).
- *Send Mixed Signals* ("America is the greatest nation on Earth and we have to change it", Candidate Barack Obama, 2008).
- *Appear to Be an Object of Desire—Create Triangles* (the Trilateral Commission, an organization that advertised its creation and intent to manage the world's economy; and the emergence of an Illuminati-Islamic Alliance against the Judeo-Christian world).
- *Create a Need—Stir Anxiety and Discontent* (encourage emotionally charged demon-

---

[20] Highbridge Audio, 2001,

strations and riots, as is currently occurring throughout the Middle East and around state capitols where collective bargaining is being debated).

- *Master the Art of Insinuation* (focus on the unreasonableness of the fiscally responsible and blame prosperous Americans—who already carry the bulk of the tax burden—for not paying their "fair share" of taxes, although the top 2% of America's prime movers already pay more than 60% of all taxes collected).

- *Enter Their Spirit* (use "entertainment" to condition the minds of the masses).

- *Create Temptation* (Promise the masses "something" for "nothing"—entitlements).

- *Keep Them in Suspense—What Comes Next?* (Gain control of the media and never reveal the truth, the whole truth, and nothing but the truth).

- *Use the Demonic Power of Words to Sow Confusion* (create pejorative terms for those identified as threats: "male chauvinist pig," "homophobe," and "infidel").

- *Pay Attention to Detail* (track all activities of those one wishes to control, with government databank).

- *Poeticize Your Presence* ("progressive" movement).

- *Disarm Through Strategic Weakness and Vulnerability* (play on the conscience of good-hearted people and politicians when they resist "change" that jeopardizes *the nation's* best interests).

- *Confuse Desire and Reality-The Perfect Illusion* (Stimulus packages that promise to "create jobs" when the jobs created are those *within* government and contribute nothing to the gross national product).

- *Isolate the Victim* (demonize leaders of the opposition party, i.e. Sarah Palin, Congresswoman, Michele Bachman, and Wisconsin Governor, Scott Walker).

- *Prove Yourself* (increase the frequency of public appearances and statements to boast about achievements—Hitler, Castro, Chaves and Obama).

- *Effect a Regression* (President's Clinton and Obama *appearing* to come to the middle when Republicans made significant gains in mid-term elections).

- *Stir Up the Transgressive and Taboo* (attempts to hang the noose of "racism" around the Tea Party Movement).

- *Use Spiritual Lures* (Obama's supposedly conversion from Islam to Christianity in order to become more acceptable to the American electorate).

- *Mix Pleasure with Pain* (extend entitlement and union benefits while driving the nation deeper into debt).

- *Give Them Space to Fall—The Pursuer Is Pursued* (the ploy to give in to Republican demands to keep the Bush Tax Cuts in place for only two years while ensuring that the economy will not improve as a result).

- *Use Physical Lures* (Republicans were totally ignored by the White House until they gained control of the House of Representatives. Suddenly, the President extended a hand for them to come to the White House for meetings and participate in the political process).

- *Master the Art of the Bold Move* (Democrats shoved legislation through Congress—and President Obama signed into law—changes in healthcare that the American people clearly did not understand ... nor want, ensuring a national debt crisis).

- *Beware of the Aftereffects* (Democrats knew that they could only push so far until the American people revolted. They took their gains and lived to fight another day. It's the socialist way).

For the sake of this discussion, I only provided one or two examples to each of Greene's secrets to seduction. I'm sure that you (the reader) can think of many others.

If one is to understand human behavior, it is important that one understands *the human being*. Not until the race comes to grips with *why* it was created can it expect to evolve into the being envisioned by its Creators (the "us" and "our" in Genesis 1:26). We have to believe that there is a greater purpose and that a greater Being is watching to see how we use the *free will* awarded to us.

When one begins to look at what is happening in the world—and who stands to gain the most by seducing the masses—all indicators point to a "supranational sovereignty of intellectual elites and world bankers," the group to which Illuminist David Rockefeller referred in his speech to the Trilateral Commission in the 1990s ... along with the I-IA, the modern-day implementers of *The Protocols*.

Never let this thought stray from the forefront of your ruminations: **The Protocols lay out a plan that is clearly intended to enslave the people of the world under a global, totalitarian government. It is this threat that looms supreme over freedom-loving people everywhere.**

I don't think that anyone who reads these words believes that human beings are *equal* in the categories that rank skill and talent. And, yet, none of us were meant to be another's slave. What is it that distinguishes a slave from a servant? The slave has no choice but to do as his master dictates. The servant serves voluntarily and is compensated justly. In that vein, all human beings are meant to be servants. But the implementers of *The Protocols* mean for the peoples of the world to have no choice in their destiny.

* * * * * * * * * *

Because the Lords of Seduction have been successful in orchestrating their plan, America is being "changed" from being "one nation under God, indivisible, with liberty and justice for all." Americans no longer know who we are; what we are supposed to do; what we are capable of doing; and how to go about doing it. We have become shackled by artfully-instilled doubt and heightened sensitivities about "offending" anyone who disagrees with us ... *including our professed enemies*. When we see a problem, we have been conditioned to be careful as to how we voice our concern. "Political Correctness" was skillfully installed by Americanism's enemies as a form of First Amendment censorship—a clever tactic in class warfare. Labels such as: "bigot" and "racist" are frequently applied to conservatives and patriots who speak out against discriminatory practices in the workplace or espouse the kinds of values that once took the U.S. to the top of the bell curve of the Cycle of Democracies.

Another result of being dumbed-down by those whose intent it is to "harm" or conduct acts of "treason," is that a vast majority of us no longer know how to recognize and develop God-given talents. Class warfare—as described in the Cloward-Piven Strategy to collapse America's economy—has been successful in making us feel guilty for the successes we have enjoyed. That it does keeps many of us from attempting to initiate the kinds of "change" that upgrade both individuals and nations for fear of being targeted by the political Left or labeled by our enemies as what many of us are—*proud capitalists.*

And I am not alone in my thoughts. Countless ideas set forth in this manuscript have been passed along to me by deep thinkers, prudent planners and effective workers. I certainly haven't been able to credit each and every one of them or to sort it all out, but my own inquisitiveness has caused me to mull over a number of fundamental questions. The question of whether to speak openly about them has been a subject of debate, too. Will it matter, and will anyone really care? That is the question which continues to be at the forefront of my mind.

Following the publication of *Shoulders of Giants* (1986), I received scores of letters and personal contacts from individuals who, after reading the book, believed it helped them address problems with greater insight and allowed them to deal with the ups and downs of life more effectively. I was encouraged to expand its scope.

After *The Oath* was published, reviewers and readers throughout America let me know how it changed—or affirmed—their views on America's problems and encouraged those readers to dig deeper for Truth.

In *The Lords of Seduction* I have attempted to balance disturbing facts with optimism and offered a number of practical recommendations for dealing with complex dilemmas that threaten America's existence as a free and fiscally sound society governed by "auto-determination." I've tried to demonstrate how people from a spectrum of backgrounds can rely upon the experiences of past achievers to establish winning attitudes, and become prime "movers and shakers" in an America of their own choosing.

I have often wondered what the historian will have to say about the choices we (as a people) are making today and the current faces sitting at the table where the Lords of Seduction plan your future ... and mine.

If America is to remain a great nation, it will have to once again become a nation ruled by good, caring *and vigilant* people who know what can be realistically achieved and set their minds to seeing that the children know how to separate truth from propaganda ... and good from evil.

CHAPTER 4

In the scheme of things, it's rather easy to identify the motives of extraordinarily ambitious people and determine if they are to be trusted with the health, welfare, and prosperity of others. The formula is simple—one I have previously referenced: pay more attention to what *they do* and less to what *they say*. The science known as "Sociology" is the study of group behavior. "Psychology" is the science of individual behavior. Both teach how to predict and understand human nature. Look at the person's (or the organizations) collective character. Look at his (its) past. Look at the people with whom he (it) associates. Learn to read body language to tell when someone is lying. Before you leap on anyone's bandwagon, look at the kinds of individuals and movements with which that person or organization has been affiliated. And even then, exercise caution and consider the long-range consequences of being affiliated with him, her, or it.

Perhaps this line of thinking is what former President Ronald Reagan had in mind when he said (about a treaty with Soviet Union over nuclear missile issues) "Trust, but verify." It is a sad statement on humanity; but for evil-minded people (as is set forth in *The Protocols* and

Communist Manifesto), "truth" is whatever needs to be said to further one's cause.

In a democracy, it is the role of *the people* to hold their elected officials and appointed leaders accountable for their actions. Perhaps, the result of the mid-term elections of 2010 makes this point.

A group of modern-day Washington overlords—with their Puppet-in-Chief at the helm—were ramming through legislation that the majority of the electorate had clearly expressed they didn't want. Poll after poll indicated that most Americans were opposed to the expanding role of government and the fact that it was mortgaging the nation's (and, in turn, it's children's) future.

When "average Americans" were given the choice to make their discontent known, they voted for "change" alright. They *voted out* many of those who—in their own, self-serving quest for power and favors—had turned a deaf ear to their bosses ... *the people.* Those who weren't voted out received a clear message from the majority of an exorcised electorate who had finally learned the definition of slavery: *"the state or condition of being held in involuntary servitude as the property of somebody else."*[21]

The previously silent majority roared. The people sent Washington a message: Government had overstepped its authority, forcing "government rule" on the American people. But, the elections of 2010 should only be viewed as "a good start," 2012 provides a chance to return to reason—reason that Americans can *truly* believe in.

Politicians often underestimate the will of the American people, the love that most Americans have for their country, and their continued ability "to rally" when faced with the return of any form of slavery to our borders.

---

[21] Bing, Web

As has been done before, if those into whose hands the future of America are in do not live up to promises and expectations, a new wave of "change" will be forthcoming. On November 3, 2010, it appeared that no one in political office was safe, regardless of party affiliation. Now that they have been awakened—and see how powerful is their voice—*the people* must continue to "change" the faces of government until they get what is demanded: prudence, reason, and accountability *from* government. On the other hand, Americans should never underestimate the resolve and power of the Hidden Hand and their ability to recruit ANY politician to their plan, regardless of stated party affiliations. Money and power talk. Though periodically "taking a shellacking"[22] the Hidden Hand is relentless. Not until it is dismembered from the body of Evil that it represents will America be free of its influence.

Remember, it is America's ability to "rally" behind high-minded causes that her enemies have always feared most ... and precisely what *The Protocols* purport to confiscate. Concern over America's ability to "rally" has driven divisive legislation and regulations from the Left that were clearly intended to feed a trusted tactic of class warfare: "divide and conquer." And, for that reason, eroding America's ability to "rally" has been at the heart of the agendas of its enemies (foreign and domestic) since a group of freedom-loving, angry and courageous colonists signed their names to a document that declared independence from an 18th century monarchy and the feudal system he represented.

---

[22] President Barack Obama, in his first conference following the sweeping his party took in the mid-term elections.

On November 3, 2010, once again, Americans from all walks of life sent a loud and clear message to the children of socialism:

> *"Mr. President and your progressive Democrat cohorts, we reject your kind of 'change'! Let's get our fiscal house in order ... before it is too late."*

Once the 2010 Election honeymoon is over—and providing that newly entrusted lawmakers continue to look out for *America's best interests*—the stage is set for more "pro-American change" in 2012. The current crisis evolved around two opposing political ideologies: cut government spending or cut, from the salaries and profits of America's prime movers, more of their earnings by imposing even higher taxes. It could be—and should be—the political showdown of this generation ... and America's best hope to restore a sense of fiscal prudence. As he and his cohorts put a new face on a Cloward-Piven socialist, it will be interesting to see what words Barack Obama reads off his Tele-prompters. The I-IA will surely employ tactics gleaned from the *Art of Seduction:*

- *Prove Yourself* (increase the frequency of public appearances and statements to boast about achievements and blame Republicans for whatever failures he's had).
- *Effect a Regression* (President Obama— as did President Bill Clinton—will appear to "change" courses, become the

voice of reason, and govern from the middle).

- *Stir Up the Transgressive and Taboo; Use the Demonic Power of Words to Sow Confusion;* and *Master the Art of Insinuation.* (Obama accused the Republicans of political terrorism, "holding legislation to address the debt crisis hostage" and talked of the "ransom" that he and his fellow Democrats were going to be forced to pay to reduce entitlements to the elderly and the poor. The American people can expect to hear how the Republicans intend to abandon the poor and elderly, when—in their Cloward-Piven Strategy— it is the *socialist Democrats* who intend to collapse the nation's economy and every entitlement program that Capitalism funds.)

When one becomes aware of tactics used by the Lords of Seduction, their words and actions become sophomorically transparent. It is doubtful that the kind of "transparency" of which Candidate Obama spoke in his run-up for the presidency will ever be displayed by his administration. And yet, it is the kind of transparency that the American people deserve.

We'll have to wait and see if the newly elected members of Congress will fall for additional tactics of seduction that will surely take place over the ensuing years and whether they will stand their ground and emerge victoriously in bringing about the kind of "change" they've been commissioned by the American electorate to orchestrate.

Congress has the power and authority to create the kind of America they so choose. Never have I seen this fact expressed so succinctly as in the final column of journalist Charley Reese, who in the Orlando Sentinel wrote:

> "Politicians are the only people in the world who create problems and then campaign against them.
>
> "Have you ever wondered if both the Democrats and the Republicans are against deficits, why do we have deficits? Have you ever wondered if all the politicians are against inflation and high taxes, why do we have inflation and high taxes? (I believe it is because the I-IA has strategically placed individuals beholding to it *in both parties*).
>
> "You and I don't propose a federal budget. The President does (or is supposed to).
>
> "You and I don't have the Constitutional authority to vote on appropriations. The House of Representatives does.
>
> "You and I don't write the tax code; Congress does.
>
> "You and I don't set fiscal policy; Congress does. You and I don't control monetary policy; the (Illuminati-owned and operated) Federal Reserve Bank does.
>
> "One hundred senators, 435 congressmen, one President, and nine Supreme

Court justices equates to 555 human beings—out of the 350 million—who are directly, legally, morally, and individually responsible for the domestic problems that plague this country.

"I excluded the members of the Federal Reserve Board because that problem was created by the Congress. *In 1913, Congress delegated its Constitutional duty to provide a sound currency to a federally chartered, but private, central bank.* (Why—except to give the ever-powerful "supranational sovereignty" the financial reins)? I excluded all the special interests and lobbyists for a sound reason. They have no *legal authority.* They have no ability to coerce a Senator, a Congressman, or a President to do one cotton-picking thing. I don't care if they offer a politician $1 million dollars in cash.

"The politician has the power to accept or reject it. No matter what the lobbyist promises, it is the legislator's responsibility to determine how he votes.

"Those 555 human beings (the bulk of whom are attorneys) spend much of their energy (doing what politicians do better than any other profession) convincing you that what they did is not their fault. They cooperate in this common con regardless of party. (The only explanation is that they answer to something other than Reason).

"What separates a politician from a normal human being is an excessive amount of gall (audacity). No normal human being would have the gall of a Speaker (Nancy Pelosi) who stood up and criticized the President (George Bush) for creating deficits, (when *she* and her senatorial accomplice, Harry Reid, controlled the *only branch of government* in which deficit spending originates).

"The President can *only propose* a budget (though President Obama has yet to propose one for fiscal year 2010-2011.) He cannot force the Congress to accept it.

"The Constitution, which is the supreme law of the land, gives sole responsibility to the House of Representatives for originating and approving appropriations and taxes ... House members, not the President, can approve any budget they want. If the President vetoes it, they can pass it over his veto, if they agree to.

"It seems inconceivable that a nation of 350 million cannot replace 555 people who stand convicted (by present facts) of incompetence and irresponsibility. I can't think of a single domestic problem that is not traceable directly to those 555 people. When you fully grasp the plain truth that 555 people exercise the complete power of the federal government, then it must follow that what exists is what they want to exist (or have been strong-armed to create).

"If the tax code is unfair, it's because they want it unfair. If the budget is in the red, it's because they want it in the red. If the Army and Marines are in Iraq, Afghanistan, and Libya, it's because they want them to be in those places.

"If they do not (pay into nor) receive social security, but are on an elite retirement plan not available to the people, it's because they want it that way. There are no insoluble government problems.

"Do not let these 555 people shift the blame to bureaucrats, *whom they hire and whose jobs they can abolish*; to lobbyists, whose gifts and advice they can reject; to regulators, to whom they give the power to regulate and from whom they can take this power. Above all, do not let them con you into the belief that there exist disembodied mystical forces like "the economy, inflation, or politics" that prevent them from doing what they take an oath to do.

"Those 555 people—and they alone—are responsible. They—and they alone—have the power. They (including the president of the United States)—should be held accountable by the people who are their bosses, provided the voters have the

gumption to manage their employees,
public servants, one and all ... "

What Mr. Reese didn't factor into his analysis is the effect of a "supranational sovereignty" in the American political system and that many of the five hundred and fifty-five he referenced are puppets, dancing to strings controlled by the Hidden Hand and its extended cabal— the Illuminati-Islamic Alliance. If the majority of these 555 people had the guts to solve America's problems, we wouldn't have the problems facing us today.

But, *The Protocols,* clearly, spelled out how America's officials, lawmakers, and judges are to be "chosen," put into office and *remain* in office:

> "We choose presidents ... we shall remake all legislatures ... our judges will be elected by us ..."

According to *The Protocols,* each of these promises was intended for the Lords of Seduction to:

> "... reconstruct all institutions and to become the sovereign lord of those who have left to us the rights of their power by laying them down voluntarily."

The power to levy taxes in a progressive manner was a crucial part of *The Protocols'* drafters. To discriminate against prosperity and promote poverty is a crucial part of Cloward-Piven Strategy and the Illuminati's policy of seduction and sedition. Syndicated columnist, Star Parker, called it a "Return to the Plantation" for poor black

Americans. She concludes her article by saying, "Americans can accept Barack Obama's invitation to move onto the (government) Plantation. Or they can choose personal responsibility and freedom."

Here's what *The Protocols* reveal about a government's ability to tax its citizens:

> "The tax upon the poor man is a seed of revolution and works to the detriment of the State ... Quite apart from this, a tax on capitalists diminishes the growth of wealth in private hands in which we have in these days concentrated as a counterpoise to the strength of their State finances. A tax increasing in a percentage ration to capital [progressive income tax] is useful to us for the sole reason that *it excites trouble and discontent* among the masses."

The last statement is a clear indication that "class warfare" is an essential part of the Illuminati's plan to destroy existing governments and replace them with a totalitarian-styled global government and that those who are supposed to be righting the Ship of State already feel the grip of the Hidden Hand around their necks. It also affirms the premise that no amount of taxation on the prime movers of a society can fund all the entitlements that the masses vote themselves. It has been said that if all the wealth of the top 2% of Americans (the super-rich) were confiscated by the U.S. Government, it wouldn't put a noticeable dent in the national debt.

If there remains any question as to the authenticity of *The Protocols of the Learned Elders of Zion* and its intent, the examples provided heretofore should erase any doubt. The secular implementers of the plan have successfully made the America of our fathers disappear right in front of our eyes—like a slight-of-hand magician.

Though the Obama White House attempted to project the image that it was capable of running the affairs of a nation, the vast majority of his cabinet were investment bankers and intellectual elite. They had never run as much as a lemonade stand. President Obama's administration is primarily comprised of career politicians and intellectuals, who—by their actions—appear to serve as "puppets" to a higher Order. It is no wonder that the administration's attempts to solve the recessionary problems of 2009-2011 failed. Or, in the Illuminati's eyes, did they achieve precisely what they were selected to do? Transfer America's wealth and resources to investment and world banks owned by the Illuminati. The story of how it all came to pass is portrayed in a made-for-television movie entitled *Too Big To Fail.* As of a result of the Cloward-Piven tactics that Barack Obama and his handlers orchestrated within U.S. financial institutions, America now faces the largest deficit and debt in history—a debt so great that many economists doubt whether it can be paid off. The result is: the American dollar will lose value against other world currencies and commodities. Most experts agree that there will be a push to create a single currency, worldwide. And, the currency of the New World Order *will not be the dollar!* It will be whatever the Illuminati choose it to be.

During the Obama Administration, "intellectual" politicians, bankers, and labor unions appear to have been driving America's Ship of State by *Mastering the Art of the Bold Move.* It is easy to point the finger of blame for

America's ills; however, our nation's current state of affairs cannot be placed on the shoulders of politicians and their puppeteers. The fault lies *with us*, the American people. Sitting still while 555 politicians, unions, and intellectuals make irresponsible business decisions on our behalf makes little sense. In fact, it borders on insanity. And now that we have seen inside the I-IA's plan, if we allow it to continue, the term, "insanity" can be aptly applied to those of us who—for too long—have remained silent ... and sat still.

If President Obama had been truly interested in stimulating the American economy, he would have assembled *the best* minds *in the business world*—successful people from small and big business, individuals who have been in the trenches and pulled themselves up by the bootstraps. He would have turned—for advice—to people who built successful businesses and managed a workforce—people who had actually created jobs. Then, he would have *followed* the recommendations of true-to-life job-creators rather than theorists and intellectuals. But after assembling panels of elitists, President Obama ignored their recommendations, proving that stimulating the U.S. economy is not the president's objective. Remaining in office for as long as possible and doing the I-IA's bidding *is*.

If President Obama had been truly interested in creating a healthcare plan that would provide quality healthcare for all Americans, he would have assembled a commission of *practicing* physicians and healthcare providers who live on the front lines of disease prevention and early detection. Instead he assembled a panel of *administrative* healthcare providers and university-based professors. But, providing affordable, quality healthcare for Americans is not the president's objective. Having government control the lives of Americans *is*, regardless of the costs in dollars ... or liberties.

If President Obama had been sincere about solving the problems on Main Street he would have assembled small-town bankers, retailers, and service-oriented professionals who actually conduct their businesses on Main Street ... not Wall Street. But solving problems that the "average Americans" are experiencing on Main Street is not the president's objective. Deceiving small town America into supporting the agenda that he was "bred and reared since early childhood" to install *is*.

The facts are: President Obama has not acted in America's best interest. He went along with the current day puppet-masters of *The Protocols,* which promised:

> "The administrators, whom we shall choose from among the public ... will not be persons trained in the arts of government, and will therefore easily become pawns in our game in the hands of men of learning and genius who will be their advisers, specialists *bred and reared from early childhood to rule the affairs of the whole world."*

It is easy to see why Barack Obama is not in touch with the average American. He was never intended to be. Though his past has previously been discussed, in the context of the preceding excerpt from *The Protocols,* Barack Obama's education and rearing must be revisited.

As a child, he never lived among us ... on the mainland. He didn't go to school with us. For much of his life, he lived outside the U.S., was reared in a Muslim family and (supposedly) attended Occidental College and two Ivy League colleges (on "foreign student" scholarships, which is one of the prime reasons he won't release his college transcripts).

The first line of Ayn Rand's *Atlas Shrugged* recurs throughout the book: "Who is John Galt?" The question that should be on every American's lips—including the mainstream media—should be *"Who is Barack Hussein Obama?"* This enigmatic character, who has deceived and seduced an entire nation of trusting people, represents the ideal "puppet" for the Hidden Hand ... as described in *The Protocols.*

Now, here's a conspiracy theory that deserves consideration. Following the Civil Rights movement and the subsequent installation of "affirmative action" and that of "political correctness," **IF** a group of atheistic despots wanted to seize the U.S. White House without firing a shot, how could they do it?

They might locate an atheistic white woman who had an affinity for non-white Muslim men and encourage her to bear a half-white, half non-white child, who could be "reared from early childhood (in a Muslim environment) to rule the affairs of the whole world."[23] And knowing that the teachings and laws of Islam would assist the group of global despots in achieving their mission: *change the world from Judeo-Christian ideologies, to Islam, then to atheism, the child would be versed in each religion—as well as in the absence, thereof.*

Realizing—*at the time*—that such a child could never be indoctrinated to Islamic ways if he were reared on the U.S. mainland, his mother would take him to some primarily Muslim country until he was ready to return to

---

[23] *The Protocols of the Learned Elders of Zion,* Ibid.

the U.S. and receive his post-graduate education in liberal U.S. universities that promoted progressive socialism and secularism. Naturally, with professors Cloward and Piven on staff at Columbia University, the tutelage of these two "specialists" would be a must. And to protect their puppet from his past, all records and collect transcripts would be sealed from the lights of publicity.

Because Chicago is a place where elections are known be manipulated in the favor of the Party of Democrats, their "puppet" would move there and—with the aid of "advisors" and "specialists"—be vaulted onto the state and national political scenes, where his ascension to the presidency would be ensured by a complicit mainstream media.

Barack Obama's short stint as a "community organizer" in lower income projects in Chicago exposed him only to a small segment of America. Most of the people Barack Obama "organized" into voting blocs neither had jobs, nor created jobs, further insulating him from mainstream America.

Facts are: The Illuminati's "puppet" lacked the experience to be president and continues to require the guidance of Illuminati advisors and handlers.

Barack Obama has yet to grasp what working Americans want ... and need. He never will. He never held a real job or supervised anyone who did. He was never meant to be a policy-maker or a prime mover ... at least not in capitalistic terms. Abdicating his responsibility as an Illinois' Senatorial decision-maker, he voted "present" the majority of the time. Barack Obama was "bred and reared" to be a pretty face on a demonic plan— to front for an I-IA plan to collapse the United States of America. And, if America is to survive Barack Obama, both the face and the plan must be exposed for what they are ... and replaced with a president and set of advisers who have the experience and audacity to lead America back to prosperity and respectability.

President Obama is surrounded by a council of men and women who are greatly responsible for the problems on Wall Street ... and Main Street. He listened to the architects of the Fannie Mae and Freddie Mac debacle, offering no solution before a near collapse of the U.S. economy. In short, the President failed to exercise the kind of leadership that the American people deserve. *He had to ignore* the admonitions of *the people.* He had no choice. Barack Obama couldn't have changed course if he had wanted to. He was—and is—owned by those who created him *in their own image*—the Illuminati-Islamic Alliance. He is their "puppet," no more ... no less.

In keeping with the seduction tactic: *Send Mixed Signals,* the President and his I-IA masters have created disarray on a number of fronts, including what the weekly numbers of Americans who apply for un-employment really means. Using Barack Obama to deliver their seductive message, The Lords of Seduction have successfully orchestrated confusion about the current status of the U.S. economy, how jobs are lost, how jobs are actually created and the role of the Obama administration in effecting both scenarios.

It doesn't take a genius to see that government may put people on the payroll and use taxpayer money to pay salaries and bonuses, such a "fix" is only temporary and continues to drain the national treasury—an example of the Cloward-Piven Strategy and, therefore, a likely intention of the Obama Administration. A better term for the kinds of "jobs" that the Obama Administration has "created" is "retribution"—payback to those who orchestrated the breeding and rearing of their "puppet" from early childhood, as well as those that supported Obama's election and promoted the socialistic ideology of the Democrat Party that he was—long ago—chosen to represent. History will record that during Barack Obama's presidency, the greatest transfer of wealth and resources in world history took place, much of it *out of the U.S.* Trillions of U.S. dollars were transferred into the Illuminati's hands ... at the expense of the American taxpayer and homeowner, never to be returned to its rightful owners.

A masterfully-executed plan it was ... the creation of Barack Hussein Obama from a Muslim-Indonesian child named Barry Soetoro.

CHAPTER 5

T he informed patriot who unashamedly votes his conscience is the world's most powerful weapon against deception and seduction. And, it is this weapon that must be used to expose and thwart the most prolific example of mass seduction that has ever been reduced to the written word: *The Protocols of the Learned Elders of Zion.* This once-secret declaration against freedom and Godliness was exposed in an 1897 book published by Philip Stepanov, a resident of a small town just south of St. Petersburg, Russia. Ever since, *The Protocols* have been the subject of much debate. But, did Stepanov really know what he had republished and how it would be revised and used in future centuries against humanity?

Some claim *The Protocols* to be a hoax—a tool used by their enemies to cast a veil of suspicion over the Jewish people worldwide, while the *real* despots worked in the shadows. From everything that I can gather, true Zionists (those who earnestly embrace and foster the "theocracy of God,")[24] could not have been involved in the drafting of *The Protocols.* The reason is that the document advocates the removal of God from the minds of men; an objective

---

[24] *Webster's New World College Dictionary, Third Edition*, 1998 Simon & Shuster Macmillan Company, New York, NY.

that runs absolutely counter to Zionism. The following excerpt states the seducer's mission as plainly as can be:

> "It is indispensable for us to undermine all faith, to tear out of the mind (of our subjects) the very principle of god-head and the spirit, and to put in its place arithmetical calculations and material needs."

From what I know about the Christians and Jews who believe in and adamantly support the "theocracy of God," I am convinced that, although the drafters of the protocols referred to its elders as "Zionists," they were anything but.

Others have said that the document represented the policy of a self-professed cabal of despots and was stolen from an Illuminati-infiltrated Masonic Lodge in Paris, France. Ostensibly, the document was then taken to Russia, just prior to the 1917 Bolshevik Revolution. Were *The Protocols* used as a war plan to replace Russia's Czar Nicholas II with V.I. Lenin's communist style of government? Was this the reason that Stepanov translated and republished them in Russian? The timing, outcome, and political motives of those behind the Revolution certainly lend credence to the possibility.

And, then there are those who are committed to protecting the true identities and ideologies of conspirators who called themselves: "Elders," a group of self-proclaimed "despots" who abandoned the religion of their birth and converted to what *The Protocols* calls a new "revolutionary faith," in which God is visibly absent. There is also evidence that suggests *for political reasons, the early founders* of Catholicism were more interested in *using*

Christianity to control the masses than to spread God's gospel. I will go deeper into this in a future chapter.

As you will come to see, *The Protocols* appear to be a living document, revered and followed by a group of modern-day audacious and atheistic conspirators who aspire to rule the world ... no matter what the cost.

While its origin may forever be subject to question, portions of the document are, clearly, consistent with the way that the world has been—and is—being strategically manipulated toward totalitarianism.

Whether the secret declaration was drafted by a small group of delusional dreamers, who set out to create a One-World Government, or fabricated as part of an equally sinister plan to falsely accuse legitimate Zionist Elders of doing so, the creators and modern-day implementers of *The Protocols* unequivocally qualify to be labeled: "*Lords of Seduction.*"

* * * * * * * * *

Deception is an age-old tactic used to gain advantage over others. In *Apollyon Rising: 2012,* author Thomas Horn provides an example of mass seduction, focusing on what he believes to be a plethora of evidence that accuses high-ranking members within Freemasonry of using false flag operations as a way to protect secrets, from the public as well as "from lower-degree Masons."

It is the identity and sinister intentions of men who would *use* "lower-degree Freemasons" for personal gain that should be the focus of attention, and not Masonry itself.

The Sovereign Grand Commander, Albert Pike, wrote in the Masonic handbook *Morals and Dogma*:

"Masonry, like all Religions, all the Mysteries ... conceals its secrets from all except the Adepts and Sages, or the Elect, and uses false explanations and misinterpretations of its symbols to mislead those who deserve only to be misled (Lucifer's disciples); to conceal the Truth, which it calls Light, from them, and to draw them (Luciferians) away from it (the Truth)."[25]

When I read the preceding statement, I was quite disappointed to see how similar the Sovereign Grand Commander's statement is to those contained within *The Protocols.*

It is more than possible that—though early Masonic leaders tried to prevent it—occult forces infiltrated Freemasonry before, during, and after the Revolutionary Era of the United States of America (*The New Atlantis*) and in the construction of its capitol city, monuments and currency. Horn believes that Barack Obama could be the prophesied antichrist or, at least, the precursor of the antichrist (what Revelation labels, *"the false prophet"*) rising from the halls of—and surrounded by—symbols of paganism and occultism.

It would be a clever ploy, indeed, if the drafters of *The Protocols* made it *appear* as though "The Elders of Zion" were official religious leaders of Jews and Christians, when in fact, they were Luciferian secularists—*Promethianists*, founders of the "revolutionary faith" of Gnostic doctrines—

---

[25] Albert Pike, *Morals and Dogma* (Charleston: Supreme Council of the 33rd Degree for the Southern Jurisdiction of the United States, 1871, 210

whose origin was solidified in occult Freemasonry and 'scientific' Marxism,[26] professing to no traditional religion and doing Lucifer's bidding on the world stage.

The last sentence of the preceding paragraph is key to understanding the message of *The Lords of Seduction*. The sinister plan outlined in *The Protocols of the Learned Elders of Zion* is not religion-based, nor does it appear that its crafters where beholding to any deity. It is the worship of power, (the kind of an ungodly nature) that holds them in its grasp.

In *Apollyon Rising 2012,* Thomas Horn also chronicles how—as individuals moved away from the religions of their youth and moved toward secular-based secret societies—the intermingling of beliefs became common place.

Rosicrucianism, a movement that grew out of the Knights Templar, became "the inner doctrine of Masonry" according to Horn. He went on to say that Freemasonry "is the mingling of Christianity with paganism."[27] Therefore, it is understandable that Promethianists seeking cover would cloak themselves with the respectability of Masonry.

Horn argues that the secret *elite* (there's that word again—the one used by David Rockefeller in his address to the Trilateral Commission) of early European Masonry—without the knowledge of lower-level, fellow Masons—cleverly crafted a document that could be used for a greater purpose:

> "... to mislead those who deserve only to be misled; to conceal the Truth ... and to draw

---

[26] *Apollyon Rising 2012: The Lost Symbol Found and the Final Mystery of the Great Seal Revealed,* Defender, Crane, Missouri, 2009
[27] *Ibid*

them (those who deserve to be misled) away
from it (the Truth)."

Adam Weishaupt, founder of a secret confederacy
that became the Bavarian Illuminati created the "blueprint
for politicized Illuminism. Though Weishaupt was born
into a Jewish family, he converted to Christianity and
became a Jesuit Priest. His "conversion" took place at *the
same time* that he was involved with Witchcraft. "Due to
pressures brought to bear by European governments,
witchcraft was put out of existence by the Pope. And so,
Jesuits had to secularize."[28]   Not only did Weishaupt
denounce his native Judaism, he also later denounced
Christianity and God Himself. This denouncement of God
is consistent with the directives contained within *The
Protocols.*

Along with some of his fellow Jesuits, Weishaupt
created a "Luciferian Movement that was used to preserve
and promote the ancient Black Arts of Babylonian and
Druid Witchcraft ... Weishaupt's goal was to use
Humanism (Atheism) to ... set up a One-World
Government ... and he *used* Freemasonry to achieve that
end."[29]

It is important to pause here for a minute and reflect
on what you have just read. The man considered to be the
father of the Illuminati, denounced God and set out to
create a One-World Government by *infiltrating
Freemasonry* pretending to be what he was not to achieve
his objective—create an Invisible Empire. Is it mere
coincidence that the *Protocols of the Learned Elders of
Zion* explains in great detail how such a One-World

---

[28] *Eight Sabbats for Witches*, Stewart Farrar, pg. 80-81
[29] *http://www.religiouscounterfeits.org/ml_adamweishaupt.htm*

Government is to be created? It would seem then that—whoever first set pen to the document—a group of professed atheists, who identified themselves as "Illuminati"— adopted *The Protocols* as an official plan of action ... hiding behind Zionism and Freemasonry all the while.

I am not a Mason; however, based upon my own research and from having first-hand knowledge of the character of my father and other Freemasons with whom he and I associated, I am convinced that the vast majority of Masons are/were unaware of how they are/were being used to promote an agenda of resident Evil ... if they are.

In his book, *The Fourth Reich of the Rich,* Des Griffin, outlined Weishaupt's "World Revolution" and the goals that Weishaupt and his cabal of self-designated Illuminists hoped to achieve:

1. The abolishment of all ordered government
2. The abolishment of all private property
3. The abolishment of all inheritance
4. The abolishment of all patriotism
5. The abolishment of all religion
6. The abolishment of all family and marriage
7. The creation of a World Government or World Order that would take that place of all of the above things that had been abolished."[30]

The list could have been lifted—almost verbatim—from *The Protocols.*

And, to give credence to an Illuminati-Islamic Alliance (I-IA), let us pause to consider how radical Islam might work into Weishaupt's plan. In a previous chapter, I wrote

---

[30] *http//www.religiouscounterfeits.org/ml_goal.htm*

that "change" involves replacing one thing with another. Therefore, using the craft of deductive reasoning let us consider that if both the Illuminati and radical Islam intended to "change" America from a Judeo-Christian nation of patriots and install another form of social structure, it is conceivable that they could find a way to change the U.S. Constitution and replace it with Sharia Law, a form of totalitarianism that could *initially* provide the basis of a One-World Government. Some might ask ... would this be such a bad thing?

Let us look at an insider's view of Sharia Law—a woman who has lived under its iron hand.

The following was written by Nonie Darwish, a product of Sharia Law. These are her thoughts thoughts—as she penned them—and not hearsay.

> "In the Muslim faith a Muslim man can marry a child as young as one year old and have sexual intimacy with this child, consummating the marriage by nine. The dowry is given to the family in exchange for the woman (who becomes his slave) and for the purchase of the private parts of the woman, to use her as a toy.
>
> Even though a woman is abused, she cannot obtain a divorce. To prove rape, the woman must have four (4) male witnesses. Often after a woman has been raped, she is returned to her family and the family must return the dowry. The family has the right to execute her (an honor killing) to restore the honor of the family. Husbands can beat

their wives 'at will' and the man does not have to say why he has beaten her.

The husband is permitted to have four (4) wives and a temporary wife for an hour (prostitute) at his discretion.

The Muslim law controls the private as well as the public life of the woman. In the Western World (America) Muslim men are starting to demand Sharia Law so the wife cannot obtain a divorce and he can have full and complete control of her. It is amazing and alarming how many of our sisters and daughters attending American Universities are now marrying Muslim men and submitting themselves and their children unsuspectingly to the law.

When will the National Organization of Women take a stand against those who practice—or would impose—Sharia Law on America ... any part of it?"[31]

It's a good question, where is the National Organization of Women? An organization that, during previous administrations, has been front and center representing *women's rights,* those of all women ... or so they pretended.

In *Ripping the West in Two,* author and lecturer Nonie Darwish also says the goal of radical Islamists is "to impose their law on the world, ripping Western law and liberty in two." She recently authored the book, *Cruel and Usual Punishment: The Terrifying Global Implications of Islamic Law.* In her latest book, Darwish warns about

---

[31] Joys of Muslim Women by Nonie Darwish

creeping law—what it is; what it means; and how it is manifested in Islamic countries.

"For the West," she says, "Radical Islamists are working to impose Sharia on the world. If that happens, Western civilization will be destroyed. Westerners generally assume all religions encourage a respect for the dignity of each individual. Islamic law (Sharia) teaches that non-Muslims should be subjugated or killed in this world. Peace and prosperity for one's children is not as important as assuring that Islamic law rules everywhere in the Middle East and eventually in the world.

"While Westerners tend to think that all religions encourage some form of the golden rule, Islam teaches two systems of ethics—one for Muslims and another for non-Muslims. Building on tribal practices of the seventh century, it encourages the side of humanity that wants to take from and subjugate others.

While Westerners tend to think in terms of religious people developing a personal understanding of and relationship with God, Sharia advocates executing people who ask difficult questions that could be *interpreted** as criticism.

It's hard to imagine, that in this day and age, Islamic scholars agree that those who criticize Islam or choose to stop being

---

* Emphasis Added

Muslim should be executed. *(This is what is confusing about Barack Obama's/Barry Soetoro's 'conversion' from Islam to a Black form of Theology.)* Sadly, while talk of an Islamic reformation is common and even assumed by many in the West, such murmurings in the Middle East are silenced through intimidation."

While Westerners are accustomed to an increase in religious tolerance over time, Darwish explains how petro dollars are being used to grow an extremely intolerant form of political Islam in her native Egypt and elsewhere.

"In twenty years there will be enough Muslim voters in the U.S. to elect the President by themselves! Rest assured they will do so ... You can look at how they have taken over several towns in the USA ... Dearborn, Michigan is one ... and there are others ...

I think everyone in the U.S. should be required to read this, but with the ACLU there is no way this will be widely publicized, unless each of us sends it on!

It is too bad that so many are disillusioned with life and Christianity to accept Muslims as peaceful. Some may be, but they have an army that is willing to shed blood in the name of Islam ... the peaceful support the warriors with their finances and own kind of patriotism to their religion. *While America is getting rid of*

Christianity from all public sites and erasing
God from the lives of children the Muslims
are planning a great jihad on America." [32]*

It is important to note that the words you have just read came directly from a woman who grew up in a Muslim culture. Her father was buried as a martyr because he led an attack on Israel. Her words affirm the suspicions of many American patriots ... that a great seduction is underway ... and the trusting American people are targets.

Using Islamists to do their bidding is consistent with the manner in which the Illuminati used Freemasonry to acquire positions of respectability throughout the world.

How the Illuminati intends to control—or do away with—the religion of Islam, once they use it to take over the world, is a question that remains to be answered, but one that has surely been addressed in Inner Circle meetings. How the Illuminati will deceive its current partner (radical Islam) could turn out to be the seduction of all seductions.

Des Griffin's aforementioned book goes on to affirm my own suspicions: "The use of deception, to make *it seem** as if the goals of the Order of the Illuminati were the same as the goals of Christianity; Adam Weishaupt wrote to his Chief Assistant, Her Von Zwack: 'The most admirable thing of it all is that the great Protestant and Reformed Theologians (Lutherans and Calvinists *who belong to our Order)** really believe they see in it the true and genuine mind of the Christian Religion."

Clearly, Weishaupt and *his* "Elders" relished in the fact that they deceived and seduced men who trusted them.

---

[32] Ibid, *http://www.religiouscounterfeits.org/ml_adamweishaupt.htm*
* Emphasis added

In another letter, Weishaupt "told of how he would *pretend* * that the Illuminati were Christians," and that he would then substitute that idea with 'The Religion of Reason' or rationalism ... "Oh man (mankind)," he wrote insultingly, "what cannot you be brought to believe?"[33]

The perplexing part of it all is: knowing that we are being seduced, the American people seem willing to ignore the consequences.

The abolishment of religion is not limited to Christianity or the Catholic Church. Investigator, William T. Still, reports that others in Weishaupt's Order wrote of difficulties in luring candidates away from other established religions. One such member, Baron Von Knigge, wrote that its recruits would abandon the cause, "... were Illuminati to let them know that our General (Weishaupt) holds all religion to be a lie, and uses even Deism (the Religion of Reason) ... *to lead men by the nose.* * "[34]

Clearly, the ancient crafts of seduction and deception are effective tools in promoting one's cause. And, they have been used to perfection by the I-IA and its predecessors. Thomas Horn and others have taken the position that the use of the secret meaning of Masonic symbols by America's founding fathers is the work of Lucifer. This author—on the other hand—believes the opposite to be the case. My conclusions are not only based upon what I observed in my father and his fellow Masons, but from an excerpt found in *The Meaning of Masonry,* composed by early 19th century mystic Mason and mystic, Walter Leslie Wilmshurst. In the *Forward* to a book which is distributed to Masons throughout the world, Wilmshurst writes: "Freemasonry is based on three great principles:

---

[33] *Ibid*
[34] *Ibid*
  Emphasis added

brotherly love, relief (of pain and suffering), and truth ... it is a *system of morality** veiled in allegory and illustrated by symbols."[35]

I truly believe that the majority of Freemasons believe this to be the intent of the organization to which they belong. I *know* that my father did. We can only hope that those who control the reins of Freemasonry, today, continue to believe in the Wilmshurst creed and stand firm against those who would use Masonry for sinister objectives. People have to be cautious. A new enemy has joined the long-standing one. Publically, Islamic leaders claim that theirs is a religion of peace. As demonstrated in the previous chapter, privately, they preach an opposing message.

From everything I can ascertain, the *true* intent of Freemasonry is in promoting good. That the "noble science" has been seized at the highest degrees by those who intend to deceive right-minded members appears to be quite likely. The founding fathers of the United States of America (many of whom were Masons) were aware of how European Orders of Freemasonry had been infiltrated by founders of what *The Protocols* introduced as a "revolutionary faith." And—from the Constitution the founding fathers drafted—they set out to prevent the same siege from occurring in the "New Atlantis" (America).

* * * * * * * * * *

The individual who translated *The Protocols of Zion* from Russian to English (Victor E. Marsden) was eminently qualified for the task. Though some modern-day

---

[35] *The Meaning of Masonry*, W.L. Wilmshurst, Wing Books a division of Random House Value Publishing, New York, NY, 1980
* Emphasis added

readers may find the English he used a bit dated, Marsden's intimate acquaintance with Russia, Russian life and the Russian language on the one hand, and his mastery of a terse literary English style on the other, placed him in a position of advantage which few others could claim. Did Marsden use literary license in translating the document? Did he insert some of his own ideology during the process? We may never know the answers to these questions; however Mr. Marsden's translation reveals a common theme that permeates the twenty-four *Protocols— world domination through deceit and seduction* (a theme that is eerily similar to that espoused by 21ˢᵗ century Islamic leaders).

It may be said that the translation was carried out at the cost of Mr. Marsden's own life's blood. Ostensibly, he told the writer of the *Preface* (of *The Protocols*) that he could not stand more than an hour at a time on his work in the British Museum, as the diabolical spirit of the matter which he was obliged to turn into English made him positively ill. This writer can identify with Marsden's sentiments ... and so might you, when you read them from the perspective of a newly enlightened follower of God.

After Stepanov published them, *The Protocols* were re-released in 1901, in a book called '*The Great Within the Small*' by Sergyei A Nilus. A copy of Nilus' book can be found in the British Museum bearing the date of its reception, August 10, 1906.

Of consequence is that all copies that were known to exist in Russia were destroyed in the Kerensky regime, and under his successors the possession of a copy by anyone in Soviet land was a crime sufficient to ensure the owner's of being shot on sight. Was this mandate intended to protect the Russian people or to protect a Marxist government that had used *The Protocols* to confiscate Russia?

Clearly, seduction and deception are tools in the hands of Communist. I once dined with a Russian Ambassador to the United States. During our discussions, the Ambassador attempted to convince me—a Christian—that the communal arrangement that existed among Christ and His disciples provided the basis upon which communism was founded. Talk about "truth" being what it needs to be ...

Upon reading *The Protocols* one can see why the Communist Party might want the book censored. It revealed a method, by which the Bolshevik's could—and did--overthrow the Czar. And, that communist Russia used many of the same tactics of despotism found in the document to create the Soviet Union of nations surrounding Russia on the world's map is unquestionable. Much of this section contains materials obtained from a website avail-able at http://www.biblebelievers.org.au. One statement found on the website is revealing: "The fact (that the book was confiscated by communists) is, in itself, sufficient proof of the genuineness of *The Protocols*," or, might it be that by confiscating the book, a great plan of deception and seduction could achieve legendary status within the underworld of conspiracy theorists?

One would also have to suspect that the butcher and despot seducer of the German people, Adolph Hitler, knew of—and used—*The Protocols* in his attempts to dominate the world. More than likely, other tyrants—before and after Hitler—have used them to their advantage, including the polished and articulate 'Sirens of the 21st century'.

Ostensibly, *The Protocols* were presented to the innermost circle of the *Lords of Seduction* at the First

World Congress of Zion, in Basle, Germany in the early
1900s—men and women who, by way of their conversion to
the new "revolutionary faith," were no longer Jews nor
Christians. They were—and are—*secularists* ("a system of
doctrines and practices that disregards or rejects *any form
of religious faith and worship**, believing that religion ...
should not enter into the functions of the state.")[36]

Does this have a familiar ring throughout America?
The U.S. Constitution's reference to separation of church
and state has been interpreted by the Illuminati's atheistic
minions on the political Left as an axe to cut Godly
references from government-supported institutions. It is
precisely because non-Judeo-Christian ideologies—or *false
flag* Judeo-Christian ideologies—have taken over governments around the world that the Illuminati-Islamic Alliance
has been able to move the world toward one-world
dictatorial governance.

A further important clue to the mysterious happenings
taking place within the framework (and under the veil of
the "noble science" of Freemasonry)[37] was discovered when
19th century British Prime Minister Benjamin Disraeli said:
*"Remember the French Revolution, the secrets of its
preparation are well known to us for it was entirely the
work of our hands."* Of importance is that Benjamin's
father, Isaac Disraeli, had written in the introduction of a
biography of King Charles I: *"It was fated that England
should be the first of a series of Revolutions, which is not
yet finished."*

The presumption is strong that *The Protocols* were
issued, or reissued in a revised format, and was seductively

---

[36] *Webster's New World College Dictionary, Third Edition,* Simon and Shuster, 1997
* Emphasis added

billed as the First Zionist Congress held at Basle in 1897 under the presidency of the late Theodore Herzl.

Protocols translator, Victor Marsden, wrote: "I participated with Dr. Herzl in the first Zionist Congress which was held in Basle in 1897. Herzl was the most prominent figure at the Congress. Herzl foresaw, twenty years before we experienced them, the revolution which brought the Great War (World War I,) and he prepared us for that which was to happen. He foresaw the splitting up of Turkey, that England would obtain control of Palestine. 'We may expect important developments in the world,' Herzl said." Perhaps, the reason Herzl "foresaw" these events is that he and his fellow Illuminists intended to orchestrate them.

If one can believe that Marsden was present *and heard* Herzl deliver the message of *The Protocols* to those in attendance, it would be difficult to refute claims *that the document he translated* for the event was fabricated.

*   *   *   *   *   *   *   *   *   *

Now, to the question that must be on everyone's mind: Who are "The Elders?" Are they merely figments of someone's imagination? Were they—are they—real people or the bogymen of someone's seditious imagination? Are they (as Thomas Horn concludes in *Apollyon Rising 2012*) *not Zionists*, but part of a demonic clan of Luciferians who are preparing the way for the prophesied False Prophet and Antichrist? A being that Horn identifies as the resurrection and reincarnation of the spirit that through several cycles of resurrection was known to earthlings by several names: Nimrod/Osiris/Apollo.[38]

---

[38] *Apollyon Rising, Ibid*

What Horn failed to see in his (incorrectly, I believe) premise (that America's founding fathers were out to *recreate* the death and resurrection of Atlantis and the risen spirit of Nimrod/Osiris/Apollo-the antichrist) is the similarities among all three of the world's "major" religions. Horn was remise in pointing out that Christianity, Judaism, and Islam expect a messiah to return to usher in a millennium of peace, and that Nimrod, Osiris, or Apollo are not names identified with the Messiah of any of the three major religions. Judaism's messiah is Elijah; Christianity's is Jesus Christ; and Islam's messiah is Mahdi. Each of these messiahs is likely to be the same entity, a metaphysical being that came to earth as a man, left as a spirit and promised to return to ensure peace on earth.

While I believe that there are certainly people in the world who reject these messianic spirits—unlike Thomas Horn—I am unable to believe that George Washington, Thomas Jefferson, Benjamin Franklin and others among the ranks of America's founders were Lucifer worshipers. Nor that England's King George (or whoever was pulling his strings) was God's disciple and fought a war to protect the world against America's founders.

At least one investigator labeled the cabal of "world bankers and intellectual elite" (who are more likely to qualify as Lucifer's disciples) "The Hidden Hand." Writing in the *Wiener Freie Presse*, December 24, 1912, the late Walter Rathenau said: "Three hundred men, each of whom knows all the others, govern the fate of the European continent, and they elect their successors from their entourage."

From all indications "The Invisible Empire" no longer limits its activities to the European continent. Today, its presence is felt in the United States, Israel, and other countries around the globe, including Arab states.

In 1844, the aforementioned former British Prime Minister Benjamin Disraeli published in his novel, *COVINGSBY*, another ominous passage: "The world is governed by very different personages from what is imagined by those who are not (privy to what is taking place) behind the scenes." Disraeli was sending the world a message. The people weren't listening then. They are not listening now.

Clearly, there are those in the entertainment and literary industries who have provided insight into the various circles of power vying for the minds of men.

On the day that these words were written, my wife and I watched the movie: *Wall Street: Money Never Sleeps*. As the plot played out, it was clear that producer, Oliver Stone, possesses uncommon insight into how international financial markets and governments can be manipulated by a few greedy men who sit on one of the Illuminati's most influential agencies: The Federal Reserve, which by the way, is neither "Federal" nor a "Reserve." It is a powerful *private* bank, wholly-owned and controlled by Illuminists and pulls the financial strings of many of the world's markets. How it came to dictate U. S. banking is another story, played out in Edward G. Griffin's book, *The Creature from Jekyll Island.*

The aforementioned movie is not the first time that Stone used a screenplay to reveal the grip of the Hidden Hand on America's policies and politics. He also produced the movie *JFK,* a behind-the-scenes look at the Kennedy assassination and a New Orleans district attorney who—though he had damning evidence—was unable to obtain a guilty verdict against one of the assassination's enablers. More on this later.

In his book, *Angels and Demons,* Dan Brown revealed how the forces of evil infiltrated the Vatican and came very close to taking control of the papacy of the Catholic Church. What Brown failed to emphasize was the role of the early *political* pillars of Catholicism (its secularist Popes, including Constantine, the Medici's, and the Borgia's) in empire-building, using religion as a false flag operation.

Perhaps, one of the most convincing conspiracy theories is the aforementioned Thomas Horn's *Apollyon Rising: 2012,* in which Horn reveals a trail of prophesies that point to how the coming son of Lucifer (the *antichrist,* whose path was paved by the "false prophet") intends to deceive the peoples of the earth through his (the antichrist's) affiliations with great religious institutions and humanist governments. Except for implementing Freemasonry, Horn's scenario is right out of the Bible, the Book of Revelation.

These are but an inkling of indications that *something* is going on behind the "lights of publicity." Is it true that a small group of families who claim to be descendants of the offspring of a marriage between the "sons of God" (angels) and "daughters of men," described in Genesis 6:4, believe that they alone were destined to exercise "dominion" over the rest of humanity? Is it possible that the families were given the charge by some great metaphysical power? Is it conceivable that these self-anointed *Lords of Seduction created the myth* that they are superhuman in knowledge and intelligence and that people—including this writer— have given them more credit than they deserve? While the answers to these questions are not yet known, it is clear that global affairs are decided behind the scenes by a few powerful and super-rich individuals who pass the baton of world domination from one generation of heirs to the next.

To those who seem bent on discrediting conspiracy theories before looking at the way things are actually playing out, I say: open your eyes and minds. Naiveté invites bondage and retreating from the truth ensures disaster. If the possibilities that I present are unfounded, the world will survive in spite of them. If they are factual, and good men–and woman–*do nothing* the world is doomed.

Consider the behavior of the ostrich. When it perceives danger, an ostrich sticks its head in the sand. The bird's actions have nothing to do with what is going on around it. It simply refuses to deal with that which it is unable to see as a result of head-burying, no matter how threatening. And, there are many Americans who are content dealing with danger as does the ostrich.

For the seeker of truth, this book should serve as a primer to new-found enlightenment. It picks up where Thomas Horn's *Apollyon Rising: 2012* leaves off and, hopefully, redirects the attention to America's true enemies–The I-IA. In his efforts to tie the Holy Scriptures to the New World Order, Horn writes that hidden in the great seal of the United States of America:

> "... is a prophecy in plain sight by the U.S. government for more than two hundred years, foretelling the return of a terrifying demonic god who seizes control of earth in the new order of the ages. This supernatural entity was known and feared in ancient times by different names: Apollo

(Apollyon), Osiris, and even farther back as
Nimrod, whom Masons consider to be the
father of their institution ... but if the reader
doubts the authority of the Scriptures
concerning the coming of Apollo as the
Antichrist or the dedication of the occult
hierarchy to the prophecy on the Great
Seal, the *'illuminated ones'* have you right
where they want you. Is it because an occult
elite knows something about the imminent
fulfillment of the Illuminati-Masonic
prophecy involving a *false Yahweh* (Zeus/
Jupiter) and his *false Christ* (Apollo)
coming with full force of pagan justice,
when Satan's reign over the world reaches
its apex in the New World Order?"[39]

While I believe that Horn is correct in many of his
assumptions, I would substitute "The Illuminati-Masonic
prophecy" with a more appropriate term: *The Illuminati-
Islamic Prophecy.* After years of contemplating how the
Scriptures describe the coming Apocalypse, I am more
prone to believe that the Anti-Christ may not be an
individual, but a group of individuals. As you have seen—
and will continue to see—the Illuminati—Islamic Alliance
meets most of the criteria and it's "puppets" qualify as
"false prophets."

Like the Great Seal of the United States (certainly since
the advent of the internet), *The Protocols* have been in
"plain sight" of the U.S. Government and other
governments around the world. A student of history would

---

[39] Thomas Horn, *Apollyon Rising 2012: The Lost Symbol Found and the Final Mystery of the Great Seal Revealed,* Defender, Crane, Missouri, 2009

be hard-pressed to deny that *The Protocols* are   being
used by *some* well-grounded hierarchy to bring about the
"full force of pagan justice, when Satan's reign over the
world reaches its apex in the coming New World Order."[40]
It still remains to be seen what kind of "world order"
freedom-loving men and women will allow to emerge and
when the true Messiah will return to harness the beast,
whoever—or whatever—it proves to be.

For those who believe that when God gave Man (*not
Lucifer*) dominion over the earth, God didn't limit
dominion *to a few men*. According to The Scriptures, He
awarded it to the whole of the human race. It is that same
"dominion" that Lucifer and his disciples are intent on
taking from us ... as they once tried to seize dominion from
God in Heaven. If *Genesis* and *Isaiah* are to be believed as
true accounts of the Heavenly battle and God's intent for
humanity, it is our duty—as members of the human race—to
not only be aware of what is going on, but to participate in
doing something about it. If you believe that you were
created in God's (not Lucifer's) image and designed to be a
part of God's plan, keep reading.

I know that some people believe Lucifer to be a
creation of man, a fictitious leader of a fictitious "out-
group" of "fallen angels" used by self-serving theologians to
frighten the masses into submission. If this belief is true,
the creation of this enemy has apparently backfired.
Religions based on God have a growing army of
adversaries. Today, satanic cults exist as a thriving
underground society, practicing all manner of demonology,
sorcery and black magic. Do these Luciferians believe that
they worship a myth ... a creation of man? I would think

---

[40] Ibid

not. *Something*—tangible and intangible—rewards their faith and loyalty.

For a conspiracy theory to have bones, it must pit one group of individuals against another—an "in-group" against an "out-group." It must incorporate a plethora of seductive techniques if it is to motivate the conspiracy's participants. Every participant in such a conspiracy is considered to be either a member of the "in-group" or the "out-group." So, it is easy to see that for any kind of espionage to transcend the ages, both sides of the issue have to be convinced that they are on the side of Truth.

The term "out-group" is a recognized sociology term used to describe any social circle looked upon with "contempt, opposition, or a desire to compete."[41]

Perhaps, the most prolific example of an in-group/out-group clash—other than the Holy Scriptures—is the *Protocols of the Learned Elders of Zion*. In the next chapter, we will dissect the document as it relates to current and past history. For purposes of demonstrating the validity of *The Protocols*, the term "out-group" (instead of "goyim") will be used to indicate the segment of humanity considered by the Invisible Empire to be targets of their seductive practices—the uninitiated, including their new-found partners—the Muslim Mafia. At the time *The Protocols* were drafted, the architects of the document considered themselves the "out-group." However, the plan that they laid out was clearly intended as a roadmap to turn the tables and have them become the "in-group," a goal that seems to most Illuminati investigators to have been masterfully engineered.

When I italicize words and phrases, I do so to emphasize some correlation with other thoughts and

---

[41] Wikipedia

examples used elsewhere in this book. And, from all indications, the term "liberalism" had a different context when *The Protocols* were drafted. Or perhaps—like confusing readers by using the "Elders of Zion" in the title —the drafters intentionally misled the un-enlightened reader, as they might have deceived loyal followers of Catholicism and Freemasonry. At that time, "liberalism" meant "a political philosophy advocating personal freedom *for the individual.*"[42] In turn-about fashion, today, "liberalism" has come to describe the ideology of the political Left ("a belief in tolerance and gradual reform in moral, religious, or political matters").[43] This "progressive" interpretation of the word is a 180 degree reversal of the original meaning of liberalism and has little to do with "freedom for the individual"—a clever tactic of seduction. And that it is constitutes a practice that is consistent with *The Protocols,* an instrument of seduction intended to have the double meaning of a cipher, yet clearly understood by—and for—those who are among the self-designated "enlightened."

In the following chapter we will examine several portions of *The Protocols* and apply them to the political and economic dilemmas faced by 21ˢᵗ century America.

---

[42] *Webster's New World College Dictionary,* Third Edition, Simon & Shuster, New York, NY, 1997
[43] Wikipedia

CHAPTER 6

Having laid a proper foundation, it is, now, time to embark upon an eye-opening odyssey—beneath—and into the lowest crypts of despotism, where Hell's Council is in session. The time is 1492, the same year that Columbus *re*-discovered the Americas. And the agenda deals with a take-over of the known world.

According to Amitakh Stanford, "The original version of *The Protocols* came out of a meeting in *Rome in 1492* (home of the Vatican). The original document certainly involved men who were not of Hebrew blood, nor were they actually followers of the Jewish faith. In fact, most of the 1492 Elders were affiliated with the Catholic Church." Stanford also confirms my earlier conclusions that: "Some parts (of *The Protocols*) contain genuine goals that are sought by the (Catholic) Elders. Other parts are intended to *mislead** people about the real intentions of the Elders. Still other parts are designed to incite emotional responses to *The Protocols* in order to achieve their agenda."[44] In the same article, Stanford contends that *The Protocols* and the plan it encapsulates are inspired by descendants of the "sons of God" (the fallen angels—Annunaki) referenced in

---

[44] *http://www.xeeattwelve.net/articles/protocols.hetml*
* Emphasis added

Genesis 6:4. As you will soon see, *The Protocols* are not words of praise or encouragement, but those promising doom and gloom for all but a few: those self-identified "despots" who—through the ages—have used the document to obtain power over people.

If you and I had been present when the newly-revised version of *The Protocols* was presented by Theodore Herzl at the first Congress of a freshly-revived Luciferian-Revolutionary Faith that *falsely concealed* itself under the cloak of authentic Zionism, here's what we would have heard an ingenious revisionist espouse:[45]

> "Political freedom is *an idea,* not a fact (the first of many proofs that the document is an instrument of seduction). Whenever it appears necessary (with the bait of an idea) to attract the masses of the people to one party for the purpose of crushing another (an example of an in-group/out-group conflict) ... the task is rendered easier if the opponent (the one to be deceived) has himself been *infected* with the idea of freedom (the second proof of seduction) ... and, for the sake of an idea, is willing to yield some of his power. It is precisely here that the triumph of our theory appears; the slackened reins of government are immed-iately, by the law of life, caught up and gathered together *by a new hand* (the Hidden Hand) ...

---

[45] Please be advised that all italicized words and phrases were *done* by the author to provide emphasis and that those enclosed with parentheses are added by the author.

"The political has nothing in common with the moral. The ruler who is governed by the moral is not a skilled politician, and is therefore unstable on his throne. He who wishes to rule must have recourse both to *cunning* and to *make-believe.* Great national qualities, like *frankness* and *honesty,* are vices in politics, for they bring down rulers (and those who appointed them) from their thrones more effectively and more certainly than the most powerful enemy ...

"The word *"right"* is an abstract thought and proved by nothing. The word means no more than: *Give me what I want in order that thereby I may have a proof that I am stronger than you ...*

"(We shall) scatter to the winds all existing forces of order and regulation, to reconstruct all institutions and to become the sovereign lord of those who have left to us the rights of their power by laying them down voluntarily.

"Our power ... will remain invisible until the moment when it has gained such strength that no cunning can any longer undermine it ... Out of the temporary evil we are now compelled to commit will emerge the good of an unshakable rule ... *The result justifies the means.* Let us, however, in our plans, direct our attention not so much to what is good and moral as to what is necessary and useful.

"Before us is a plan in which is laid down strategically the line from which we cannot deviate without running the risk of seeing the labor of *many centuries* brought to naught. (Keep in mind that these words were presented to Herzl's "Congress" in Basle, Germany in 1897.)

"A satisfactory form of government for any country is one that is concentrated in the hands of one responsible person. Without an *absolute* despotism there can be no existence for civilization ..."

The following is among some of the more disconcerting statements lifted from *The Protocols:*

"Our countersign is *force* and *make-believe* (deceit and seduction). Only force conquers in political affairs, especially if it be concealed in the talents essential to statesmen. Violence must be the principle, and *cunning* and *make-believe* the rule for governments ... This evil is the one and only means to attain the end ... Therefore we must not stop at *bribery, deceit* and *treachery* when they should serve towards the attainment of our end. In politics one must know how to *seize the property of others* without hesitation if by doing so we secure submission and *sovereignty.*

"Our State, marching along the path of peaceful conquest, has the right to replace the horrors of war by less noticeable and more *satisfactory sentences of death*, necessary to *maintain the terror* which tends to produce blind submission ... for the sake of victory, we must keep to the program of violence and make-believe ... by the **doctrine of severity** that we shall triumph and *bring all governments into subjection to our super-government.*

"In all corners of the earth the words *"Liberty, Equality, Fraternity,"* have been brought to our ranks, thanks to our blind agents, whole legions which bore our banners with enthusiasm. And all the time these words were canker-worms at work ... putting an end everywhere to peace, quiet, solidarity and destroying all the foundations of "out-group" States (nations).

"Our triumph has been rendered easier by the fact that in our relations with the men, whom we wanted (to do our bidding,) *we have always worked upon the most sensitive chords of the human mind* ... upon the insatiability for material needs of man ...

"It is indispensable for our purpose that wars, so far as possible, should not result in territorial gains: war will thus be brought on to the *economic ground* ... and this state of things will put both sides at the mercy of our international (machinery of politics). Our *international rights* will then *wipe out national rights* ..."

The last sentence squares with Illuminist, David Rockefeller's statement before the Trilateral Commission one hundred years later. Another troublesome part of *The Protocols* deals with individuals, groups, and nations that the Illuminati select to front their plan.

> "The administrators, whom we shall choose from among the public ... will not be persons (or clerics) trained in the arts of government, and will therefore easily become *pawns in our game in the hands of men of learning and genius* who will be their advisers, specialists bred and reared from early childhood to rule the affairs of the whole world ...

Does the recruitment of radical Islamic clerics by the Illuminati follow what you have just read? Does the seismic rise of Barrack Obama? Think about it.

Now, to controlling what *the people* think they know about *the news* and indoctrinating the masses to a particular ideology:

> "We are constantly, by means of *our press*, arousing a blind confidence in these theories (of selecting those with blind ambitions and the need for power and recognition).
>
> "Do not suppose for a moment that these statements are empty words: think carefully of the successes *we arranged* for
>
> - Darwinism (Evolution),
> - Marxism (Communism), and

- Nietzscheism (Socialism) ...

"There is a great force that creates the movement of thought in the people, and that is *the press*. The part played by the press is ... to create discontent. (The press) has fallen into our hands. Through the press we have gained the power to influence while remaining ourselves in the *shade* (from the lights of publicity).

"Our goal is now only a few steps off. There remains a small space to cross (the Atlantic Ocean and the destruction of the United States of America) and the whole long path we have trodden is ready now to close its cycle of the Symbolic Snake (the Luciferian serpent of Eden described in Genesis) ... We have set all forces in opposition one to another, breaking up their tendencies towards independence. To this end we have armed *all* parties (including radical Islam) ... we have set up authority as a target for every ambition. A little more, and disorders and bankruptcy will be universal ..."

A close look at the state of the world in 2011 seems to be consistent with the afore-referenced promises.

"We have included in the constitutions (of nations) such rights as to the masses appear *fictitious* (a reference to the art of political seduction) and not actual rights. All these so-called *"Peoples' Rights"* can exist

only in idea, an idea which can never be
realized in practical life ... Once the
(electorate) has only those pitiful crumbs
which we fling them from our table in
return for their voting in favor of what we
dictate—in favor of the men we place in
power ... (the economy will become
dependent on (labor) strikes by (the "out-
group's") comrades or lockouts by their
masters.

At the time of this writing, organized labor is up in
arms about the fact that states can no longer afford to pay
the benefits that were obtained through collective
bargaining. And, because the matter has been driven into
the courts, the will of the people—and the people's duly
elected representatives—will be decided by judges. Just wait
until you learn what *The* Protocols say about how judges
are elected/appointed. Now, read what is likely to be the
next step in the "collective bargaining"   battle.

"We (shall) appear on the scene as
alleged saviors (a reference to the art of
seduction) of the worker from this
oppression when we propose to him to
enter the ranks of *our fighting forces—*
Socialists,   Anarchists,   Communists—to
whom we always give support in accordance
with an alleged brotherly rule (of the
solidarity of all humanity).

"We are interested in the killing out of
the "out-group" (God-fearing, law-abiding
private citizens). Our power is in the

chronic shortness of food and physical weakness of the worker because by all that this implies he is made *the slave of our will*, and he will not find in his own authorities either strength or energy to set against our will ..."

The use of the term "slave of our will" should enrage anyone or group subjected to any form of slavery or bondage, including African Relief Funds, the NAACP, National Organization of Women (NOW) or women in Islamic cultures.

"By *want* (and the envy and hatred which want engenders) we shall move the mobs (masses) and with *their hands* we shall wipe out all those who hinder us on our way."

"... with their hands ..." sends a strong message that the Lords of Seduction will rely on the "shortage of food" and other commodities as well as the "weakness of the worker" to take over governments—and in turn—entire nations. Now that you have read the statements above, consider the demonstrations and riots taking place around the world, including those within the U.S. and in Muslim nations.

"When the hour strikes for our sovereign lord of *all the world* to be crowned (the antichrist) it is these same hands which will sweep away everything that might be a hindrance thereto (including all

who assisted the Illuminati in achieving
their objective)."

And because of the "great force" (the press) that
"creates movement"—or the lack thereof—the people
remain clueless to the I-IA's mission. *The Protocols*
describe how a "supranational sovereignty" and their
emissaries intend to unravel the social institutions that
allowed them to ready the masses for one-world
governance:

> "The (out-group) has lost the habit of
> thinking unless prompted by the suggestions
> of our specialists. Therefore they *no longer*
> see the necessity ... to teach in national
> schools the knowledge of the structure of
> human life, of social existence (which
> requires division of labor) and
> consequently, the division of men into
> classes and conditions. It is essential for all
> to know that owing to difference in the
> objects of human activity *there cannot be
> any equality* ... The true knowledge of the
> structure of society ... would demonstrate to
> all men that the positions and work must be
> kept within a certain *circle* (The Inner
> Circle of the Illuminati)."

The message here is: *anyone*—or any group—who has
been given special privileges by the Lords of Seduction will
have them taken away.

> "Thanks to promptings intended to mis-
> lead and to its own ignorance (we will
> orchestrate) a blind hatred towards all
> conditions which (a social class) considers
> above itself (class warfare), for ('the out-
> group') has no understanding of the
> meaning of class and condition."

And, in case one still doubts how portions of *The
Protocols* are used today by an Invisible Empire to create
the economic troubles currently affecting the U.S. and the
rest of the world, consider the following:

> "Hatred will be still further magnified
> by the effects of *an economic crisis*, which
> will stop dealing on the exchanges and bring
> industry to a standstill. We shall create by
> all the secret subterranean methods open to
> us and *with the aid of gold, which is all in
> our hands, a universal economic crises*
> whereby we shall throw upon the streets
> whole mobs of workers simultaneously in
> all countries ... These mobs will rush
> delightedly to shed the blood of those
> whom, in the simplicity of their ignorance,
> they have envied from their cradles, and
> whose property they will then be able to
> loot."

The price of gold and silver is approaching an all-time
high. It has been reported that globalist and Illuminist-
want-to-be, George Soros, just purchased $800 billion
dollars of gold. The value of the U.S. dollar will continue

to shrink and as the value of gold, silver, oil, wheat, and corn rise, America's debt is approaching an insurmountable ceiling. Uprisings throughout the Middle East and around state capitols throughout America seem to fit what is promised by the drafters of *The Protocols.*

In addition, the Rodney King/ Los Angeles Riot issue in the 1990s seemed to follow this portion of *The Protocols* to the letter (more on this incident later).

> "Ours (property) they will not touch, because *the moment of attack (fiscal and physical) will be known to us* and we shall take measures to protect our own.
>
> "When the populace has seen that all sorts of concessions and indulgences are yielded it in the name of freedom (Lyndon Johnson's welfare state) it (the populace) has imagined itself to be sovereign lord and has stormed its way to power. (Watch out Tea Party. This reference could also be applicable to the 2010 mid-term election sweep of the House of Representatives. Prepare to be seduced—or worse, the target of the Rothschild Formula). But, naturally like every other blind man, it (the retaliatory movement) has come upon a host of stumbling blocks. The French Revolution was wholly the work of *our hands* (a reference to the Philadelphes, or French branch of the Illuminati).
>
> "Ever since that time (The French Revolution) we have been leading the peoples (of the world) from one

disenchantment to another ... At the present day we are, as *an international force*, invincible, because if attacked by some, we are supported by other States. Unification must be accomplished only under *our sovereign rule* ...

"The word *'freedom'* brings out the communities of men to fight against every kind of force, against every kind of authority, even against God and the laws of nature. For this reason we, when we come into our kingdom, shall have to erase this word (freedom) from the lexicon of life as implying a principle of brute force which turns (the masses) into bloodthirsty beasts (for a while). These beasts fall asleep again every time when they have drunk their fill of blood; and at such time *can easily be riveted into their chains* (affirmation of Thomas Jefferson's admonition: "A government powerful enough to give the people everything they want is also powerful enough to take it away.") But if they be not given blood they will not sleep and continue to struggle (against us—The Illuminati).

"Every republic passes through several stages (The Cycle of Democracies). The first of these is comprised in the early days of mad raging by the blind mob, tossed hither and thither, right and left: the second is demagogy from which is born anarchy, and that leads inevitably to despotism (a tyrannical state of behavior).

"Thanks to continual *changes* (in their Constitutions) the plan of action of our force remains (for the people) an unknown mystery."

Now comes the affirmation that the architects of *The Protocols* dissolved all ties with the theocracy of God in favor of a secular-based "revolutionary faith." More than any other passage, it reveals the true theosophy of the men who authored *The Protocols*—Luciferian atheists, one and all, regardless of the cloaks, robes, or aprons they displayed in public. What you are about to read could well come from metaphysical beings that Genesis and Isaiah identify as defiant "sons of God" or "fallen angels"—the Annunaki.

"We shall destroy God ... The very laws of creation have established subordination ... It is indispensable for us to undermine all faith, to tear out of the mind of the 'out-group' the very principle of god-head and the spirit, and to put in its place arithmetical calculations and material needs.

"All the nations will be *swallowed up* in the pursuit of gain and in the race for it will not take note of their common foe (today, the Illuminati-Islamic Alliance) ... The intensified struggle for superiority and shocks delivered to economic life will create, nay, have already created, disenchanted, cold and heartless communities (dictatorships) ...

"Then will the hour strike when, not for the sake of attaining the good, not even to win wealth, but solely out of *hatred towards the privileged*, the lower classes will follow our lead against our rivals for power ... (Clearly, radical Islam has demonstrated "hatred" toward Jews and Christians.

"We shall create an intensified centralization of government in order to *grip in our hands* all the force of the (world) community. We shall *regulate* mechanically all the actions of the political life of our subjects by *new laws* (judicial reinterpretations of the U.S. Constitution). These laws will withdraw, one by one, all the indulgences and liberties which have been (previously) permitted (including affirmative action, government financed entitlements and political correctness) ...

"When we have also robbed them of their faith in God the might of power was flung upon the streets into the place of public proprietorship and was seized by us.

"The art of directing masses and individuals by means of *cleverly manipulated theory and verbiage* (Black Liberation Theology, affirmative action, political correctness, etc.) by regulations of life in common and all sorts of other quirks ... belongs likewise to the specialists of our administrative brain ... We have set one against another the personal and national reckonings of the "out-group" religious and race hatreds, which we have fostered into a huge growth in the course of *the past twenty centuries* (proof that policies fleshed out in *The Protocols* are of ancient origin and not the creation of 15th, 18th, and 20th century fictionists and could coincide with Constantine's founding of what became the Catholic Church of Rome, incorporating many pagan principles that emerged from the Nicean Council). This is the reason why there is not one State which would anywhere receive support (fiscal, physical, and militarily) if it were to raise its arm, for every one of them must bear in mind that any agreement against us would be unprofitable to itself. *We are too strong—there is no evading our power.* The nations cannot come to even an inconsiderable private agreement without our *secretly having a hand in it.*

"The intensification of armaments, the increase of police forces—is essential for the completion of the aforementioned plans. There should be in all the States (nations) of the world, besides ourselves, *a few* millionaires (or, today, billionaires—the Order of the 300) devoted to our interests ...

"We must create ferments, discords and hostility. Therein we gain a double advantage. In the first place we keep in check all countries, for they will know that we have the power whenever we like *to create disorders* or *to restore order.* All these countries are accustomed to see in us an indispensable force of coercion. In the second place, by our *intrigues* we shall tangle up all the threads which we have stretched into the cabinets of all States by means of the political, by economic treaties (Cap and Trade,) or loan obligations (The Federal Reserve, International Monetary Fund and World Bank). In order to succeed in this we must *use great cunning* and penetration during negotiations and agreements ... We shall keep to the opposite tactics and *assume* (by seduction) *the mask of honesty and complacency*. In this way the peoples and governments of the "out-group," whom we have taught to look only at the outside whatever we (and our press) present to their notice, will still continue to accept us as the benefactors and saviors of the human race."

How much more specific could the drafters of this document be about their intent to seduce, deceive, and then enslave the "human race?"

"We must be in a position to respond to every act of opposition by war with the neighbors of that country which dares to oppose us (to entice a neighboring nation or an opposing ideology to launch a war ... and finance both sides). But if these neighbors should also venture to stand collectively together against us, then we must offer resistance by a universal war (World Wars

I, II, and the dreaded War of all Wars,
World War III. Either way, the Illuminists
win. The condition of the world with which
they end up is another matter).

"The principal factor of success in the
political is the *secrecy* of its undertakings ...
We must compel (the governments of the
out-group) to take action in the direction
favored by our widely conceived plan,
already approaching the desired consum-
mation, by what we shall represent as public
opinion, *secretly promoted by us through
the means of the press*, which, with a few
exceptions that may be disregarded, *is
already entirely in our hands.*"

If I were a member of the press, I'd be outraged that
any group of individuals sought to control me or the
institution I had devoted—or intended to devote—my life to.

"To sum up our system of keeping the
governments (of the world) in check, we
shall show our strength to one of them by
terrorist attempts ... (This is a *directed* role
of radical Islam ... an unsuspecting, newly-
recruited "puppet" in The Invisible
Empire's masterfully-designed ploy).

"Our directorate (Inner Circle) ... will
surround itself with publicists, practical
jurists, administrators, diplomats and,
finally, with persons prepared by a special
super-educational training in our special
schools."

Consider for a moment the names of colleges and universities that are steeped in liberalism on both eastern and western coasts. The Cloward-Piven Strategy was born at New York's Columbia University. Consider the socio-political persuasions of their graduates, including the sitting president of the United States of America. Look at the diplomas of those currently assisting Barack Obama and his handlers in running the U.S. government, at a time when it appears that *The Protocols* represent the "order of the day."

"These persons ("intellectual elites") will have consonance of *all the secrets of the social structure,* they will know all the languages that can be made up by political alphabets and words; they will (become) acquainted with the whole underside (seductive side) of human nature, with all its sensitive chords on which they will have to play ... their tendencies, short-comings, vices and qualities, the particularities of classes and conditions.

"Around us will be a whole constellation of *bankers, industrialists, capitalists* and *—the main thing—millionaires,* because in substance everything will be settled by the question of figures (thus, the need to gain control of lending institutions, (those deemed by the governing class to be "too big to fail") the world's financial markets, *and debt)* ... It will be of assistance to us when we come to consider *the* *division of property*—of the dwelling, of taxation, of the reflex force of the laws. All these questions are such as ought not to be touched upon directly and openly before the people (thus, Obama's *promise* of transparency and, yet, his administration's refusal to live up to the promise). ... The reason of keeping silence in this respect is that by not naming a principle (or policy) we leave ourselves freedom of action, to drop this or that out of it without attracting notice."

Just minutes prior to editing this portion of manuscript, I listened to Frank Luntz's analysis of the 2011 budget crisis and the stand-off between the Republicans and the Democrats. Luntz said "Democrats were successful in not revealing their hand." They never said which parts of the *un*balanced budget they would—or would not—be willing to cut in the next round of negotiations. The Democrat Party followed suit during debt ceiling negotiations. *The Protocols* continue:

"We count upon attracting all nations to the task of erecting the *new fundamental structure* (a One-World Government,) the project for which has been drawn up *by us*. This is why, before everything, it is indispensable for us to arm ourselves and to store up in ourselves that absolutely reckless audacity (no matter how ridiculous the claims or how invalid the statistics are which we shall quote) and irresistible might of the spirit which in the person of our active workers will break down all hindrances on our way.

"When we have accomplished our coup d'etat we shall say then to the various peoples (of the world): 'everything has gone terribly badly, (we inherited a terrible situation that was uncorrectable) all have been worn out with suffering. We are destroying (or going to destroy) the causes of your torment—nationalities, frontiers, differences of coin-ages and create some-thing better.'"

Pay close attention to the rhetoric coming from the Obama Campaign during the run-up to the 2012 elections. At the time of this writing, the replacement of multiple international currencies with a single currency is being floated as a trial balloon in world markets. The arrogance of the drafters of this document is uncovered in the following excerpt:

"You are at liberty, of course, to pronounce sentence upon us (after we have strapped you with debt and onerous regulations), but can it possibly be a just one if it is confirmed by you before you make any trial of what we are offering you ... (if you re-elect us). ... Then will the mob (people of the world) exalt us and bear us up in their hands in a unanimous triumph of hopes and expectations (Talk about arrogance)?

Voting, the instrument which will set us on the throne of the world by teaching even the very smallest units of members of the human race to vote ... (keep in mind that these words were written long before The United States became a nation and the voting rights act of the 1960's was passed) will then have served its (voting's) purposes and will play its part then for the last time by a unanimity of desire to make close acquaintance with us before condemning us (thus, completing the cycle of democracies, *back* to bondage).

"To secure this we must have *everybody vote* without distinction of classes and qualifications, in order to establish an absolute majority, which cannot be got (outsmarted) from the educated propertied classes ..."

The preceding sentence speaks to what the Illuminati think about civil rights, education, and upward mobility of the classes. It also gives insight as to why the powers that be refuse to secure our southern borders.

"We shall destroy among the "out-group" the importance of the family and its educational value and remove the possibility of individual minds splitting off, for the mob (masses,) *handled by us*, will not let them come to the front nor even give them a hearing (the intent of class warfare). It (the entitlement state) is accustomed to

> listening to us who *pay it* through government programs, only for obedience and attention. In this way we shall create a blind, mighty force which will never be in a position to move in any direction without the guidance of our agents (who have been strategically) set at its (the entitlement society's) head *by us* as leaders."

Consider the names, backgrounds, and qualifications of some of the individuals and organizations that have been appointed as "agents" of the Illuminati. Like me, you've probably questioned why they were chosen ... and remain as forces with which to be dealt.

> "The people will submit to this regime because it will know that upon these leaders (us) will depend its earnings, gratifications and the receipt of all kinds of benefits."

How visionary for the drafters of *The Protocols* to have predicted how successfully their plan would be implemented.

> "We want our schemes to be forcibly and suitably *concocted.* Under various names (Invisible Empire, Illuminati, Hidden Hand, Shadow Government, U.S. Federal Reserve, Trilateral Commission, Council of Foreign Relations, OPEC, ACLU, NAACP, National Organization of Women, Centers for Disease Control (CDC), Global Warming Prevention Organizations, Food and Drug Administration

(FDA), Greenpeace, Global, Rainbow/PUSH Coalition, Environmental Organizations, ACORN, and ambassadors to the United Nations) there exists in all countries approximately one and the same thing ... These institutions have divided up among themselves all the functions of government: administrative, legislative and executive, wherefore they have come to operate as do the organs in the human body, controlled by an administrative brain. *If we sufficiently injure one part in the machinery of State, the State falls sick, like a human body, and ... will die.*

"When we introduced into the State organism the poison of (socialism/progressivism) its whole political complexion underwent a change. (There's that word again). States have been seized with a mortal illness—blood poisoning. All that remains is to await the end of their death agony. At first, (the will to be free) produced Constitutional States."

The Protocols, then, go on to mock a constitutional form of government:

"A constitution, as you well know, is nothing else but a school of discords, misunderstandings, quarrels, disagreements, fruitless party agitations, party whims—in a word, a school of everything that serves to destroy the personality of State activity ... It was that the *era of republics* become possible of realization (the United States of

America;) and then it (a free and independent republic) was replaced by *a caricature* of a government (of our own choosing)—by a president (of our choosing), taken from the (masses,) from the midst of our *puppet creatures, or slaves*" (How "puppets" are chosen and "slaves" are created is the topic of the next section).

The following promises to be one of the most enlightening and revealing parts of *The Protocols,* especially when applied to the sudden rise to power of Barack Obama and the sustaining power and influence of Bill and Hillary Clinton and Jimmy Carter—Social Democrats, all.

"*We name presidents* ... we shall establish the responsibility of presidents ... We shall be in a position to disregard forms (formalities) in carrying through matters for which our *impersonal puppet* will be responsible. In order that our scheme may produce this result *we shall arrange elections* (yes, "arrange elections") in favor of such presidents as have in their past some dark, undiscovered stain; then they will be trustworthy agents for the accomplishment of our plans out of fear of revelations (exposure) and from the natural desire of everyone who has attained power, namely, the retention of the privileges, advantages and honor connected with the office of president. (The question of Barack

Obama's citizenship, his "foreign student"
college scholarships, and Muslim upbringing and Social Security Number come
to mind).

"The chamber of deputies (that we shall
arrange) will provide cover for, will protect
(the president we choose) ... but *we shall
take from* it (the president's protectorate or
political party) the right to propose new, or
make changes in existing laws, for *this right
will be given by us* to the responsible
president, *a puppet in our hands.* Naturally,
the authority of the presidents will then
become a target for every possible form of
attack (by the 'out-group,) but *we shall
provide him with a means of self-defense* in
the right of an appeal to the people (Bill
Clinton's impeachment and yet his ability to
remain in office,) for the decision of the
people over the heads of their representatives (the   House   of   Representatives
impeached Clinton and, yet, did not strip
him of his presidency) ... that is to say, an
appeal to that same *blind slave of ours*—the
majority   of   the   (electorate   and   its
representatives).

"Independently of this we shall invest
the president with the right of declaring a
state of war. We shall justify this last right
on the ground that the president as chief of
the whole army of the country must have it
at his disposal, in case of need for the
defense of the new constitution (the one

that the Hidden Hand is effecting through "change.")

"The key of the shrine (of government) will lie *in our hands*, and no one outside ourselves will any longer direct the force of legislation ... we shall instigate ministers (advisors) and other officials of the higher administration about the president to evade his dispositions by taking measures of their own, (Leon Paneta's orchestration of the raid on Osama Bin Laden's compound) for doing which they will be made the scapegoats in his place (as were Barack Obama's scapegoats, "spiritual advisor, Jeremiah Wright, and political advisor, professed communist, Van Jones).

"We are compelled to introduce into the constitutions of States (State, with a capital "S" as well as those with a small "s") to prepare for the transition to an imperceptible abolition of every kind of constitution (rule of law by which may be *temporarily* replaced by Sharia Law—and then totalitarianism) and then the time is come to turn every form of government into our despotism (a One-World, Auto-cratic Government void of God).

"To produce the possibility of the expression of such wishes by all the nations it is indispensable to trouble in all countries the people's relations with their govern-ments so as *to utterly exhaust humanity with dissension, hatred, struggle, envy and even*

by the use of torture, by starvation, by the
inoculation of diseases, by want, so that the
('out-group' sees) no other issue than to
take refuge in our complete sovereignty in
money and in all else (implementation of
the aforementioned "Doctrine of Severity").
But if we give the nations of the world a
breathing space the moment we long for is
hardly likely ever to arrive."

I urge you to ponder the preceding paragraphs and
make sure that you have a firm grasp on what the drafters
and revisionists of this document have in store for
humanity.

"What we want is: that from the first
moment of its promulgation (while the
peoples of the world are still stunned by the
accomplished fact of the revolution that we
shall orchestrate [today, with the assistance
of the Muslim Mafia] and while they are still
in a condition of terror and uncertainty)
they should recognize once and for all that
we are so strong, so inexpugnable, so super-
abundantly filled with power, that in no case
shall we take any account of them, and so
far removed from paying any attention to
their opinions or wishes, we are ready and
able *to crush with irresistible power* all
expression or manifestation thereof at every
moment and in every place, *that we have*
seized at once everything we wanted and
shall in no case divide our power with them

> [radical Islam, environmentalists, unions, and the entitlement society] ... Then in fear and trembling they (the people of the world) will close their eyes to everything, and be content to await what will be *the end of it all.*"

The preceding statement provides insight into how the Illuminati intend to deal with radical Islam and other "puppets" once the conquest of the world's governments is accomplished.

"The end of it all"–is *this* "the end" that the Illuminati and its Annunaki guides want–to destroy the world that God created and recreate it with Lucifer on the throne? Could it be that the original–and revisionist–drafters of *The Protocols* knew precisely what they were doing, spreading propaganda that the document was false (and getting others to agree with them) while using its scare tactics to create an air of mysticism around it and intimidate the prime movers of the world into submission? Clearly, this cabal of despots were/are intent on dominating their fellowman by whatever means necessary? Let's see what the author(s) of the document say about the abolition of freedom:

> "The word *'freedom,'* which can be interpreted in various ways, is defined *by us* (the Elders) as follows. Freedom is the right to do whatever the law (we impose) allows. This time will be of service to us, because (when we change the laws to our liking) all *freedom will thus be in our hands*, since the (newly-changed) laws interpretation of the

word will at the proper will abolish or create only that which is desirable for us according to the aforesaid program."

And, what did the Elders who lived in the 15th, 18th, and 20th centuries think about a "free press?" Here's what their version of the document says:

> "We shall deal with the press in the following way: what is the part played by the press? It serves to *excite and inflame those passions which are needed for our purpose* ... We shall saddle and bridle it with a tight curb ... The pretext for stopping any publication will be the alleged plea that it is agitating the public mind without occasion or justification."

I'd be willing to bet that that Juan Williams, Glenn Beck, Rush Limbaugh, Michele Bachman, and Sarah Palin might be able to identify with the last excerpt from *The Protocols.* And, if this book finds its way into the hands of the Illuminati, I will become a target. The way I look at is: there's a price to pay for calling Evil what it is.

The document goes on to say:

> "I beg you to note that among those making attacks upon us (the Hand that rules the press) will also be organs established *by us*, but they will attack exclusively points that we have pre-determined to alter (after they are revealed)."

Now, this is troubling. Surely, Rupert Murdoch's FOX News is not an instrument of the Illuminati? It's a scary thought. Perhaps, the architects of *The Protocols* didn't foresee cable television.

Telling the press—and the public that it is intended *to serve*—that the press is owned is a clever tactic of seduction (*Use Demonic Power of Words to Sow Confusion; Disarm Through Strategic Weakness and Vulnerability;* and *Master the Art of the Bold Move*)[46] and is indeed a bold move. Consider this possibility as you read the following:

> "We control the press. Not a single announcement will reach the public without our control. (And, it doesn't end with television and radio). Literature and journalism are two of the most important educative forces, and therefore our government will become proprietor of the majority of the journals. This will neutralize the injurious influence of the privately-owned press and will put us in possession of a tremendous influence upon the public mind ... "

This is one reason why self-published books that challenge the Illuminati's agenda are sometimes difficult to get into major bookstores. They, too, are under the influence of the heavy hand of the Illuminati.

> "All our newspapers will be of all possible complexions: revolutionary aristo-

---

[46] *The Art of Seduction*, Robert Greene, Highbridge Audio, 2001

cratic, republican, even anarchical—for so long, of course, as the constitution (of the Illuminati—*The Protocols*) exists ... Like the Indian idol *"Vishnu"* they will have *a hundred hands*, and every one of them will have a finger on any one of the (instruments of) public opinions as required. When a pulse quickens, *these hands* will lead opinion in the direction of our aims, for an excited patient loses all power of judgment and easily yields to suggestion. Those fools who will think they are repeating the opinion of a newspaper of their own camp will be repeating *our opinion* or any opinion that seems desirable for us. In the vain belief that they are following the organ of their party they will, in fact, follow the flag which we hang out for them.

   " *We shall have a sure triumph over our opponents* (true soldiers of freedom) since they will not have at their disposition organs of the press in which they can give full and final expression to their views ... "

In keeping with the adage: "To say it is so doesn't make it so," we need to keep in the back of our minds the possibility that *The Protocols* are no more than the *ultimate instrument of seduction* and the possibility that you and I are being seduced as we read them. Even so, let's continue with our examination:

   "Until such time as we are in the plenitude power, the capitals (of states and nations) should find themselves stifled by the provincial opinion of the nations (that we already control, i.e., of a majority of the votes in the United Nations) arranged by our (global machinery of politics).

"When comes the time of our overt rule, the time to manifest its blessing, *we shall remake all legislatures*, all our laws will be brief, plain, stable, without any kind of interpretations, so that anyone will be in a position to know them perfectly. The main feature which will run right through them is *submission to orders*, and this principle will be carried to a grandiose height ...

"Not a single case of illegality or abuse of power will be left without exemplary punishment (as is the case with Sharia Law). *Our judges* will know that whenever they feel disposed to plume themselves on foolish clemency (unlike the tenor of current-day American courts) they are violating the (newly installed) law of justice ..."

It is important to keep the preceding paragraph in mind as you see how America's courts are being used by the ACLU and the Obama Administration to overrule the people's will.

"Our legal staff will serve not beyond the age of 55, firstly because old men more obstinately hold to prejudiced opinions, and are less capable of submitting to new directions (a jab at senior citizens), and secondly because this will give us the possibility by this measure of securing elasticity in the changing of staff, which will be thus the more easily bent under our pressure: he who wishes to keep his place (in the judicial, legislative, or executive branch of our form of governance) will have to *give blind obedience to deserve it.* In general, our judges will be elected *by us* only from among those who thoroughly understand that the part they have to play is *to punish and apply (our) laws* ... The young generation of judges will be trained in certain views regarding the inadmissibility of any abuses that might disturb the established order of our subjects ...

"We shall abolish the right of appeal, which will be transferred exclusively to our disposal—to the cognizance of him (our puppet) who rules, for we must not allow the conception among the people of a thought that there could be such a thing as a decision that is not right of judges set up by us. Our government will have *the appearance* of a patriarchal paternal guardianship ... The *entitlement electorate* will be rejoiced that we have regulated everything in their lives as is done by wise parents who desire to train children in the cause of duty and submission. For the peoples of the world, in regard to *the secrets of our policy (The Protocols,)* are

ever through the age's only children ...
precisely as are also their governments.

*"We are obliged without hesitation to
sacrifice individuals,* who commit a breach
of (our newly) established order, for in the
exemplary punishment of evil lies a great
educational problem."

The next part of *The Protocols* appears to have been
in the works throughout America, especially in Ivy League
Universities, those in the Berkley, California area and
school of journalism, nationwide. Ask any graduate of
either of these schools about his or her political views.

"In order to effect the destruction of all
collective forces *except ours* we shall
emasculate the first stage of collectivism—
*the universities—*by re-educating them in a
new direction. Their officials and professors
will be prepared for their business by
detailed secret (and socialist-leaning)
programs of action from which they will not
with immunity diverge, not by one iota.
They will be appointed with especial
precaution, and will be so placed as to be
wholly dependent upon the government (or
government unions and protected by
tenure). The universities must no longer
send out from their halls milk sops (a new
name for young American patriots) con-
cocting plans for a constitution, like a
comedy or a tragedy, busying themselves
with questions of policy in which even their

own fathers never had any power of thought.

"When we are in power we shall remove every kind of disturbing (to our plan) subject from the course of education (school prayer and recitation of the Pledge of Allegiance) and shall make out of the youth *obedient children of authority*, loving him (the antichrist) who rules as the (false) support and hope of peace and quiet."

And, in case you have been led to believe that the content of school textbooks is unworthy of parental oversight, consider the following excerpt from *The Protocols:*

"We shall replace (the study of ancient history) with the study of the program of the future (that we have created). *We shall erase from the memory of men all facts of previous centuries which are undesirable to us* ... (entire months dedicated in public schools to the teaching of the history of only one segment of the American population is a way to "erase from the memory of men all facts of previous centuries ... and insert those that serve the Illuminati's purpose)

"*We shall abolish every kind of freedom of instruction.* (We shall see to it that) learners of all ages have the right to assemble together with their parents in the educational establishments as it were in a club: during these assemblies, on holidays, (our) teachers will read what will pass as

free lectures on questions of human
relations, of the laws of examples, of the
philosophy of new theories not yet declared
to the world (such as Global Warming—a
modern-day invention of World Government Advocates). These theories will be
raised *by us to the stage of a dogma* of faith
as a traditional stage towards *our faith* (in
the fallen angel, Lucifer and his One-World
Government) ...

"*We shall swallow up and confiscate to
our own use the last scintilla of
independence of thought,* which we have
for long past been directing towards subjects
and ideas useful for us. *The system of
bridling thought is already at work* in the so-
called system of teaching by object lessons."

If there is still doubt in your mind about the multi-
cultural—reach of the Hidden Hand, consider a report by
Robin Simcox, a research fellow at the Centre for Social
Cohesion in London. It is yet another example of how *The
Protocols* are a living document.

"In Sweden (prior to 9-11-01) an Iraqi-
born young man by the family name,
Abdaly, played sports, went (night) club-
bing, worked as a DJ, and *even had an
Israeli girlfriend.* But that was then; on
December 11, the 28-year-old launched a
suicide bomb attack in the center of
Stockholm, Sweden, killing himself and
injuring two others. So, what happened to

Abdaly during the last decade? Un-
fortunately, what turned a regular Muslim
adolescent into a fanatical jihadist is plain
for everyone to see—*it is the British
educational system.*

"Abdaly moved to the U.K. in 2001 to
study at the University of Bedfordshire in
Luton, near London. A friend of Abdaly's
told London's Daily Telegraph that once he
started studying there, "everything changed
... Someone had taken advantage of him
and had brainwashed him." And so Abdaly
becomes another name on the growing list
of those who have passed through British
schools and gone on to commit Islamist
terrorist attacks. If the Battle of Waterloo
was won on the playing fields of Eton, *the
war on terror is being lost in the labs and
lounges of our universities.*

"A report that I," said Robin Simcox,
"co-authored" with Hannah Stuart and
Houriya Ahmed for the Centre for Social
Cohesion earlier this year showed that of all
Islamism-inspired terrorists convicted in
British courts or responsible for suicide
bombings in the U.K. between 1999 and
2009, at least 31 percent attended a British
university. Among the more famous, Omar
Sheikh attended the prestigious London
School of Economics before he masterminded the 2002 kidnapping and
beheading of Daniel Pearl. And then
there's Omar Sharif, who went to King's

College London before his 2003 suicide bombing at a Tel Aviv pub called Mike's Place that killed 3 and wounded 50.

"Furthermore, as we noted in our study, *five terrorists have been senior members of a university Islamic society* (ISOC). These include Waheed Zaman, part of the al Qaeda cell that aimed to set off homemade liquid bombs on transatlantic flights in 2006, and Umar Farouk Abdulmutallab (the '*underwear bomber*,') who attempted to detonate a bomb concealed in his underpants on a flight to Detroit last Christmas Day.

"It was (the 'underwear bomber's') case that opened a window onto British academia's culture of denial. As president of the University College London (UCL) Islamic society, ("the underwear bomber") was known to have organized extremist events and exhibits, one of which juxtaposed images of mujahedeen fighters against the collapse of the World Trade Center. One student who attended said that he was shocked. "It seemed to me like it was brainwashing," he told the press, "like they were trying to indoctrinate people."

"How could 'the underwear bomber's' views have escaped the school's attention? Under pressure from the media, UCL established an internal inquiry. Not surprisingly, the investigation concluded that UCL was in no way culpable for failing to notice either 'the underwear bomber's (Abdulmutallab's) radical beliefs or the attempts of his ISOC to influence students.

'Sometimes even when the school is paying attention it seems not to matter. Consider the case of Mohammed Atif Siddique, a student that Glasgow Metropolitan College staff saw accessing terrorist websites on several occasions. According to British court documents, school officials were 'reluctant to do anything for fear of some accusation of racist conduct' (the intent of "political correctness" and a common Leftist tactic to silence speakers of truth). In 2007, Siddique was charged with terrorism-related offenses, like providing instruction or training for the purpose of assisting, preparing for, or participating in terrorism; and distributing or circulating a terrorist publication.

"Of course, the reluctance, or inability, to describe things as they truly are is the price paid for *political correctness.* No one would hesitate to condemn a campus culture in which students were inspired by neo-Nazis to carry out terrorist acts in the name of white supremacy. And yet the *liberals and leftists who typically fill faculty and administrative positions* would never dream of holding the Muslim community to the same standards. Instead, they are much more likely to invent a convenient narrative, one in which, for example, Muslim threats

of violence and terrorism are really just
responses—and quite understandable ones
at that—to Western war-mongering."

At this point in Simcox's article, I feel compelled to
raise the matter of an Islam-Illuminati Alliance (I-IA).
Along with the liberalization of the universities and courts
of the free world and the advent of "political correctness,"
it has become increasingly difficult to draw attention to
perpetrators who seem to be doing the I-IA's bidding.
Now, back to Simcox's article.

"Suicide bombing" according to Leftist
(I-IA disciples,) "is a legitimate defense of
Muslim lands against the neo-imperialism
of the West (a clever way to justify a policy
with which the Illuminati and the press it
controls agree). The Islamists loudly
denouncing British, as well as American,
foreign policy, insulting our soldiers, and
glorifying terrorism are just exercising their
rights to freedom of speech (and yet, should
conservatives resort to the same behavior,
they would be facing "hate crime"
allegations).
"And by hosting clerics like Murtaza
Khan (and Iran's dictator/president
Mahmoud Ahmadinejad at New York's
Columbia University—President Obama's
alma mater), universities are admirably
defending these (Islamic) rights—even as
Khan advocates stoning women for
adultery, preaches that Jews and Christians

are the "enemies" of Muslims, and claims that it was the West, rather than al Qaeda, that slaughtered nearly 3,000 people on 9/11.

"In the end, it is the moral bankruptcy of our academic intelligentsia that has allowed and now empowered radical clerics like Khan to operate on British (and U.S.) campuses. At some point in the near future, another young Muslim educated in the U.K. will take what this cleric and many others say to heart. This student will try to murder as many people as possible because he thinks his religion demands it and the West deserves it. And university authorities (who—as you recall—were "educated" by the Illuminati's "puppets" in a "new direction") will once again look the other way. Perhaps at some point British (and hopefully American) society will put its foot down, and complain that it's sick of our tax money funding factories that turn young Muslims into terrorists. At the time of this writing, New York Congressman, Peter King, is doing just that, with hearings that are designed to expose the radicalization of Islam in America). But in the meantime, we Brits (or Americans) can no longer feign surprise that our universities are churning out al Qaeda's foot soldiers."

I don't know that the case for using radical Islam and educational institutions as places to indoctrinate young people toward the I-IA's agenda could have been made any better. Ms. Simcox's article is a clear and present example of how the drafters of *The Protocols* have implemented the part of their plan, which says:

> "When we come into power, we ... shall make out of the youth *obedient children of authority,* loving him (the antichrist) who rules as the (false) support and hope of peace and quiet."

Keep in mind that it was an exorcised youth movement that fell in behind Barack Obama's candidacy for president. And, in 2012, many will have attained the age to vote ... legally.

Clearly, *The Protocols* are not the work of any particular religious group—at least not one based on the theocracy of God. The more one studies the document, the more it will be obvious that *The Protocols* is anything *but* the work of godly people. It is the product of *anti-religion* disciples of Lucifer who have denounced God. The following sections affirm these conclusions.

> "Our ruler (the promised antichrist) will always be among the people and be surrounded by a mob of apparently curious men and women, who will occupy the front ranks about (the antichrist) to all appearance by chance, and will restrain the ranks of the rest out of respect as it will appear for good order ... "

The kind of protection of the antichrist mentioned above was well-portrayed in two movies by the titles of *The Omen I, II (Damien)*, and *The Omen III*.

For centuries, Man has anticipated the coming of the antichrist. Though the Revelation to St. John the Divine provided clues, the identity of the antichrist remains a mystery. Is it possible that the antichrist is not a single human being, but a group of human beings that have banded together to do Lucifer's bidding—The Invisible Empire, Shadow Government, Illuminati or the Islamic-Illuminati Alliance? Keep this thought in the back of your mind as you read on.

> (When we have established a New World Order, as began to take place during the U.S. presidency of Woodrow Wilson, (we) "... will be enabled to resort to the lawful confiscation of all sums of every kind for the regulation of their circulation in the State (a One-World Government). From this follows that taxation will best be covered by a *progressive tax* on property." (Such a tax was implemented under the administrations of Herbert Hoover and Franklin D. Roosevelt. At one time incomes over $100,000 were taxed at 90%. And if President Obama has his way, taxes will head upward in that direction).
>
> "The rich must be aware that it is their duty to place a part of their superfluities (wealth) at the disposal of the State (for redistribution to the masses) since the State guarantees them security of possession of

the rest of their property and the right of
honest gains ..."

Of course, the super-rich members of the Illuminati
considered themselves exempt from the redistribution
policies they demand of the rest of us. Social progressives
choose which segment of the wealthy they will discriminate
against. *The Protocols* provide a pre-emptive word of
warning to the Illuminati's appointed "puppets" in houses
of government.

> "The tax upon the poor man is a seed
> of revolution and works to the detriment of
> the State ... (Consider President Obama's
> rhetoric on taxing only the prosperous
> segment of the American society). Quite
> apart from this, a tax on capitalists dim-
> inishes the growth of wealth in private
> hands in which we have in these days
> concentrated it (growth of wealth among the
> 'out-group') as a counterpoise to the
> strength of (democracies and) their State
> finances. A tax increasing in a percentage
> ratio to capital (progressive income tax) ... is
> useful to us now for the sole reason that *it
> excites trouble and discontent* among the
> 'out-group,' (thus the *original* Tea Party in
> Boston Harbor and the Tea Party move-
> ment of 2010 and the continuing push on
> the part of the Democrat Party to tax
> successful Americans at ever-increasing
> rates).

"Purchase, receipt of money (income) or inheritance will be subject to the payment of a progressive tax. Any transfer of property, whether money or other, without evidence of payment of this tax which will be strictly registered by names, will render the former holder liable to pay interest on the tax from the moment of transfer of these sums up to the discovery of his evasion of declaration of the transfer (the drafters of *The Protocols* envisioned the Internal Revenue Service more than one hundred years before it was created by their "puppets") ...

"Any kind of stagnation of money acts ruinously on the running of the State machinery, for which it is the lubricant; a stagnation of the lubricant may stop the regular working of the mechanism (as has been orchestrated by the Federal Reserve, enabling the global recession of 2009-2010 and the massive "stimulus" initiatives that immediately followed). ... Economic crises have been *produced by us* by no other means than the withdrawal of money from circulation."

In 2011 American banks are sitting on trillions of dollars that they refuse to lend. Huge capitals (personal incomes and wealth) have stagnated, withdrawing tax money from States as well as the federal government, which were constantly obliged to apply to those same stagnant capitals for loans. The U.S. was, therefore "forced" to borrow trillions of dollars from China, producing a huge movement of capital from nation to nation ... as the Illuminati smiled all the way to The World Bank, which they own. Could it be that the economic tsunamis faced by various state and national governments were orchestrated by the Hidden Hand in order to create discord in the Middle East, as well as that within financially-strapped U.S. State Governments? Let's return to *The Protocols* for the answers.

> "These loans (to cover a state's or nations mounting debt) burden the finances of the State with the payment of interest and made them (nations) the bond slaves of these capitals (financial resources controlled by the Illuminati) ..."

Note once again the reference to the word "slave" in the Illuminati's plan of action. And, on the matter of how the wealth of nations is manipulated, *The Protocols* offer:

> "We have removed gold from circulation as far as possible. (This is precisely what happened during the presidency of Franklin Delano Roosevelt [and why George Soros is trying to silently corner the gold markets]. Americans were ordered to turn in to the U.S. Government all the gold they had accumulated). *That the peoples may become accustomed to obedience* it is necessary to inculcate lessons of humility and therefore to reduce the production of articles of luxury ... A people of small

masters knows nothing of unemployment and this binds him closely with existing order, and consequently with the firmness of authority. For us its part will have been played out the moment authority is transferred into our hands (by our emissaries—government union bosses, the Muslim Mafia, and the ACLU) ... Subjects give blind obedience only to *the strong hand* which is absolutely independent of them for in it they feel the sword of defense and support against social scourges ...

"The supreme lord (Lucifer and his One-World Government) who will replace all now existing rulers, dragging in their existence among societies demoralized by us, societies that have denied even the authority of God, from whose midst breeds out on all sides the fire of anarchy, must first of all proceed to quench this all-devouring flame. Therefore he (the mortal Supreme Ruler of a global government, a Luciferian disciple *that the Illuminati chooses*) will be obliged to *kill off* those existing societies (thus the reason for the Islamic-Illuminati Alliance,) though he should drench them (non-compliant societies) with his own blood, that he (Lucifer's surrogate) may resurrect them again in the form of regularly organized troops fighting consciously with every kind of infection that may cover the body of the State with sores.

"The object of this mode of action is that all may know *that government cannot be entrusted to those who have not been inducted into the secret places of its art* ... The king's plan of action for the current moment, and all the more so for the future, will be unknown, even to those who are called his closest counselors."[47]

The excerpts from *The Protocols* that I have included should stir your emotions. Whether it is was originally drafted as a hoax or a cipher, clearly, someone or some ungodly group of individuals has reduced the document's ideologies to print and adopted it (The Protocols) as their master plan. I do not believe—for one moment—that the works of the Lords of Seduction represent the sentiments of any one race, religion, or creed. They appear to be a mix of individuals who no longer subscribe to any organized religion or creed that is remotely based on God's laws.

And, anyone who attempts to hang the yoke of *The Protocols* around the necks of true Zionists is as guilty of sedition and unholy acts as the architects of the document, themselves. Though the identity of its author(s) may forever remain a mystery—as you will come to see in future chapters—*The Protocols* appear to be a living, breathing document.

I have personal experience in dealing with such a document. Mine involved a long-standing conflict between two plastic surgery societies. For suspected anti-trust violations, the authors of a "white paper" entitled "Intergroup Conflict" were investigated by the U.S. Federal

---

[47] http://www.biblebelievers.org.au

Trade Commission. During the investigation, secret documents of the offending party (the American Society of Plastic and Reconstructive Surgeons) were confiscated by the FTC. Later—through the Freedom of Information Act—my group (The American Academy of Facial Plastic and Reconstructive Surgery) was able to obtain copies of those documents. We discovered in the documents a detailed and sinister plan (conceived and conducted in the same vein as *The Protocols*) in which the ASPRS intended to "stall, frustrate, and destroy" the "out-group" (as they referred to the AAFPRS) by using "guerilla warfare" tactics, "similar to those used in Viet Nam" and reminiscent of tactics outlined in *The Protocols.*

When the document reached the light of day, however, the governing body of the ASPRS claimed that the document represented "random ruminations of one of their executive officers and was never adopted as the policy of the organization." However, the evidence refuted those claims. Numerous examples could be documented in which the modus operandi stated in the ASPRS' "Intergroup Conflict" document were carried out by members of the organization throughout the world.

Were it not for my own experiences in such sinister matters, I would be more inclined to doubt that *The Protocols* represent the premeditated plan of any group or organization.

After reading through *The Protocols* and reviewing debates over their authenticity, I was led to dig deeper. Additional evidence of their implementation came to light when an Illuminist, David Rockefeller, addressed the Trilateral Commission in 1991. As previously presented in this   manuscript, Rockefeller said,

"We are grateful to the Washington Post, The New York Times, Time Magazine and other great publications whose directors have attended our meetings and respected their promises of discretion for almost forty years. It would have been impossible for us to develop our plan for the world if we had been subjected to the lights of publicity during those years. But, the world is now more sophisticated and prepared to march towards a world government. *The supra-national sovereignty of an intellectual elite and world bankers is surely preferable to the national auto-determination practiced in past centuries.*"

I want to repeat my conviction that *The Protocols do not* represent the opinions and policies of godly men. After months of research, I believe that they represent the sinister dreams (and perhaps a masterful instrument of seduction) expressed by of a small cabal of newly-professed members of a "revolutionary faith"—secularists who are blinded by their own quest to be the gods overseeing their newly created "supranational sovereignty." That—throughout the centuries—this "supranational sovereignty" has entered into alliances with various groups to do its bidding, is more than a possibility.

Regardless of identity of the original authors, a modern-day, self-designated "supranational sovereignty of intellectual elites and world bankers" has seemingly used *The Protocols'* to create dissention and distrust among the various peoples of the world and to use despotism to create the makings of a global government of the Illuminati's own liking. They also know that the path to such an end leads directly through the heartland of the United States of America. And, based on history, they know that the spirit of the American patriot must be broken before the "land of the free and home of the brave," is firmly in their grasp.

CHAPTER 7

Now that "the problem" has been identified, let us move on to possible solutions. To bring about remedy, we have to look no further than the White House and Congress. America is starving for the kind of leadership that sustains a nation's might on the world stage. We are in need of journalists who are willing to seek the truth and bring it to the people when they find it. We can't seem to move beyond the War Between the States. And, that we cannot plays into the hands of the Illuminati. It is also a major reason why America's government is being run by a growing number of lesser qualified individuals than at any time in its history. This, too, is no coincidence. America's enemies have been creating divisions between segments of our society and using those divisions to the Illuminati-Islamic Alliance's strategic advantage. Many patriotic and forward-thinking Blacks see how race is used to further both a *greater* and *lesser* cause—the undoing of America. One speaker of such truth is Lloyd Marcus.

In his March 27, 2010 article, *"A Black Man, the Progressive's Perfect Trojan Horse,"* Marcus wrote:

> "... Recently, I have come to believe that perhaps I am wrong about Obama's race

not being an issue. In reality, Obama's presidency has everything to do with racism, but not from the Tea Party movement. Progressives and Obama have exploited his race from the rookie senator's virtually unchallenged presidential campaign to his unprecedented bullying of America into Obama*Care*. Obama's race trumped all normal media scrutiny of him as a presidential candidate ... (Remember what *The Protocols* said about protecting their 'puppet' president?) Obama*Care* forces all Americans to purchase healthcare, the constitutionality of which will be decided by the U.S. Supreme Court. "No white president could get away with boldly and arrogantly thwarting the will of the American people and ignoring laws. President Clinton tried universal healthcare. Bush tried social security reform. The American people said 'no' to both presidents' proposals and it was the end of it. So how can Obama get away with giving the American people the finger? The answer: He is black.

"The mainstream liberal media continues to portray all who oppose Obama in any way as racist. Despite a list of failed policies, overreaches into the private sector, violations of the Constitution and planned destructive legislation too numerous to mention in this article, many Americans are still fearful of criticizing our first black president. Incredible!

"My fellow Americans, you must not continue to allow yourselves to be 'played' and intimidated by Obama's race or the historical context of his presidency. If we are to save America, the greatest nation on the planet, Obama's progressive agenda must be stopped."

The article was then signed, "Lloyd Marcus (black) Unhyphenated American, Singer/Songwriter, Entertainer, Author, Artist & Tea Party Patriot." At the end of his article, Marcus wrote: "SHARE THIS WITH AMERICA!!!!" I just did.

America owes as debt of gratitude to Mr. Marcus and anyone who will speak the truth and not be intimidated by those who are quick to hang the yoke of racism or bigotry around our necks. The Left's plan to "hush" free-speaking Americans and instill double standards has worked quite successfully ... and, now that America is gasping for its fiscal breath, the practice of double standards must be contested.

According to Illuminist, David Rockefeller, the main-stream media (the supposed *institution of truth* in a free society) has allowed his "supranational sovereignty" to use racism as a way to quiet the opposition, all while modern-day Elders have artfully avoided being "subjected to the bright lights of publicity."

I realize that it is unfair to cast the shroud of suspicion over all members of the press. And, to the innocent, I offer my apologies. I know many of them personally and do not believe—for one minute—that the ones I know would knowingly misrepresent the facts. It is my contention that many members of the media have been seduced. They have learned from their editors and producers what kind of reporting will be acceptable in the eyes of their superiors. I don't think that it's a surprise that the majority of the press and *big three* network pundits lean far leftward and apply different standards to politicians with whom they agree. It's the only way they can survive in modern media circles.

Perhaps the following list of incidences will demonstrate how the mainstream media has circled the wagons to protect President Obama, providing cover for sophomoric decisions and a long list of gaffs.

What if any Republican president had preempted negotiations between Israel and Palestine by "siding with the Muslims" on border issues? In an internationally-broadcast speech President Obama stated that it was "the United States' position" that Israel should voluntarily give back control over territories of which it gained control while driving back its Muslim invaders in the Six Day War of 1967? Would Jewish members of the Democrat Party and a liberal press have overlooked the President's position *for* Palestinian Muslims and *against* Israel on the border issue, suggesting what Israeli Prime Minister, Benjamin Netanyahu called an "indefensible" Israeli concession?

What if President George W. Bush (or any Republican president) had declared that a law passed by Congress, signed by

President Clinton and reviewed by the Supreme Court was "unconstitutional," would the press have asked for him to be impeached?

If President Bush had sat on his hands and done nothing when pirates killed four Americans, would the press have remained silent?

If President Bush had sent the Republican National Committee and his own campaign team to Madison, Wisconsin to harass duly elected officials would the press have remained silent?

If any other U.S. president had said that the "We are not at war ..." with a country while our military were—at that same moment—shooting down Libyan aircraft, launching missiles into that country and killing soldiers loyal to the nation's dictator, would the press would have called him out as a liar?

If any other U.S. president had expended billions of dollars intervening in a civil war of a middle-eastern country (without the approval of Congress) at a time when the U.S. debt threatened U.S. sovereignty, would the press have demanded impeachment?

If any other U.S. president doubled a national debt that had taken more than two centuries to accumulate, *in one year*, would the press have remained silent?

If any other of our presidents had then proposed to double the debt *again* within ten years, would the press have protected him from fiscal conservatives?

If any other U.S. president had publically criticized a state law that he admitted he *never read*, would the mainstream media have called him irresponsible?

If any other U.S. president were to side with a foreign country and sue a state in the United States to force that state to continue to allow illegal immigration, would the press have questioned his patriotism and compliance with the oath he took to "protect and defend the United States of America and its Constitution?

If any other president's administration had told border patrol officers to send back—and not arrest—illegal foreigners that had already crossed the border in order to boast of a "reduction in the number of illegal's arrested," would the press have questioned the veracity *of anything* the administration reported?

If any other president's administration had sold automatic weapons—that they are trying to outlaw in the U. S.—to Mexican drug lords who used those same guns to kill U. S. Border Patrol officers, would the press have not called for the head(s) of the person(s) who sanctioned the sale?

If any other of our presidents had pronounced the Marine "Corps" like Marine "Corpse," would the press have made an issue of it? (Remember Dan Quayle's misspelling of "potato" while reading the misspelled word from a cue-card that had been presented to him?)

If any other U.S. president had been the first President to need a Teleprompter to be able to get through a press conference, would the mainstream media have laughed and said this is more proof of how inept he is on his own and is really managed by smarter men behind the scenes?

If any other president refused to allow domestic drilling for oil and gas, while the cost of gasoline at the pump soared to record levels, would the press have accused him of siding with OPEC (a Muslim cartel)?

If during one of the deepest recessions in modern history any other of our presidents had put **eighty-seven thousand** workers out of work by arbitrarily placing a moratorium on offshore oil drilling on domestic companies that have one of the best safety records of any industry because *one foreign* company had an accident, would the press have questioned his judgment at a time when the price of oil on the global market is skyrocketing?

If any other of our presidents had used a *forged document* as the basis of the moratorium that would render eighty-seven thousand American workers unemployed would the press have questioned his veracity?

If any other U.S. president had spent hundreds of thousands of dollars to take his First Lady to a Broadway play in New York City, at a time when America's economy is in trouble, would the press have questioned whether he is in touch with reality?

If any other U.S. president berate the use of corporate jets by businessmen while flying Air Force One just a few hundred miles to deliver a campaign speech and raise money for his re-election, would the press have pointed out the hypocrisy?

If any other U.S. president had reduced American citizen's retirement plan holdings of General Motors stock by ninety percent *and given* the unions a majority stake in GM, would the press have questioned his concerns for the rest of America's middle class, *non-union* workers?

If any other U.S. president had made a lame joke about his bowling score at the expense of the Special Olympics, would the press have ignored it?

If any other U.S. president had given British Prime Minister Gordon Brown a set of inexpensive and incorrectly formatted DVDs, when Gordon Brown had given him a thoughtful and historically significant gift, would the press have brushed it aside?

If any other U.S. president had given the Queen of England an iPod containing videos of his speeches, would the press have called him arrogant?

If any other U.S. president had bowed to the King of Saudi Arabia, would the press have questioned his allegiance of—and respect for—the U.S. presidency?

If any other U.S. president had visited Austria and made reference to the non-existent "Austrian language," would the U.S. press have brushed it off as a "minor slip?"

If any other U.S. president had stated that there were *fifty-seven* states in the United States, would the press have questioned his knowledge of the nation he sought to lead?

If any other U.S. president had flown all the way to Denmark (at great expense to the U.S. taxpayer) to make a five minute speech (to the Olympic Selection Site Committee) about how the Olympics would benefit *him* walking out his front door in his home town, would the press have labeled him 'self-centered, conceited, and egotistical'?

If any other U.S. president (or vice-president) had been so Spanish illiterate as to refer to "Cinco de Cuatro" in front of the Mexican ambassador when it was the 5th of May (Cinco de Mayo), and continued to flub it when he tried again, would the U.S. press have ignored it? (No wonder Barack

Obama needs a Teleprompter and a team of handlers to package his remarks.)

If any other U.S. president had burned **nine thousand** gallons of jet fuel to go plant a single tree on Earth Day, would the press have called him a hypocrite?

If any other U.S. president's administration had okayed Air Force One (followed by a jet fighter) to fly low over downtown Manhattan while millions of people watched, causing widespread panic, would the press have questioned if he understood what happened on 9-11-2001?

If any other U.S. president had failed to send relief aid to flood victims throughout the Midwest, with more people killed or made homeless than in New Orleans, would the press have made it into a major ongoing political issue with claims of racism and incompetence?

If any other U.S. president had created the position of thirty-two Czars who report directly to him, bypassing the House and Senate on much of what is happening in America, would the press have questioned his attempts to circumvent Congress and the Constitution?

If any other U.S. president had ordered the firing of the CEO of a major corporation, even though he had no constitutional authority to do so, would the press have remained silent about it?

So, what is it about Obama that causes the U.S. mainstream media to overlook his ineptness to lead? Is it the fear of justifiable criticism of the first U.S. black president? The American people have a right to know the answer to this question. It can be found in *The Protocols*...in black and white. The Illuminati "owns" the press and can direct it to crucify or glorify any one of its "puppets" at will. Never before has media bias been so blatant.

While mainstream reporters and their editors protect Left-leaning politicians—especially President Barack H. Obama and his administration—they seem obsessed with negativism toward conservatives ... especially *conservative women*.

In the run-up to the 2012 presidential election, Michele Bachman's headaches have been used by the mainstream media to question her ability to hold the office of president. There was a time when a woman's menstrual cycle was used to raise the same question—a question that the National Organization of Women summarily squelched. Where is N.O.W., now? The answer is: in the tank for those who Bachman's candidacy threatens ... and their identities should be quite obvious.

Once again, let's look at a segment of *The Protocols* for affirmation.

> "... exhaust humanity with dissension, hatred, struggle, envy and even by the use of torture, by starvation, by the inoculation of diseases, by want, so that (they) see no other issue than to take refuge in our complete sovereignty in money and in all else."

As far back as the 1600s the Illuminati intended to control the press. Another part of *The Protocols* proclaim:

> "*Not a single announcement will reach the public without our control.* Even now this is already being attained by us inasmuch as all news items are received by a few agencies, in whose offices they are focused from all parts of the world. These agencies will then be already entirely ours and will give publicity only to what we dictate to them."

Those who have bought into the Hidden Hand's entitlement agenda have been vaulted into mind-shaping positions—in art, in entertainment, in classrooms, boardrooms, and in reporting "the news." At the same time, revered institutions and conservative values are being blasted. Bias and hypocrisy tend to overshadow objectivity. This is why FOX News has enjoyed such high ratings in the industry. Conservative Americans feel that they—at least—have one media outlet that is attempting to be "fair and balanced" ... or so it seems.

A quieter, but equally effective campaign of seduction is mixed with an unhealthy dose of mind-pollution in what is being sold as "entertainment" and/or "art." Individuals who "package" such information control a powerful arsenal; and anyone in the industry who represents time-tested standards appears to be at risk of being passed over.

The reason that the Illuminati have gained such a foothold in America is the "Judge" of social conscience (mainstream America) temporarily took its hands off the controls. While distracted by national and global conflict, regulatory ropes are consistently being slipped around the hands and necks of those who advocate traditional and time-tested values. Double standards are unapologetically being imposed. As "liberties" are being expanded *for some Americans*, they are being taken away from others—especially from many of the people who do the work, provide the jobs and pay the lion's share of taxes.

The spirit of the legendary Robin Hood lives. At the behest of the Illuminati-supported ACLU, a band of modern-day bureaucrats and judges are confiscating and redistributing liberties right before our eyes. The ACLU appears to be able to chip away at the U.S. Constitution and avoid being subjected to the "lights of publicity." Did anyone ever ask where the ACLU's funds come from? It must require an enormous budget to employ such a huge staff of attorneys, paralegals, secretaries, etc and to see all the suits that the ACLU prosecutes through the legal system. Now that's an "investigative reporting" story that would serve America well.

Until the mid-term elections of 2010, the sleeping giant (mainstream America) had fallen prey to the Illuminati's seduction. It had come to believe that *"We, the people"* are powerless. The I-IA's power-brokers were setting agendas. The democrat*ic* system was turned upside down. Small numbers seemed to have the advantage. "Affirmative action" had been shown to promote the most blatant example of discrimination imposed upon the American people since the War Between the States.

When was the last time that you visited the public school that the children in your community attend; *your* City Hall, *your* state Capitol, or *your* government buildings in Washington? Remember, as a tax payer, the people that you encounter there *work for you*. After you have visited places supported *by* your tax dollars, visit places that have to compete in the marketplace *for* your *after-tax* dollars—places like Disney World, Disney Land, or Publix Foods and see   difference in the people who operate these *private sector* businesses and how they treat you. What you will quickly realize is that the houses of government (local, state and federal) are not necessarily operated by the most qualified, hospitable, and appreciative people. In fact one can often detect an air of arrogance among government employees. Yet, *government* employees enjoy salaries and benefits that exceed those earned by non-government employees. Many have jobs protected by tenure or "affirmative action," and cannot be fired except for heinous indiscretions, which do not include incompetence or insubordination. It is important to keep in mind that government jobs are financed by the very individuals who are *excluded* from those workplaces because of the unfair practices of "affirmative action."

There is a reason for all this. For the Illuminati's plan to work, "affirmative action" could not be limited just to government (as was originally promised by President Lyndon Johnson.) Socialist "intellectual elites" had to see that onerous penalties would be levied against *private* business and industry should the private sector choose to ignore "affirmative action" in their hiring and retention practices and hire the most qualified workers, admin-istrators or teachers. Parkinsonian practices of *sanctioned incompetence* permeate government, where mediocrity—not excellence—is the mandated norm ... even the highest seats of government.

America was sufficiently warned by the noted British economist (Northcote Parkinson) that this was the natural history of big government. Enough of us didn't listen. Are we listening now?

If one wanted to unravel a nation, "affirmative action" would be a necessary part of the plan. In an affirmative action government, the masses of high-minded, hard-working, tax-paying Americans would be excluded from participation in many of the programs that their efforts build and support. And if affirmative action hires, appointees, or elected officials weren't as qualified as other candidates—in time—a nation becomes less competitive in the global arena. So, if a group of us were to set out to tear America apart at the seams, here's what we would do:

- Make Americans feel a sense of guilt for expecting opportunity and pay to be based on merit, i.e. on the "content of one's character."[48]

- Insist that hires and promotions be based upon the color of skin, sexual orientation, or gender.

- See to it that a *minority* of socialist-leaning disciples controlled headlines, and cast a shroud of bigotry over anyone who disagreed with them.

- Make patriotic, tax-paying Americans feel guilt for demanding that our borders be protected.

- Demonize successful American entre-preneurs.

- Have Americans feel guilt for demand-ing that their taxes be spent wisely and

---

[48] Martin Luther King, *I Have A Dream,* Washington, D.C., 1963.

that their government live by the same budgetary principles as we are forced to exercise in our homes or businesses.

- Make Americans feel guilt for demanding that our armed forces be supplied with whatever they needed to keep the peace and secure our borders and only sent into harm's way when national security is at stake.

- Ensure that hard-working Americans feel guilt for expecting fellow countrymen and women to contribute to America's defense and prosperity—in whatever way he or she is able.

If you and I were part of The Illuminati (or advising them) these are some of the things we would surely recommend. Collectively the installation of these measures would go a long way toward creating a One-World Government ... at America's expense. Remember what I said earlier: *To defeat the enemy; think like the enemy thinks.*

Seduction has become "big business." The misinformed are being led by contemporary "Pied Pipers" along a path of ruination—and patriots are made to feel guilt if we point out the fact that we are. The guilt is not limited to adults.

Young Americans are being sent mixed messages about role-playing. Some of the confusion arises from camps where it seems that women want to be more like men, and men want to be more like women. Children are confused. That's part of the I-IA's plan—confuse them; then capture their minds.

Another excerpt from *The Protocols* makes the point:

> "We have fooled, bemused and corrupted the youth ... by rearing them in principles and theories which are known to us to be false (and decadent)."

Clearly, confusion is a natural component of the art of seduction. Conflict follows closely behind; then comes chaos; finally, indoctrination and servitude. And the disturbing fact is that seemingly-intelligent people have been desensitized to the dangers of ignoring the obvious.

To give away—without a fight—what was bought with the life blood of young men and women in the air, on the land and at sea is *an insult* to those who made the ultimate sacrifice so that Americans—like you and me—can raise our voices and take up the mantle of freedom.

A look back at the failed democracies should cause us to choose only the kinds of "change" that bring about prudence. But as Mark Twain said, "... Man is incurable foolish."

Today's version of the human race is easily swayed by seductive promises of prosperity and has bought into the "more is better" attitude that naturally causes human beings to choose between masters. In recent times, the "masters" that we have chosen have taken us in the wrong direction ... and toward the cliff overlooking a Great Abyss.

* * * * * * * * *

How did America lose its way? Let's explore some of the possibilities. As humankind evolved into culturally sophisticated animals, parents delegated more of their parental responsibilities.

It wasn't that long ago when sunset signaled a family gathering at the dinner table to discuss the day's events while nourishing their bodies with home-cooked (and in many cases home-grown) food. Reports and recognition were often followed with rewards. Unacceptable behavior resulted in embarrassment and/or disciplinary measures. Accountability abounded. That was a time now reserved for the history books, but if America is to survive the Cycle of Democracies, one that can—and must--be revived.

A recent survey reported that in the late 1940s, nine (9) of ten (10) households contained both parents. By contrast, at the turn of the 21st century only four of ten family units contained both father and mother. A number of factors are responsible, but until *"We the people"* recognize that promoting and rewarding *separateness* is destructive and that programs which reward *togetherness* is rewarded, the downward slide will surely continue.

In 21st century America, interpersonal exchanges have been replaced with electronic media boxes whose one-way speakers deny debate. Airway intruders fill the family-room with opinions and values generated around the corporate tables of media and marketing directors. Sound and visual "bytes" deliver premeditated messages designed to influence the way we think ... more often than not, focusing on conflict. That this is the case is not an accident. It is an orchestrated plan of the Hidden Hand, whose *Protocols* promise: "... we shall make out of the youth obedient children of (our) authority ..."

One such Illuminati "child of authority" appears to be the man currently occupying the Oval Office. His Muslim heritage and secret past raises a lot of questions.

Since Barack Obama vaulted onto the scene, the world has learned a lot about Dhimmitude and Muslim Sharia Law. It dictates that conversion *from* Islam to Christianity is a crime punishable by death. This fact is substantiated by the words of a Muslim judge who presided over the trial of an Afghani convert. At trial, the judge said: "It is a crime to convert to Christianity from Islam." The prosecutor in the case said: "We are Muslims and becoming a Christian is against our laws. He (the convert) must get the death penalty."

One has to wonder how Sharia Law squares with the conversion of Barack Obama from an Indonesian Muslim to Black Liberation Theology. The President has admitted that while growing up in Indonesia as Barry Soetoro, he was raised as a Muslim. His school application form affirms this fact. Obama claims that—under the tutelage of Reverend Jeremiah Wright, he converted from Islam to a little understood form of Christianity. If this is the case, why has Barack Obama escaped the ire of Muslim clerics and remained in the good graces of the leaders of Islamic nations? There can be only two possibilities: Barry Soetoro (a/k/a Barack Obama) never truly converted to Christianity or, if he did convert, holding Sharia Law at bay (in Obama's case) is consistent with the Illuminati-Islamic Alliances' policies of seduction, including those published in *The Protocols of the Elders*, which say:

> "The chamber of deputies will protect
> ... we shall provide him (the president) with
> a means of self-defense."

Since the I-IA's plan is to rule the world, it is conceivable that the current group of "Elders" (the Inner

Circle) has cut a deal with Islamic clerics and judges, providing Barack Obama with a reprieve until he once again—and publically—"sides with the Muslims." Another possibility is that Muslims do not consider Black Liberation Theology a Christian religion. One way or the other, President Obama's "conversion" raises a lot of questions.

Earlier I referred to an old Mafia motto that applies to the unholy alliance between Islam and the Illuminati: "The enemy of my enemy is my friend." Both Islam and The Elders of the Illuminati have stated that eliminating the Judeo-Christian "god-head" is essential to bringing their plan to fruition.

Under the section of *The Protocols* entitled: "We Shall Destroy God," the authors wrote:

> "... it is indispensable for us to undermine all faith, to tear out of the mind of the out-group the very principle of god-head and the spirit, and to put in its place arithmetical calculations and material needs."

This is—without question—one of the more disturbing portions of *The Protocols.* It spells out the atheistic views of the Hidden Hand. Could Barack Obama be the tie that binds the enemies of the Judeo-Christian God—a Muslim who converts to a religion that claims to be a different kind of Christianity—Black Liberation Theology?

According to www.politicalislam.com, before he became a candidate for president, Barack Obama, "... closely aligned himself with Reverend Jeremiah Wright," Wright's Trinity United Church of Christ and—through

Reverend Wright—Black Liberation Theology (BLT) and Louis Farrakhan's Nation of Islam.

In January, 2008, *Israpundit* reported that a month before, "Wright's Trinity United Church of Christ bestowed its highest social achievement award upon ... Louis Farrakhan, the head of the Nation of Islam ... The award dubbed the 'Lifetime Achievement Award' is named the 'Dr. Jeremiah A. Wright, Jr. Trumpet Award," after the pastor that married Barack and Michelle Obama." It would be interesting to ask Jeremiah Wright, Louis Farrakhan, and Barack and Michelle Obama the color of the skin of the "Christ" worshipped in Wright's Church of Christ.

It is important to note that Farrakhan's Nation of Islam (NI) promotes separatism between blacks and whites. Wikipedia lists The Nation of Islam's objectives, among which are to:

- Be allowed to create a separate nation of their own within the confines of the United States of America;
- Establish separate schools for boys (up until age 16) and girls (up until age 18) as well as women's colleges and universities;
- All black children should be taught by *black* teachers;
- Free school equipment, provided by the U.S. government;
- Intermarriage or race mixing should not be allowed."

Clearly, Louis Farrakhan is not interested in *a united* America. He wants his own Islamic nation *within* the United States—a nation donated by and financed by the American taxpayer, ninety-percent of which are white and who adhere to Judeo-Christian ideologies. I know that Farrakhan's demands are factual because a man who once worked for me attended Farrakhan's "Million Man March" (of which only about a third of that number were present.) He listened to Farrakhan's speeches and brought back with him literature circulated at the event by Farrakhan's minions. One of the publications my employee brought home outlined the plan that is summarized above. An added demand that Farrakhan intended to place on the U.S. government is that it give an *existing state* to the Nation of Islam and finance his plan with U.S. tax-payer dollars.

So, two questions deserve the rational consideration of all freedom-loving Americans: **Why Obama? Why now?** Barack Obama has common roots with many individuals who admittedly don't like the United States of America (or the God, "In Whom We Trust") and intend to "change" it.

The cozy relationship between Farrakhan, Wright, Black Liberation Theology's founder, James Cone, and the Obama's should give Americans reason for pause. The paths of all these men (and one woman) converge at a Chicago church. It is for Farrakhan's work in furthering the mission of the Nation of Islam that the church, which President Barack and (First Lady) Michelle Obama attended and were married in, honored the leader of the Nation of Islam with a "Lifetime Achievement Award." Clear-thinking Americans should be asking: *isn't it a bit strange that a church that presents itself as "Christian" would honor a professed enemy of Christianity: Islam?*

About revolutionist James Cone's Black Liberation Theology and Islam, another *Israpundit* writer reported:

> "When viewed from the Christian point-of-view, Black Liberation Theology is a strange creed, but when seen from the standpoint of Islam, there is a **very strong parallel**[49]. Islam and BLT are theologies that have a political goal of making all politics submit to their demands. Submission is the political goal. (So, if you haven't already been convinced that Islam and the "supranational sovereignty" share common goals, the preceding statement should bridge the gap).
>
> "Islam and Black Liberation Theology are both based upon the principle of duality (a philosophy that the world is composed of two opposing entities ...)"

The foregoing statement should explain why the Illuminati and Islam joined forces to create what I have labeled the Illuminati-Islamic Alliance (I-IA), thereby dividing the world into "two opposing entities—the I-IA, and everyone else. The *Israpundit* article goes on to say:

> "The Koran divides up humanity into Muslims and the kafirs (Christian and Jew). *Black Liberation Theology has a "god" that divides humanity into blacks and whites.* But the duality is not the division, but a

---

[49] In this section, as before, the author has italicized certain words and phrases for his own emphasis.

complete separation that is ethical, political, cultural and religious. The believer (Muslim or BLT convert) has nothing in common with the kafir (Islamic) or white (BLT) non-believer.

"According to Islam, Allah loves the Muslim and according to Black Liberation Theology, a black god loves the Blacks. Allah preaches violence against the kafirs (Christian and Jew) and (Allah) helps Muslims to kill them (Christian and Jews).

"The Koran says that cruelty and hatred of the kafir (Christian and Jew) is a sacred duty for Muslims."

If Black Liberation Theology believes God and His Son are black and that God and Christ only love Blacks (and for twenty years Barack and Michelle Obama sat in the pews of Jeremiah Wright's church and listened to this theology being preached from its pulpit) it could explain why President Obama denounced his white mother's race and said, "America is not a Christian nation." At least, the America he came to know as a young man growing up in a Muslim or atheistic home was not painted by his teachers as a traditionally Christian nation. No rational person would question that America is clearly a predominately white nation (by an 80%/20% ratio). If the president believes that God is black and knows that the majority of Americans don't distinguish the color of the God they worship, it is no wonder that he believes America is not the kind of nation that Black Liberation Theology envisions ... at least *not yet*. Back to the *Israpundit* article:

"Black Liberation Theology does not preach violence against whites, but excuses and justifies it (violence) ... as does Islam. BLT also justifies black crime as a legal way for oppressed blacks to strike back at the white oppressors. It sees a rapist or killer of whites as 'a revolutionary' committing a legitimate act of a just war (As does Islamic jihad).

"A quote from James Cone, the father of Black Liberation Theology, is revealing: 'What we need is the divine love as expressed in black power, which is the power of blacks to *destroy** their oppressors, here and now, by *any and all means at their disposal*"[50]

Let's take a closer look at James Cone, the man who founded BLT. When one analyzes his teachings, one might conclude that he—too—has studied *The Protocols* ... or at least been indoctrinated by those who have. In his book, *"A Black Theology of Liberation,"* he writes:

"Black theology refuses to accept a God who is not identified totally with the goals of the black community. If God is not for us and against white people, then he is a murderer, and we had better kill him. (Does this have a familiar ring? Remember

---

[50] *A Black Theology of Liberation*, James H. Cone, p. 70).
* Emphasis added

that *The Protocols* say: "We will destroy God.")

"The task of black theology is to kill Gods who do not belong to the black community ... Black theology will accept only the love of God which participates in the destruction of the white enemy. ('Enemy' is a strong word, one that should give every white American pause. Again, the spirit of *The Protocols* emerge "... we shall wipe out all those who hinder us on our way.")

"What we (the BLT faithful) need is the divine love as expressed in Black Power, which is the power of black people to destroy their oppressors here and now by any means at their disposal (this is right out of *The Protocols)*. Unless God is participating in this holy activity, we must reject his love."[51]

For *two decades* Barack Obama sat in Jeremiah Wright's congregation and listened to him deliver sermons based on the creed of James Cone's Black Liberation Theology. If Barack and Michelle Obama weren't in agreement with this unorthodox form of "Christianity," reason dictates that they would have done what most in disagreement would do—walk out and join another church. But, they didn't—at least not until the teachings of Wright's church came into the lights of publicity.

Neither Islam nor Black Liberation Theology ever acknowledges the suffering of its enemies. Jihad (more

---

[51] *beliefnet,* Rod Dreber

appropriately labeled *The Mother of All Holocausts*) has killed over *Two Hundred and Seventy Million* kafirs (Christians and Jews) over the last one thousand four hundred years, but there has never been any acknowledgment of the atrocities. Adolf Hitler's dastardly Crusade to rid the world of Jews killed six million Jews and four million Christians ($1/27^{th}$ of the numbers that Muslims have killed in the name of Islam). While Hitler is aptly remembered as a butcher, history remains silent about the evils of Islam's *ongoing* Jihad (at least until now).

In Mohammed's official biography, *The Sira*, there are hundreds of pages devoted to jihad against the kafirs (Christians and Jews). There is not one single time when Mohammed expressed remorse about the beheading, torturing, killing, raping and robbery of innocent non-Muslims. Indeed, there are many occasions when he laughed at the kafirs' suffering.

While President Obama made his global "victory lap" and apologized for the actions and policies of the United States of America, he remained visibly silent on the atrocities committed by a religion that is his heritage.

The *Israpundit* article provides additional insight into the glaring similarities between Black Liberation Theology (BLT) and Islam. For purposes of affirming linkage between BLT and Islam, I will use dual nouns (kafir/white or Allah/Black God).

> "The duality of total separateness from the kafir (Islam's term for Christians and Jews) and white (BLT) creates an ethical position. Ethics become dualistic (means that what is ethical for one group is unethical for the next). The kafir/white is

treated differently from the (Muslim or black) "brother/sister." Since Allah/Black God hates and plots against kafirs/whites there is no empathy with the victims of the aggression. There is no remorse and, therefore, there is never an apology. There is nothing to apologize for. Allah/Black God *wanted* them (*white* Christians and Jews) dead, so there is no need to weep.

"This dualism in ethics means that the kafir/white can be deceived, robbed, insulted, raped, brutalized and killed in the name of good (as defined by BLT and   Islam)."

After reading the above, I was reminded of a line from Shakespeare: "O, what men dare do! What men may do! What men daily do, not knowing what they do!" When it comes to the intent of modern-day despots who seem to be following *The Protocols*, however, a reincarnated Shakespeare might write: *Oh, what men dare do! What men despotically do, knowing, well what they do!*

If deceiving, robbing, insulting, raping, brutalizing and killing members of other religions in the name of one's own version of God is the definition of "good," Americans have every right to be concerned. The President of the United States of America has been both a Muslim and student of Black Liberation Theology protagonists. Add to that his relationship with anti-American Weather Underground terrorist, Bill Ayers, and professed communist, Van Jones, and the picture of the "Real Barack Obama" becomes even clearer.

Whoever is pulling the strings of Barack Hussein Obama had to know that they selected the "perfect (affirmative action) puppet." Rather than living up to the oath he took to "defend the U.S. against all enemies, foreign and domestic," President Obama's actions suggest that he might well be siding with and defending America's, Israel's, and the Judeo-Christian God's enemies.

How could one conclude such things? Look at his stance on prosecuting Muslim extremists who hijacked and flew American planes into the World Trade Centers. Look at his bowing to a Saudi Muslim Prince. Look at his apologizing for America's stance on independence and freedom against Muslim terrorists. Look at how he misrepresented to the people of Indonesia America's motto (saying it is "e pluribus unum" rather than "In God We Trust;) how he misquoted the Declaration of Independence (refusing to recognize that the founders referred to "inalienable rights" granted by a colorblind God ("the Creator")—not once, but on three different occasions; and how he said that America is united "under one flag," when the pledge of allegiance states that we are one nation united "under *(one) God*" ... and the list of questionable misrepresentations goes on.

There are other reasons for concern. Barack Obama is said to be a graduate of both Columbia University and Harvard Law School, yet the speeches he delivers are carefully scripted and read from Teleprompters. The chance that the gaffs referenced earlier were oversights is slim. It appears that President Obama is seductively "changing" the fundamental tenets of the nation he was elected to lead and presenting a different America to the world than most Americans believe they live in ... or would get during an Obama presidency.

It is time that patriotic Americans demand from its President the audacity to present history *as it actually occurred.* There is reason to look more closely at those who would reinvent God (as Black Liberation Theology or Islam has) or "destroy" him (as *the Protocols* suggest). There is reason to consider *The Protocols* as a living document. There is reason to turn ones back on the Lords of Seduction (and their puppets) and rebuild America from the pieces that remain.

Admittedly I have been/will be hard on President Obama. As Commander-in-Chief of the greatest fighting force in world history, a lot of people depend upon his judgment and allegiance. And that I questioned the president's policies, associates, and loyalty to the oath he swore will be viewed by the liberal Left as a "racist" attack on the President and his advisors. As *The Protocols* stress, this is how the Illuminati's "Chamber of Deputies" protect the people they've vaulted into positions of prominence. In parts of this book, I published what many free-thinking Black Americans have said about using the race card against anyone who expresses disagreement with BLT or with Black agendas and their leaders.

Truth is: my remarks are not intended to cause undue attention against people with any particular skin color, but to ideologies which run counter to the Great American Dream described by the U.S. President Thomas Jefferson, President Abraham Lincoln, President John F. Kennedy, President Ronald Reagan, and Dr. Martin Luther King. At the behest of these leaders, Americans from all walks of life, "bought" into an even-handed dream to create "one nation, under God, indivisible, with liberty and justice for all," in which citizens would be judged by "the content of their character."

The toe-stepping observations that are herein revealed are intended to open the reader's mind to a world in the throes of premeditated totalitarian "Change." No matter what one's color, religion or creed, it is time to take a closer look at the kind of "changes" happening in America, in Israel and throughout the free world. Based on the teachings of Islam and Black Liberation Theology, an *unholy* war has been declared on anyone who is white or not Muslim. And, who is the holy wars' apparent champion—a man who has proven his allegiance to both Islam and Black Liberation Theology—Barack Hussein Obama, the I-IA's Siren-in-Chief.

The answer to the question: **"Why Obama? Why now?"** should becoming clearer.

Crowning a pseudo-American "Prince of Jihad" has long been in the works. Even though Obama's place of birth has been questioned—as described in *The Protocols*—his legal right to become the president has been aptly handled by the Illuminati's "... chamber of deputies," whose role it is to "protect him (the president of their choice) with a means of self-defense." To be specific, *The Protocols say:*

> "In order that our scheme may produce this result *we shall arrange elections in favor of such presidents as have in their past some dark, undiscovered stain* ... then they will be trustworthy agents for the accomplishment of our plans out of fear of revelations and from the natural desire of everyone who has attained power, namely, the retention of the privileges, advantages and honor connected with the office of the president. The *chamber of deputies*[*] will

---

[*] Emphasis added

provide cover for, will protect, will elect
presidents, but we shall take from it the
right to propose new, or make changes in
existing laws, for this right will be given by
us to the responsible president, *a puppet in
our hands*. Naturally, the authority of the
presidents will then become a target for
every possible form of attack, but we shall
provide him with a means of self-defense in
the right of an appeal to the people, for the
decision of the people over the heads of
their representatives, that is to say, an
appeal to that same blind slave of ours—the
majority of the mob (masses)."

Clearly, President Obama is beholding to a *"chamber
of deputies"* who groomed him to become president of the
only remaining bastion standing between a global
government and free, independent nations governed by
"national auto-determination." Is he beholding to the heirs
of the men who wrote—or revised—*The Protocols?* That is
another question that history may be left to answer.

As Commander-in-Chief, President Obama could
provide political cover for Islamic nations (like Iran) while
they developed arsenals that are capable of massive jihad
— specifically a nuclear attack on Israel and terrorist attacks
on the United States of America, a historical Judeo/
Christian nation. He could assist Palestinians in their
ongoing conflict with Israel.

If I am wrong about President Obama, I hope that he
and all his supporters will accept my most sincere apologies
and that the one true God and all the peoples of Earth will
forgive me. If I am right about President Obama, I trust

that he will be exposed for what he is and be dealt with directly.

Whether I am right or wrong about Barack Obama, I am certain of Islamic leaders' intent on destroying the bastions of Judaism and Christianity—the U.S. and Israel. And, I am certain that he wrote in one of his books (*Audacity of Hope*) that he would "stand with the Muslims should the winds of change begin to blow in an ugly direction." Both the U.S. and Israel—targets of Islamic Jihad—stand in the I-IA's way of ruling the world. Based upon what I have learned about its founder, I feel certain that Black Liberation Theology is a likely partner (or ally) to radical Islam. I also feel certain in saying that the Illuminati will "use all means necessary" to get its way and that an Illuminati-Islamic Alliance is one way to that end.

So, it stands to reason that the entities who shared common "enemies" would be allies. It certainly appears that much of the discord in the world is being orchestrated. Remember: *"There are no coincidences."* Someone, somewhere, is following the kinds of policies and procedures that are contained within *The Protocols* ... and resurfacing through many of the individuals and organizations with which Barack and Michelle Obama and the *Council of Deputies* have been/are linked.

* * * * * * * * * *

According to a Wall Street Journal report (9/1/1993) the (then) "Prince of Jihad" (Sheikh Omar Abdel-Rahman) and some of his followers who lived in Brooklyn, N.Y., were linked to a series of terrorists acts ranging from the assassination of Egypt's former leader, Anwar Sadat, to the *first* attempted destruction of New York's International

Trade Center and similar landmarks. The (terrorists) group's actions seem to arise from the teachings that martyrdom, earned through killing either a Christian or Jew, ensures passage to paradise. Their commitment to rid the world of "infidels" (Christians and Jews) carries over from reports of persecution of Mohammed thousands of years ago.

According to Sheikh Omar in his Ph.D. dissertation, "jihad (the holy war) was the only way to vanquish the enemies of Islam." (His intentions were known years before he moved to the U.S. and masterminded the first terrorist attack on Americans). How could this have been allowed to happen? Surely, the United States Intelligence community was aware of the Sheikh's intentions. Who provided cover for him?

The Sheikh's followers have stated publicly that they know what they are supposed to do. That's frightening stuff. On 9/11/2001 the sheikh and a small army of radical Muslims delivered on his threats. Since then several other attempts to kill Americans in mass numbers have been thwarted; but, make no mistake about it. Jihad is real.

And, the United States of America—along with Israel— are in the crosshairs. Yet, Obama Administration Attorney General, Eric Holder, made the decision to move Sheikh Omar's trial out of a military court setting into an expectedly more forgiving venue—a *civilian-comprised federal court,* overseen by judges that might have been Illuminati "puppets." More surprising to the American people is that Holder chose New York City—of all places— as his venue, throwing salt in the wounds of a grieving city, still recovering from the slaughter of thousands of its citizens and heroes.

Obama's attorney general appeared to be using the power of his office to treat terrorists as "criminals" rather than terrorists, thereby awarding them certain rights not traditionally provided to terrorists.

As far back as the early 1990s the handwriting was on the wall. Americans and their government didn't believe that terrorism would land on our shores. We were wrong. Today, new warnings as to America's ability to survive are being issued. Hopefully, this time the American people and their leaders will listen ... and not ignore the melodious rhetoric of "change" issuing from the mouth—of the Illuminati's Siren-in-Chief, who continues to downplay the threat and—until the people of New York City shouted a resounding "NO"—provide Islamic terrorists with under-served rights, living up to the President's promise to "side with the Muslims."

.

* * * * * * * * *

How involved should you and I become in calling out fanaticism and those who defend it? More involved than ever, the survival of our nation and way of life depend on it.

Who is "the enemy" that our Commander-in-Chief— according to the oath he took—*should be* protecting us against?" We now know *part of* the answer to this question. In addition to radical Islam, the Illuminati (world bankers and intellectual elites) appear committed to destroying us from within, employing white collar terrorism to collapse financial institutions and the U.S. dollar on world markets.

There was a time when "the enemy" resided *outside* the borders of the United States. In 2011 that no longer appears to be the case. I believe the infamous cartoon character may have been right. Pogo said, "We have met the enemy, and it is us." At least, the enemy *lives among us.* Regardless of what the Illuminati's Sirens say publically, the "*enemy*" is not the other race, the other sex, the other religion or the other anything or anyone. Humanity's enemy is Evil, itself—Luciferian Evil.

It is difficult for us to admit that we, Americans, have fallen victim to a masterfully-designed plot. We were once the envy of the world. As Alexander Tyler warned in his Cycle of Democracies, we have become apathetic and allowed our might to be whittled away by those who envied—or loathed—us. We have allowed our enemies to cause us to be so focused on the problems that exist *among us* that we let our guard down on the dangers emanating from a coalition that was behind the orchestration of our demise. Was this a coincidence? Let's once again turn to what *The Protocols* say about it:

> "We count upon attracting all nations to the task of erecting the new fundamental structure (One-World Government,) the project for *which has been drawn up by us.*
>
> "This is why, before everything, it is indispensable for us to arm ourselves and to store up in ourselves that absolutely reckless *audacity* (a word that Barack Obama used in the title of his book: *Audacity of Hope*) and irresistible might of the spirit which in the person of our active workers (the Left-leaning members of the Democrat Party) will break down all hindrances on our way.
>
> "When we have accomplished our coup d'état, we shall say then to the various

peoples: everything has gone terribly badly, all have been worn out with suffering. We are destroying the causes of your torment (coming to your rescue) ... Then will the mob exalt us and bear us up in their hands in a unanimous triumph of hopes and expectations."

This scenario seems to accurately describe the role of the antichrist that was prophesized two thousand years ago by the writer of the Book of Revelation. And, now, we find the prophesied plan—along with a description of its implementer(s)—in *The Protocols*. The masters of chaos and despotism, who drafted the document, knew full well what they were doing and how they intended to go about gaining control of the world. Now that these "revelations" have come into the "lights of publicity," what shall we do? For how much longer will we ignore what is happening and who is behind it?

For centuries, the Lords of Seduction have been successful in keeping *the people* under the thumbs of their Hidden Hand. They have used a number of the tactics of seduction: *Isolated the Victim* (the trusting nature of the American people); *Entered Our Spirit* (by controlling the media and entertainment industry); and have *Given Us Space to Fall*. Theirs is the masterful execution of a plan that was exported to this side of the Atlantic shortly after the founding fathers created a Constitution which was intended to defend America *against* just such enemies.

Forgetting the basics of "sticking together," those of us who should know better often let talking heads on electronic screens tell us how we feel about issues that affect our very existence. Investigative polls collated from interviews of a smattering of the population tell you and me how we view each other and those who lead us. We allow pollsters to categorize our thought processes—to fit your opinion (and mine) into a tiny box on a prepared questionnaire used to measure the effectiveness of agenda-promotion and to create "news."

The power to edit is omnipotent. "Creative" editing is capable of converting "news" into propaganda, and friends to enemies.

If you doubt what I say, the next time you watch "the news," keep this list of tactics in front of you. And, keep in mind that—before a word is read by a newscaster—an editor has previously scripted the broadcast. In addition, an editor/producer communicates with the newscaster or interviewer through an in-the-ear device during the broadcast. He or she can insert thoughts on a "live" basis or prompt questions that he/she wants to be asked. For the most part, the person on the screen of your television set is an actor, a mouthpiece for what was written for him or her and displayed on a Teleprompter, a similar device used by Barack Obama and his handlers.

* * * * * * * * *

That the American economy and the American worker are targets of manipulation and seduction is also addressed in *The Protocols:*

> "We shall raise the rate of wages which, however, will not bring any advantage to the workers, for, at the same time, we shall produce a rise in prices of the first necessaries of life, alleging that it arises from the

decline of agriculture and cattle-breeding: we shall further *undermine* artfully and deeply sources of production, by accustoming the workers to anarchy (labor union demonstrations) and to drunkenness and side by side therewith taking all measure to extirpate from the face of the earth all the educated forces of the 'out-group' (the American patriot).

"In order that the true meaning of things may not strike the out-group (you and I) before the proper time *we shall mask it* under an *alleged* ardent desire to serve the working classes and the great principles of political economy about which our economic theories are carrying on an energetic propaganda (thus the grip of labor unions on the U.S. economy ... and the grip of the Hidden Hand on the unions)."

Does this not sound like the platform of the Democrat Party and its Left-wing, "progressive" supporters?

For how much longer will the patriotic American worker tolerate this kind of seduction? How long will U.S. business and industry tolerate it? Labor disputes and commodity shortages (oil, food, etc.) are all about redistribution of power and wealth. According to *The Protocols,* minimum wage laws are an intentionally perpetrated hoax on the American worker. And labor union bosses are empowered to carry out the hoax.

Those who earn more are paying more and having less. As strange as it sounds, legislative and industrial "gridlock" could be America's best hope. If you haven't read Ayn

Rand's *Atlas Shrugged* or seen the movie, you must do so. The timing of the movie made about her book couldn't be more appropriate. The message is profound and on target. The Lords of Seduction are not going to like it—not a bit. That's why it took a Libertarian man of means to produce the movie. Mainstream Hollywood wouldn't touch it. Well-known actors and actresses wanted to play the role of the movie's heroin, but were advised by their handlers that doing so could jeopardize their careers. The story and message runs counter to the political Left's agenda.

Truth is: America is in trouble because the tail has been wagging the dog.

CHAPTER 8

" **C**onservatives are not *for* anything ... just against communism."[52] These disturbing words were uttered by Ayn Rand, the aforementioned author of *Atlas Shrugged* and *Fountainhead*. Coming from anyone's mouth the statement would be disturbing ... but from Ayn Rand's? The reason why I question Ms. Rand's motives is that she was a professed *anti*-socialist and *anti*-communist, who escaped from the iron hand of totalitarianism as a young adult. At the time she published these interesting words, communism—Russia's replacement government that had been ushered in by the Bolshevik Revolution—was America's greatest threat. Today, the threat of communist domination hails from China, who controls much of the U.S. debt ... and all that goes with it. Ayn Rand's writings are based on the theme that human beings should act in their own best interest and resist being governed by those who would enslave bodies or minds. With that thought in mind, it would have been quite appropriate for patriotic conservatives to be adamantly "against communism." Ms. Rand's most ardent student, Leonard Peikoff, explained (in the introduction he wrote to *Atlas Shrugged*) that Ayn Rand:

---

[52] Who Was Ayn Rand?—a biography, Playboy interview 1964

"Wanted to show who the prime
movers are and why and how they function.
Who are their enemies and why, what are
the motives behind the hatred for and the
enslavement of the prime movers; the
nature of the obstacles placed in their way,
and the reasons for it."[53]

Though it is unlikely that she could have envisioned
the global threat posed by Islam, perhaps by stirring the
emotions of America's historical "prime movers" (political
conservatives) Ms. Rand was acting as a catalyst, trying to
light a fire in minds of free men and women who—if they
chose to do so—could prevent the U.S. from falling deeper
into socialist—and then—communist hands. Don't forget
that China is ruled by communists and that these
communist—by owning much of our debt—already exercise
a lot of control over us Americans. Today, the threat of
communism has cleverly taken back seat to radical Islam.
The Bear of Russian Communism has merely gone into a
state of hibernation. Another movement has taken its
position on the battlefields of freedom and independence.
The faces of the warriors have changed, but the target is the
same—Judeo-Christian principles and the auto-determination of democracy. America is being attacked on several
fronts.

I have often wondered if taking a page from *Atlas
Shrugged* might be a solution to America's apparent
demise. If conservatives went on strike and joined—en
mass—the Tea Party, it would ensure a Republican defeat.
Every conservative American entrepreneur and business

---

[53]*Atlas Shrugged,* A Plume Book, Penguin Group, USA, New York, NY, 1999

owner would, first, withdraw all monies from America's banks and transfer it "off shore," and then refuse to pay federal income tax, ensuring the collapse of an out-of-control U.S. government. After the collapse, a *John Galt-like Party* of patriots could emerge and take back the country on its own terms. Don't discard the possibility. It could happen.

While it is true that conservatives are *against* any form of totalitarian governance (communism, its precursor: socialism, and also totalitarianism-like Sharia Law), we are unashamedly *for*—and willing to enthusiastically support—old-fashioned American capitalism, the kind of relationship between a government and its people that was ingeniously installed by the founding fathers of the United States of America when they drafted the Declaration of Independence and the U.S. Constitution:

- We are *for* telling the truth to the American people, even if it is not good news.
- We are *for* transparency in government.
- We are *for* free enterprise.
- We are *for* balanced budgets and living within our means.
- We are *for* presidents, judges and lawmakers who uphold their oaths of office—to "protect the U.S. and its Constitution against all its enemies, foreign and domestic. "
- We are *for* preserving what needs to be preserved in the name of American sovereignty and bringing "change" to

bear on anything—and anybody—that that poses a threat to that sovereignty.

- We are *for* safe streets, clean neighborhoods, clean entertainment and clear thinking.

- We are *for* keeping the Hidden Hand off our backs, out of our homes and hip pockets, places of business, schools, churches and synagogues.

- We are *for* having the people who finance "change" (by performing productive work each day) to have more say in what needs to be changed.

- We are *for* fair equitable tax laws that allow those who worked both hard *and smart* on their way to realizing the American Dream to be able to keep the bulk of what they earned.

- We are *for* eliminating the "Death Tax," and allowing an American citizen to pass to his heirs—and not his government—the bulk of his or her assets.

- We are *for* governing *our government*— and not the other way around.

- We are *for* thwarting the efforts of those who are out to establish a One-World Government at the expense of the United States of America.

- We are *for* preserving the value of the U.S. Dollar and seeing that it remains the world's most valued currency.

- We are *for* exposing the way a "supra-national sovereignty of intellectual elites and world bankers" select U.S. presidents (and advisors) who are beholding to the Illuminati and its stated mission—to replace Americanism with socialism ... and socialism with totalitarianism.

- We are *for* thwarting the efforts of the architects of a One-World Government that promise to exercise control over the minds and bodies of human beings.

- We are *for* bringing into the light, the agenda of the Hidden Hand of Lucifer and the identities of his disciples.

- We are *for* publically acknowledging the source of our being and fulfilling the task assigned at the time of our genesis: Create a heaven-like colony on Earth and bring the Greatest Experiment ever conceived to a happy conclusion.

- We are *for* spreading this message to the four corners of the Earth in hopes that the human race will rise up against the Lords of Seduction and create, instead, a world in which every human being can find his or her way back to what it, once, was: a creature, made in the image of God and His angels, a miraculous creation comprised of genetic "dust," intelligently gathered from life forms that have long existed in other galaxies.

So, if conservative, God-glorifying Americans are *for* all of these John Galt-type of things, it stands to reason that we are *against* the policies and procedures of *The Protocols of the Learned Elders of Zion* and those who are committed to their implementation.

Facts are: Lucifer's incarnates (the Lords of Seduction) have awakened a sleeping giant. Patriotic Americans have seen enough of the kinds of "change" that are intended to drive the United States of America and its God into oblivion. We will no longer roll over while a virtual army of despots work—and/or buy—their way into our sacred houses of government, mock of our Declaration of Independence and Bill of Rights, and replace the Constitution drafted by America's founding fathers with a Constitution of the Illuminati-Islamic Alliance's (I-IA's) creation—*The Protocols of the Learned Elders of Zion.* But the exorcism will not be easy. Once inside, demons resist being ousted. Consider depictions of an exorcism that have been depicted on the silver screen.

Though the present is laden with what might seem to be insurmountable challenges, in the long run over-the-top progressive "puppets" and "pawns" of The Hidden Hand have done America a favor. They continued to shove their despot agenda down our throats and tighten the nooses around our necks until patriots finally said: *enough!*

The results of the 2010 mid-term election demonstrated that independent/conservative Americans will no longer sit quietly and be played for fools. It appears that a new kind of "change" is coming to America—the kind intended to *change it back* to "... one nation, under God, indivisible, with liberty and justice for all," the antithesis of the kind of world that the I-IA has in mind.

No longer is the identity of America's enemies a secret. We now know who wants her to fail and we have a copy of their game plan. It is known as: *The Protocols of the Learned Elders of Zion.* And, America's enemies are everyone who embraces them. For the sake of emphasizing this point, I feel the need to repeat some of the most disturbing sections of the document. The seductive overlords who crafted it wrote:

> "Our countersign is *force and make-believe.* Only force conquers in political affairs, especially if it be concealed in the talents essential to statesmen (that we select).
>
> "Violence must be the principle, and cunning and make-believe the rule for governments which do not want to lay down their crowns at the feet of agents of some new power. This evil is the one and only means to attain the end (that we desire). Therefore we must not stop at bribery, deceit and treachery when they should serve towards the attainment of our end (global governance, controlled by The I-IA).
>
> "In politics one must know how to seize the property of others without hesitation if by it we secure submission and sovereignty.
>
> "Our (global) State, marching along the path of peaceful conquest, has the right to replace the horrors of war by less noticeable and more satisfactory sentences of death, necessary to maintain the *terror* which

tends to produce blind submission. Just—but merciless—severity is the greatest factor of strength in the (global) State: not only for the sake of gain but also in the name of duty, for the sake of victory, we must keep to the program of *violence and make-believe* ... Therefore it is not so much by the means themselves as by the *doctrine of* severity that we shall triumph and *bring all governments into subjection to our super-government.*."

As you ponder what you have just read, remember the excerpts from *The Odyssey* that I included in the introductory pages of this book, especially the admonitions of Circe as Odysseus embarked on his journey. It is only because the hero of the story was forewarned—and heeded the warnings—that he safely made it to a destination of his choice. Great wisdom lies in the teachings of yesterday's sages. And, that is my only purpose in writing the book you are now reading—to bring some of them to the forefront to hold out a flag of caution, and encourage you think about how you, your family, and your nation are targets of the Illuminati-Islamic Alliance.

Don't just take my word for it. Come with me as we examine what men smarter than I have concluded and see how we can fit their ideologies and admonitions into American "change" under Barack Obama and the power-thirsty puppeteers who pull his strings.

* * * * * * * * * *

In 1750, Alexander Tyler wrote an essay that should have been warning enough for America's leaders and lawmakers:

> "A democracy cannot exist as a permanent form of government. It can only exist until the voters discover they can vote themselves largess ('generous giving')[54] from the public treasury. From that moment on, the majority always votes for the candidates promising them the most benefits from the public treasury, with the result that a democracy always collapses over loose fiscal policy, always followed by a dictatorship. The average age of the world's greatest civilizations has been 200 years."

Tyler further described how great democracies (as did ancient Greece and Rome) tend to *progress* toward anti-democratic states. Today, we would call such a transition one from the "abundance" of free-market capitalism to the "austerity" of socialism and then to the "bondage" of totalitarianism. We should also note an important word in Tyler's Law: the verb, *progress.* Is it a coincidence that Left adopted a noun derived from the verb, *progress,* to put a new face on an old socialistic ideology: *"progressive,"* a new label for what used to be called "Social Democrat."

Masters of the art of word-crafting, *progressives* are quite familiar with the Rothschild Formula:[55] the practice of casting aspersions on the credibility of anyone—or group—

---

[54] Webster's New World College Dictionary, Third Edition, 1997
[55] The Creature from Jekyll Island, G. Edward Griffin, American Media, Westlake Village, California, 2002

that doesn't agree with them or threatens to expose the seductive practices of the in-group (The Illuminati). By attaching pejorative labels, such as "right-wing radicals," to well-meaning American patriots, public opinion can be swayed into believing that anyone who is not a liberal or progressive is either a "red neck" or a member of the "non-progressive radical right."

Nothing could be farther from the truth. Radicalism shows no favoritism. It weighs in on both sides of political scales. And, that is does, is a critical factor in Tyler's Law. For, in a democracy, it is possible for *the masses* to vote themselves into the grasp of whatever state of ideology they can be persuaded—and incited—to favor. This is why *The Protocols* emphasized control over the media. Such control is essential for a progressive, socialistic agenda to be installed. *Without* the complicit participation of a mainstream media, progressivism would die a slow death. *With* the mainstream media at its back, *progressivism* has become a driving force in the last fifty years for changing both policy and laws in America.

And, when it serves the Illuminati's agenda, the press will turn against Islam. But for now, it serves the Illuminati's agenda to "side" with a president who sides with the Muslims.

Recent revelations from a general in the North Viet Nam army underscore the press's role in driving America into the arms of its professed enemies.

General VoNguyen Giap was a brilliant, highly respected leader of the North Vietnam military. The following quote is said to be from his memoirs, currently found in the Vietnam War memorial in Hanoi:

"What we still don't understand is why you Americans stopped the bombing of Hanoi ... You had us on the ropes. If you had pressed us a little harder just for another day or two, we were ready to surrender! It was the same at the battle of TET. You defeated us! We knew it, and we thought you knew it. But we were elated to notice *your media**was helping us. They were causing more disruption in America than we could in the battlefields. We were ready to surrender. You had won!"

General Giap has published his memoirs and confirmed what most Americans knew. The Vietnam War was not lost in Vietnam—it was lost at home. The same slippery slope, sponsored by the US media, is currently underway. It exposes the enormous power of a biased media to cut out the heart and will of the American public.

And while some have challenged the veracity of Giap's comments, China's Ho Chi Min (who pulled the strings of North Viet Nam) is quoted as saying,

"We didn't need to win military victories. We only needed to hit them (Americans) until they gave up and got out ... every day our leadership would listen to the radio to follow the growth of the (American) anti-war movement. Visits to Hanoi by people like Jane Fonda, and former (U.S). Attorney General Ramsey Clark and ministers (Jesse Jackson) gave us

---

* Emphasis added

confidence that we should hold on in the
face of battlefield reverses. We were elated
when Jane Fonda, wearing a red
Vietnamese dress, said at a press conference that she was ashamed of America's
actions in the war and that she would
struggle along with us ... Those people
represented the conscience of America.
The conscience of America was part of its
war-making capability, and we were turning
that capability in our favor ... America lost
because of dissent and protest. It lost the
ability to mobilize the will to win ... We had
the impression that American commanders
had their hands tied by political factors.
Your generals could never deploy a
maximum force for the greatest military
effect."[56]

Clearly, Hollywood—though the people who comprise
the Screen Actors Guild Union believe they do—*do not*
represent the "conscience of America." They represent a
very Left Wing section of it. Those pulling the strings
during the Viet Nam war never intended for America to
win, including the anti-war demonstrators at home—young
Americans who were seduced by America's enemies to do
their bidding on home front battlefields where Wars of
Minds are decided. The "organizers" and financiers of the
anti-war demonstrations certainly appear to have understood the policies of persuasion that are presented in the
Protocols of the Learned Elders of Zion.

---

[56] Snopes.com

What is more disturbing is that some of the group who didn't appear to want America to win had taken an oath to protect and defend her citizens against "all enemies, foreign and domestic," an oath they failed to honor. The greater question is: who was pulling the anti-war demonstrators strings during Lyndon Johnson's Administration? The best answer is: the same group of world bankers and intellectual elites (The Hidden Hand /Illuminati) who also appear to be pulling the strings of the sitting President and his administration, as well as those of demonstrators across the Middle East and union demonstrations in America.

We have to ask ourselves: in dealing with terror, did the powers that be really want Osama Bin Laden and the other terrorist leaders captured ... or killed? Perhaps, this is why President Obama resisted his CIA Director (Leon Paneta's) plan to take out Bin Laden and why Paneta didn't inform the president that the raid was to be carried out until *after* it had begun. The President would have to have gone against his pledge to "side with the Muslims" as the winds of change began to "blow in an ugly direction," ... for Muslim terrorist leader, Osama Bin Laden.

Are the problems in Egypt, Tunisia, Libya, Yemen, Saudi Arabia and Jordan merely the next in a series of conflicts being orchestrated by the men and women sworn to carry out a plan that is outlined in *The Protocols?* Are the Illuminati—through the Muslim Brotherhood—merely flexing its muscles in these Arab states to convince the leaders there that small-time dictators are vulnerable? Is there a plan to establish a United Arab Union with the Muslim Brotherhood serving as the Illuminati's newly-empowered puppets? And, why do American's continue to tolerate the lies and half-truths being spewed by a media that allows the Hidden Hand to operate without being subjected to the "lights of publicity?" Why do America's media protect the cozy associations of prominent political leaders such as Jesse Jackson with America's sworn enemies? Was Vietnam a test case to see how the U.S. press, entertainment industry, and special interest organizers could be used for an enemy's advantage?

According to the *Daily World*, May 7, 1985 edition, Jackson was the keynote speaker at a 1985 commemoration of the 10th anniversary of "the liberation of Vietnam," and event sponsored by the Communist Party USA,[57] a fact that has been kept from the American public by a complicit press.

In the January 1984 edition of *Political Affairs*, "the theoretical journal of the Communist Party USA," self-described "Harlem organizer for the New York Communist Party" Kevin Mercadel boasted, "Our 1984 electoral activity began with the formation of the Rainbow Coalition in Harlem in support of Jesse Jackson's campaign for the presidency." Mercadel added that the Communists were not only allowed to work in the coalition, "but, indeed, it was expected of us (the Communist Party)."[58]

Clearly, there has been cooperation from America's media in covering up Jackson's association with—and support from—the Communist Party worldwide.

An anonymous visionary once said, "Do not fear the enemy, for they can take only your life. Fear the media, for they will destroy your honor." What say you ... the "voice of the people?"

---

[57] *Between The Lines*, Joseph Farah WorldNetDaily March 27, 2001
[57] http://www.wnd.com/news/article.asp?article, "Comrade Jesse Jackson"

Has America already crossed her last great frontier? Are we now a puppet in the hands of the Invisible Empire? According to Alexander Tyler, the bell-shaped cycle takes the people who comprise a democracy:

> "... from bondage to spiritual faith; from spiritual faith to great courage; from courage to liberty; from liberty to abundance; from abundance to complacency; from complacency to apathy; from apathy to dependency; from dependency back again into bondage."

It is the intent of the stated architects of *The Protocols* to bring the peoples of the world into "bondage."

How could a race of people, now celebrating a century and half of emancipation, allow its professed leaders (Jesse Jackson, James Cone, Jeremiah Wright, and Barack Obama) sell them back into the hands of masters whose mission it is to create a global plantation—one in which people of all colors, religions and ideologies—will become slaves to the Lords of Seduction? When will responsible leaders from the entitlement segment of the Black and Hispanic Community realize that the next step from dependency is bondage? And, who—other than this writer— will speak out and plant a seed of Truth among those who have been seduced into believing that government is their savior?

In addition to bell-shaped curves, there are two related laws of physics that apply to the stage of political science and the puppets who dance on it. One is called the *Law of Cause and Effect*, which states: "for every action, there is an equal and opposite reaction." Another physical law that plays in the political arena is the *Law of Inertia*. Allow me to address their significance in political circles.

In reference to the rise and fall of democracies the term "inertia" may refer to the "amount of resistance to *change* exerted by people who are being manipulated. To make the point, I have substituted "nation" for "object."

> Unless a nation/ethnic class of the citizenry is subjected to an external force, it moves in the same direction ... and at a constant velocity toward whatever end it was originally directed. Thus a nation/ethnic class of the citizenry will continue moving at its current velocity until some *external* force causes its speed or direction to *change*. A nation/ethnic class of the citizenry that is not in motion will remain at rest until some force causes it to move.

Now, how does physical science apply to political science and to the theme of the book that you hold in your hands? Clearly America has moved along the bell curve as Tyler described. And, in keeping with Laws of Inertia, the farther down the slope an object/nation/ethnic class of the citizenry goes, the faster it races toward the bottom. At each stage in America's evolution some "force" acted on the direction in which the object/nation/ ethnic class of the citizenry moved. In fact there have been two forces at work ... at the same time. One is the desire to create and perpetuate a free, capitalistic republic (commonly known as The Political Right). The other is an "equal and opposite" desire to create an autocratic, socialist empire in which the people are ruled by one or more powerful governing overlords (commonly known as The Political Left).

At each turn these two equal and opposite forces have battled to see in which direction the Cycle of Democracies would trend. As a result, there has been an ebb and flow of freedom and independence. At each tide, one side celebrated while the other licked its wounds. To use a football analogy, a glance at the scoreboard of democracies reveals the fourth quarter score, with only a short time remaining on the proverbial clock: The Left 28, The Right 21. Though there is still time enough to pull the game out, it will take an all-out effort and a two-minute drill for the ages.

As I understand it, there is a big difference in the ideologies and political tactics of The Left and The Right. Though the Illuminati has a hand in both of America's political parties, the Right is primarily comprised of men and women committed to the same values as those who signed the Declaration of Independence; constitutional patriots who have seen The Left as "puppets" of modern day slave traders (The Order of the Illuminati). In football terms, the Right has been in a "prevent defense." The Left—on the other hand—has been in a hurry-up offense, pulling out all the trick plays and gadgets in their play book (*The Protocols,*) changing the rules (the U.S. Constitution) as they go. And the conflict between the two parties creates the kind of conflict and unrest that plays directly into the Illuminati's hands—the kind of political unrest that distracts the voters away from the Left's agenda of undermining and re-writing the Constitution to the liking of America's enemies.

Even among those who identify themselves as "Independents," it becomes the duty of each and every

American to vote for the candidate who agrees with one's own political ideology and values. The patriotic thing to do is: decide which of the two factions you agree with and join—or cheer—for that side. At the end of the game, there can be only one winner—one champion of human rights. Which will it be?

As you will come to see, The Right has a plan for America—one that has been openly published and played in the light of day. It is called *The Constitution* of the United States of America.

The radical Left also has a plan for America. It is known as the *Protocols of the Learned Elders of Zion.* It was crafted in secret and for centuries was hidden from of the "lights of publicity."[59]

The authenticity of *The Protocols* has been debated by scholars for more than a century. Some believe it to be a forgery of an 1864 book of fiction by French political satirist Maurice Joly, titled *Dialogue aux enfers entre Machiavel et Montesquieu* or *Dialogue in Hell Between Machiavelli and Montesquieu.*[60]

Having authored books of fiction, I can attest to the fact that "fiction" is the way authors often communicate their own beliefs and experiences to others. So, even if the meat of *The Protocols* surfaced in a novel, it does not necessarily mean that they are fictional. In fact, Machiavelli's *The Prince* was written in 1513 as a satirical political treatise. Machiavelli had been arrested, tortured and banished by the powerful Medici Family, the patriarchs that became "political popes" of the Catholic Church when they took control of Florence. Machiavelli

---

[59] David Rockefeller, The Bilderberger Meeting, 1991
[60] Segel, Binjamin W. *A Lie and a Libel: The History of the Protocols of the Elders of Zion* (translated and edited by Levy, Richard S.), p. 97 (1996, originally published in 1926), University of Nebraska Press

believed that if he could convince the **Medici** that he was a brilliant strategist, they would release him from prison and bring him into their court as an adviser. It didn't happen. Yet Machiavelli's work became incorporated in the strategic planning of all kinds of warfare, including those conducted in secret, by Shadow Governments ... and so have *The Protocols of the Learned Elders of Zion.*

Once *The Protocols* were brought into the light, The Left claimed that it was the work of a small group of insignificant zealots and died with them. However, as you have already seen, reading each pronouncement of *The Protocols* is like reading the annals of history and current headlines of events. In them (*The Protocols*) you will better understand how your ancestors, your immediate family, your children and children's children *have been, are, and will be* manipulated by a cabal of global overlords.

Clearly, America has moved down Tyler's bell curve, from abundance to complacency, apathy, and dependency. Though those who despotically carry out *The Protocols'* pronouncements deny its authenticity, it is laced with liberalism, progressivism, socialism and totalitarianism. Call them by either name you choose, *The Protocols* embody an ideology of people who intend to seduce the masses— despots who are committed to "changing" the world to their liking.

These Lords of Seduction are not only powerful, they are clever. Not only do they know how to manipulate the puppets they put in office, they know how to seduce the masses into believing that *their* presidents are independent thinkers.

During the first two years of the Obama Admin-istration, the Hidden Hand moved at a breakneck pace to undermine the foundations of America ... and it worked. A huge "stimulus bill" that created an immediate escalation in U.S. debt was followed by the gutting of American healthcare and replacing it with an unaffordable socialist health system known as "Obama *Care*." Violating the Constitution of the United States, the Democrat Party audaciously rammed through the kind of "change" that will be difficult to overcome and impossible to pay for.

At the time of this writing, the future of Obama *Care* has been driven into the hands of America's legal system. Two left-wing federal judges have ruled in its favor. In December, 2010, a Virginia-area federal judge ruled that the portion of the Obama *Care* bill *requiring* Americans to purchase health insurance was "unconstitutional." Shortly thereafter, a Florida-based Federal Judge agreed with the one in Virginia.

The constitutionality of Obama *Care* will surely be decided by the Supreme Court of the U.S. *One* Supreme Court Judge will more than likely decide the fate of America's healthcare system and fiscal stability for decades to come. Let us hope that the *one* judge is independent of the Hidden Hand and understands the consequences of his or her vote.

Clearly, "change" has come to America. Ever since President Obama took office, the world has witnessed the greatest example of "bulldozer politics" (as well as racially and ideologically-based cronyism) in recent history.

Following the 2008 elections, The Left controlled both houses of Congress and the White House. They didn't *need* Republican support to install sweeping social "change" in the way government operates. As a result, Democrats pushed their agenda through Congress, ignoring the Republican's appeal for prudent input.

Then came the midterm elections of 2010 and the Republicans won control of the House of Representatives. Suddenly, the political brakes were temporarily applied to the Democrat's agenda—and "change" once again came to Capitol Hill and the White House. A president that had turned deaf ears to the Right suddenly changed political masks and (in the Clintonesk fashion) Barack Obama *appeared* to move more to the middle of the political spectrum. In fact, the two men suddenly began to appear together in press conferences in order to seduce Americans into believing that Obama and Clinton were ideological equals. Once again, a children's story provides a lesson: "Beware of wolves in sheep's clothing."

Though they sometimes seem to ignore Tyler's Cycle of Democracies, Democrats are also students of history. Bill Clinton *re-invented* himself (politically) after Republicans took control of Congress away from Democrats in the midterm elections of his first term. A left-of-center U.S. President suddenly came to the middle. In political terms, the "truth" about Bill Clinton came out of a Karl Marx memoir. As defined in 1887 in the *Communist Manifesto,* Bill Clinton's "truth" became: "whatever leads to success." And, at the behest of his far-Left supporters, so shall Barack Obama's.

The Hidden Hand can see the falling popularity of *their* president. So, in order to get him "re-elected," they will re-invent him, further seducing the American people into believing that he has abandoned his far Leftist agenda.

Let us hope that Conservative Democrats, along with intelligent Republican and Independent voters and their elected officials are able to see through the seductive "change" taking place in the I-IA's Siren-in-Chief's new "false flag" image.

When Obama and his backers saw the handwriting on the wall, the terms, "compromise" and "common ground" began to appear on the President's Teleprompters—terms that (until Republicans took control of the House) were absent from the vocabulary of Democrats.

The lesson to take away from the example of political seduction is: the Right tends to believe in the good and the positive. It trusts that people mean what they say and do as they say. And, that they do is the Right's greatest weakness when dealing with the Illuminati-Islamic Alliance and their poppet-in-chief.

As affirmed in *The Communist Manifesto,* The Left seems to believe that Truth is: whatever needs to be said— right now—in order to further its agenda. Those same sentiments are found in Islam and in Black Liberation Theology. In fact, the Father of Socialism (and socialism on steroids—communism) promoted the ideology that "all contents of our consciousness are determined by our economic needs. It follows equally that each social class has its own science and its own philosophy." Note that Marx debunked the absolute truths found in Nature. He added, "... *the truth is whatever leads to success.*" It is crucial to the cause of America's survival that this statement be imprinted within the mind of every journalist that reports what leaders say and every individual who shall enter into political or business relationships with Left-leaning citizens, teachers, reporters, pundits, and politicians. Equally as vital is the constant reminder that Islam and Black Liberation Theology foster the same teachings.

This is why (to Conservatives) the U.S. Constitution (as it was originally drafted) represents the *One Truth* of American law. To left-leaning "progressives," however, the

U.S. Constitution—like *The Protocols*—is a "living document," meant to be "changed" to comply with whatever leads to the successful accomplishment of the Hidden Hand's One-World mission. And this difference in the two principle political ideologies that exist in American politics is simply not understood by the majority of U.S. citizens. That's where a patriot's duty kicks in. It is the responsibility of those who cherish the American Way to ensure that every child in the U.S. learns to distinguish between the absolute "Truth" and the socialists' (and Islamists'/BLT's) self-serving versions of "Truth."

In Luke, the Gospel teaches: "Unto whom much is given, much is required." Clearly, a lot has been given to people living in the 21st century version of America. Therefore, much is required. It is our duty to expose the content of The *Protocols of the Learned Elders of Zion*, (the living Constitution of a socialist-based One-World Government). It is our duty to teach children of all races and religions how the *Protocols* precisely describe the manner in which professed disciples of Lucifer intend to seduce them and their counterparts around the globe. If America's media weren't under the heavy hand of the I-IA, the front page of every American newspaper and the open remarks of television news broadcast would lead with the following excerpts and credit both its original authors and modern-day disciples of America's enemies:

> "We (the Hidden Hand of Lucifer) will choose presidents of nations. We shall establish the responsibility of presidents ... we shall arrange elections in favor of such presidents as have in their past some dark, undiscovered stain ... then they will be

trustworthy agents for the accomplishment
of our plans out of fear of revelations and
from the natural desire of everyone who has
attained power, namely, the retention of the
privileges, advantages and honor connected
with the office of president. The chamber
of deputies (the president's Cabinet and
advisers) will provide cover for, will protect,
will elect presidents, but we shall take from
it the right to propose new—or make
changes (there's that word, again) in existing
laws, for this right will be given *by us* to the
responsible president, *a puppet in our
hands.*"

If the American media truly wanted to do a yeoman's
job in investigative reporting, it could delve deeper into the
sinister declaration rather than summarily dismissing it
because it confronts what they have been indoctrinated to
believe ... and champion. The document further describes
the kinds of individuals with whom the Hidden Hand
would surround its "puppet" president.

"The administrators, whom we shall
choose from among the public ... will not
be persons trained in the arts of
government, and will therefore easily
become *pawns* in our game in the hands of
men of learning and genius ('intellectual
elite') who will be their advisers, specialists
bred (affirming that a small group of Ruling
Families control the destiny of the human

race) and *reared from early childhood to rule the affairs of the whole world."*

How much more explicit could the drafters of the Illuminati's Constitution be? And, to argue that the document is a fraud or the work of an insignificant dreamer is the ultimate admission of having been seduced.

A press in search of truth would leave no stone unturned about the identity of a man who aspired to be—and became—a U.S. president.

According to Robert Riegler:

> "The birth certificate that the White House released lists Obama's birth as August 4, 1961. It also lists Barack Hussein Obama as his father. No big deal, right? At the time of Obama's birth, it also shows that his father is aged 25 years old, and that Obama's father was born in "Kenya, East Africa." This wouldn't seem like anything of concern, except the fact that *Kenya did not even exist until 1963*[*], two whole years after Obama's birth, and 27 years after his father's birth. How could Obama's father have been born in a country that did not yet exist? Up and until Kenya was formed in 1963, it was known as the "British East Africa Protectorate." But, this is not the only thing that I found that does not jive.
>
> The other item I looked into was the hospital that Obama was born in. On the birth certificate released by the White

---

[*] Emphasis added

House, the listed place of birth is "Kapiolani Maternity & Gynecological Hospital." This cannot be, because the hospital(s) in question in 1961 were called "Kauikeolani Children's Hospital" and "Kapiolani Maternity Home," respectively. The name did not change to Kapiolani Maternity & Gynecological Hospital until 1978, when these two hospitals merged. How can this particular name of the hospital be on a birth certificate (original and authentic) dated 1961 if this name had not yet been applied to it until 1978?"

Except for those who read *The Lords of Seduction*, Riegler's findings may never reach the national "lights of publicity." It appears that the President's protectors have successfully squelched the "birth issue"... at least for now.

Barack Hussein Obama, his administration and the Left-leaning leaders of the Democrat Party appear to have leaped right off the pages of *The Protocols*. Where are Watergate's Bob Woodward and Carl Bernstein? Where are their protégés? The plot of political seduction that could be uncovered by a focused reporter would make Watergate look like a nursery rhyme. But such a story would not serve the Illuminati's or political Left's agenda.

Though *The Protocols* had existed (in secret) for centuries, they were presented at the First Zionist Congress held at Basle, Germany in 1897 under the presidency of the late Theodore Herzl. Toward the end of his life Herzl was a decorated hero of Zionism and a Zionist State. It is just what led to his rise to prominence that is not widely understood. According to Wikipedia, Theodore Herzl "grew up as a "thoroughly emancipated, anti-traditional, secular, would-be German boy who dismissed all religion, and spoke of Judaism with 'mocking cynicism.' He had exhibited a secularist disdain toward religion, which he saw as 'uncivilized.' Like George Soros a/k/a György Schwartz, Herzl became interested in 'The Jewish Question' (how Hitler's Nazis intended to do away with the Jews). The subtitle of one of Herzl's early books is *Proposal of a Modern Solution for the Jewish Question.*[61]) To the dismay of Jews who appreciated his work in bringing about the State of Israel, Herzl's writing retained traces of Jewish self-contempt."[62]

What the majority of his readers didn't (and don't) know was (is) that Herzl seduced them. And, like George Soros, he used the trust that he had garnered among his own people to vault himself and a small group of former Jews and Gentiles into positions of power that could only have been imagined during Hitler's reign of terror and despotism.

When asked by CBS' Steve Kroft (during a "60-Minute" interview if Soros "... helped in the confiscation of property from fellow Jews, friend, and neighbors, Soros answered, "Yes, Yes". And, when Kroft asked, "Was it difficult"? Soros replied, "No, not at all. Not at all, I rather enjoyed it." Then Kroft asked "No feelings of guilt?" Soros answered, "No, only feelings of absolute power." And, this is the man who played a major role in Barack Obama's election and appears to be pulling at least some of his strings now that Obama is in The Oval Office.

---

[61] *Der Judenstaat*, the Jewish State. 1896, Leipiz, Germany and Vienna, Austria, M. Breitenstein's Verlags-Buchhandlung
[62] Elon, Amos (1975). *Herzl*, p.23, New York: Holt, Rinehart and Winston

While Herzl's motives may have been a noble act of devotion to his people, his methods were quite consistent with those contained within *The Protocols.*

In his diaries, Herzl wrote:

> "When we occupy the land ... We must expropriate ("take from its owner"[63]) gently the private property on the estates assigned to us. We shall try to spirit the penniless population across the border by procuring employment for it in the transit countries, while denying it any employment in our country. The property owners will come over to our side. Both the process of expropriation and the removal of the poor must be carried out discretely and circumspectly ..."[64]

The question is: To whom were these suggestions directed—to The Third Reich or to the Jewish people? Who were Herzl's "we" and "our?" Did he know Soros in those days? Where did Herzl's loyalty truly lie? There can be little or no doubt that the *Protocols of the Elders of Zion* and Herzl's diaries arose from the same philosophical schools of mass seduction. Though it appears that in his later life Theodore Herzl became more of a diplomat (and was buried a hero of Zionism), his early associations and writings indicate that he was greatly influenced by the philosophy and practices of the authors of *The Protocols.*

My purpose in addressing Theodore Herzl is not to belittle the good he did (toward the end of his life) in

---

[63] Webster's New World College Dictionary, Third Edition, 1997
[64] *The Complete Diaries of Theodor Herzl*, vol. 1 (New York: Herzl Press and Thomas Yoseloff, 1960), pp. 88, 90

helping establish the State of Israel. Anyone who knows me will attest to the fact that I am no anti-Semite. In fact, I married into a Jewish family and understand the challenges they and their ancestors have faced over the centuries.

Though I remain a Christian, I am keenly aware that my religion is based on Jewish Principles and Laws. A fact that many of my Christian brethren sometimes forget is that Christ was raised a Jew. He practiced all the rituals of Judaism. The "Last Supper" was a Seder, the Jewish meal celebrating Passover. The Scriptures tell us that Christ challenged *the politics*—not the religious principles—of the Temple and its hierarchy of priests. In fact, Jesus was a devout Jew.

Let it also be known that I am a staunch supporter of America's truest ally, the State of Israel. After reading about Theodore Herzl, I am not quite sure that I understand exactly where he stood on religion and politics. His writings contain mixed messages. His early writings and practices suggest that he was more politically oriented than he was interested in Jewish tradition and theology.

The Zionist Congress in Basle, Germany (that Herzl organized) was attended by some two hundred participants from seventeen countries, sixty-nine of whom were delegates from various Zionist societies ... Seventeen women attended the Congress, some of them in their own capacity, others accompanying representatives. While women did participate in the First Zionist Congress, they did not have voting rights; they were accorded full membership rights at the Second Zionist Congress, the following year, 1905.[65]

---

[65] Wikipedia, First Zion Congress

It is believed that this was the first time the Inner Circle of the Hidden Hand openly shared its plan with anyone outside the original thirteen families.

The Protocols go on to say:

> "The idea of freedom is impossible of realization because no one knows how to use it with moderation. It is enough to hand over a people to self-government for a certain length of time for that people to be turned into a disorganized mob. From that moment on we get internecine strife which soon develops into battles between classes, in the midst of which States burn down and their importance is reduced to that of a heap of ashes."

And, yet Israel was clearly established as a free and democratic form of governance. The stated intent of the so-called "intellectually enlightened" is clear: "to reconstruct all institutions and to become the sovereign lord of those who have left to us the rights of their power by laying them down voluntarily ..."

As one of the principle movers in establishing the State of Israel, I still wrestle with where Herzl stood on democracy. He is said to have played a major role in establishing Israel's form of government and yet in the above passage from the document Herzl introduced at the First Zionist Congress speaks against democracy.

Clearly, the drafters of *The Protocols* were familiar with Herzl's diaries and yet took aim at democracy as a model for the World Government they intend to impose. In fact, *The Protocols'* description of how they intend to rule humanity is right out of the *Communist Manifesto* (or vice versa) and explicitly expressed in the statement: "Out of the temporary evil we are now compelled to commit, will emerge the good of an unshakable rule: *The result justifies the means."*

Drafters of *The Protocols* appear to have been more than familiar with the principles of Tyler's Law. They were aware of the fact that Tyler hadn't said *how* a free people can slow—or stop—the slide back toward dependence or how the people within a democracy can press the "re-set button" every time forces of ruination begin to take them back in the direction of bondage.

And, if you are still not convinced that those at the center of a "supranational sovereignty" are to be taken seriously, the following statement from *The Protocols* should leave no room for doubt:

> "Therefore we must not stop at bribery, deceit and treachery when they should serve towards the attainment of our end. In politics one must know how to seize the property of others (by taxation or any means necessary) without hesitation if by it we secure submission and sovereignty."

This brings us to perhaps the most egotistical part of *The Protocols*:

> "It is indispensable for us to undermine all faith, to tear out of the mind the very principle of god-head and the spirit, and to put in its place arithmetical calculations and material needs."

Is there evidence that each of the statements presented above have come to pass? While the authenticity of the document continues to be debated, only fools could deny that *someone* (or some alliance) in a very powerful position is following both the spirit and letter of *The Protocols* and its literary cousin—*The Prince,* a treatise on political seduction written by 16th century scholar, Niccolo Machiavelli. "Founding a wholly new state, or even a new religion, using injustice and immorality has even been called the chief theme of the *Prince.*"[66]

Knowing that both *The Protocols* and *The Prince* advocate seduction, tyranny, and revolutionary faiths as a means to an end that the course of history seems to follow both their context and content, it becomes the responsibility of those of us who have now been fore-warned to call into the light the practices of whoever is behind the seductive and nefarious plots expressed in both of these treatises. The survival of the U.S. depends on it.

It is difficult for a trusting people to believe that a small group of powerful men and women (by whatever name or title they are known) would conspire to deceive and drive fellow human beings into bondage. However, world events are playing out *precisely* as described in *The Protocols.* And, the current President of the U.S. seems to fit the mold of the kind of "puppet" that the architects of *their* Constitution said they would place in positions of power.

It is hard to remain focused on the uphill swing of the cycle (from spiritual faith, to courage, to liberty and to abundance,) knowing that a circle of men are willing to commit tyrannical acts such as "bribery, deceit and treachery," all of which are designed to "undermine all

---

[66] Strauss, Leo (1958), *Thoughts on Machiavelli*, University of Chicago Press

faith, to tear out of the minds of men the very principle of god-head and the spirit ..."

While it will not be an easy task, bringing down Evil is entirely possible. The solution is laid out in the Bible. In the great battles of the Old Testament, God's people defeated its enemies by trusting in His infinite power and wisdom.   Joshua won at Jericho. A shepherd boy, David, defeated the giant, Goliath; and the fleeing Israelites watched as the Egyptian army was consumed when the walls of the Red Sea collapsed upon them.

So vanquishing Evil is not a new thing. In fact, Lucifer was driven out of heaven. In a like manner, he and his "enlightened" disciples can be driven out of America's institutions and venerable halls of government. It's a matter of bringing the Satanic plan into the light of day, gathering the necessary resources, trusting in God, fighting fire with fire, and turning the Illuminati on its heels.

Throughout America there are patriots every bit as intelligent and capable as those who devised (and have been orchestrating) the *Protocols of the Learned Elders of Zion*. Over my life I have learned that "good" or "bad" is neither defined by the color of one's skin, name, place of origin, or religious preferences. Though some of the drafters of *The Protocols* may have been Jewish by the nature of their birth, they didn't practice the kind of Judaism or Christianity that I have come to know and respect.

After realizing what America's founding fathers were up against, I can understand why they were so adamant in the stance they took against imperialism and why they placed God at the center of their creation. In fact, the term "Annuit Coeptis" means *"Providence (God) has favored our undertakings."* The founders boldly placed this phrase on the most circulated piece of American currency—the dollar bill. For good reason, they didn't specify a Jewish God or a Christian God, they went back to the roots of the Bible—the guiding light they used in declaring all men free.

Though at the time *The Protocols* had been a closely-held secret, the framers of the U.S. had to know about them. Both Jefferson and Franklin had spent time in France—home of the Rothschild's. From the founders' actions as well as the content of the documents they drafted, they risked everything to keep a government *of* patriots, *for* patriots, and *by* patriots from falling prey to the Hidden Hand's seductive practices. That's why the Judeo-Christian God became the cornerstone of the government that the U.S. founders established—a cornerstone laid by Freemason-in-Chief George Washington.

Nearly two and a half centuries later, the question is: Do enough of us believe what the founders believed: that the United States of America can defy Tyler's Law and turn back the political and fiscal onslaught of The Illuminati? If so, how can we make it so? These are some of the questions that this book hopes to answer.

As we continue our tortuous odyssey into identifying and then rejecting the kind of "change" that is being championed by The Hidden Hand's current cast of "puppets" and "pawns," let us first examine some of the obstacles in our path.

CHAPTER 9

I t's a long-documented fact: *big government rarely solves the people's problems, but it surely is capable of creating, confounding, and expanding them.* And, we don't have to go that far back in history for proof. We only need to revisit the conclusions of 20th century British economist, C. Northcote Parkinson, author of the principle—and book—known as "Parkinson's Law."

The law states: *Work expands so as to fill the time available for its completion.* After reading Parkinson's book, I wondered if—when it applies to government—his "law" also means: *"Waste expands so as to consume the dollars available to be spent ... or borrowed."*

From his years in the British Civil Service, Parkinson noted the rate at which bureaucracies expand and that the increase in the number of government employees had little to do with the amount of work that needed to be done.

Since Barack Obama took office, the number of government employees making over $150,000/year rose by one hundred (100%) percent in the first two years of his government. As promised, he *created jobs*; however, many of the "jobs" he boasts of "creating" were federal bureaucratic jobs that resulted in a further drain on the U.S. budget and the American taxpayer.

As unemployment and wages tanked throughout America, one part of the country flourished. Many of Obama's newly-created jobs are linked to administrating Obama*Care,* the largest single socialistic program in American history, one that promises to break the American Treasury, unless it is repealed. However, it appears that—once again—the American people were duped. From all indications, the monies used to build, outfit, and staff the new Obama*Care* administrative building was not part of the massive Obama*Care* expenditures, but part of the "stimulus plan." Perhaps, this is where billions of unaccounted for dollars in the "stimulus plan" went. If this is true, President Obama and his Party have misled the American people. While, the facts are still being gathered, one part of the nation has benefited by having Barack Obama in the Oval Office. Since President Obama took office, three counties immediately surrounding Washington, D.C. have become the richest per capita in the U.S. Big government, those who administer it, and those who promote it are thriving, while the rest of the nation is struggling.

And, we now know where some of the jobs "created or saved" came from. They were created by—and for—the sole benefit of First Lady Michelle Obama (a/k/a Michelle LaVaughn Robinson). It is revealing that in the First Lady's (now, Top Secret) Princeton University senior thesis she described herself as "black first and a student second". Perhaps, some independent-minded reporter will ask Mrs. Obama how she views herself now that she is the First Lady of the most powerful nation in the world.

Since becoming America's First Lady, Ms. Obama's servant list exceeds—in numbers and costs to the American tax payer—that of any previous president's wife. A look at the numbers is staggering. The First Lady, herself, requires more than twenty attendants, whose salaries are posted before their name and titles:

- $172,200—Susan Sher,
  (Chief of *Michelle Obama's* Staff)
- $140,000—Jocelyn C. Frye,
  (Deputy Assistant to the President and Director of Policy and Projects for the First Lady)
- $113,000—Desiree G. Rogers,
  (Special Assistant to the President and White House Social Secretary)
- $102,000—Camille Y. Johnston,
  (Special Assistant to the President and Director of Communications for the First Lady)
- $100,000—Melissa E. Winter,
  (Special Assistant to the President and Deputy Chief Of Staff to the First Lady)
- $90,000—David S. Medina,
  (Deputy Chief Of Staff to the First Lady)
- $84,000—Catherine M. Lelyveld,
  (Director and Press Secretary to the First Lady)
- $75,000—Frances M. Starkey,
  (Director of Scheduling and Advance for the First Lady)
- $70,000—Trooper Sanders,
  (Deputy Director of Policy and Projects for the First Lady)

- 65,000—Erinn J. Burnough,
  (Deputy Director and Deputy Social
  Secretary)
- $64,000—Joseph B. Reinstein,
  (Deputy Director and Deputy Social
  Secretary)
- $62,000—Jennifer R. Goodman,
  (Deputy Director of Scheduling and
  Events Coordinator for the First Lady)
- $60,000—Alan O. Fitts,
  (Deputy Director of Advance and Trip
  Director for the First Lady)
- $57,500—Dana M. Lewis,
  (Special Assistant and Personal Aide to
  the First Lady)
- $52,500—Semonti M. Mustaphi,
  (Associate Director and Deputy Press
  Secretary to the First Lady)
- $50,000—Kristen E. Jarvis,
  (Special Assistant for Scheduling and
  Traveling Aide to the First Lady)
- $45,000—Tyler A. Lechtenberg,
  (Associate Director of Correspondence
  for the First Lady)
- $43,000—Samantha Tubman,
  (Deputy Associate Director, Social
  Office)
- $40,000—Joseph J. Boswell,
  (Executive Assistant to the Chief Of
  Staff to the First Lady)
- $36,000—Sally M. Armbruster,
  (Staff Assistant to the Social Secretary)

- $35,000—Natalie Bookey,
  (Staff Assistant)
- $35,000—Deilia A. Jackson,
  (Deputy Associate Director of Corre-
  spondence for the First Lady)

Remember what you read on the previous pages about *Parkinson's Law.* Even this First Lady's assistants have assistants. All of these salaries add up to a staggering *six million, three hundred sixty four thousand dollars* ($6,364,000) for the four (4) years the President and First Lady Obama are in office.

Surely President and Michelle Obama know that America is in a belt-tightening recession. What's more, the above-referenced costs do not include 'First Make-up Artist' Ingrid Grimes-Miles and "First Hairstylist" Johnny Wright, both of whom traveled aboard Air Force One on Michelle Obama's $242,000 vacation in Spain.

Going along with the First Lady for her *European* vacation were her daughter Sasha, several long-time family friends, personal staff, various guests, and 70 Secret Service personnel. Surely, there are a lot of resorts *in America* that could have used the revenues spent on the First Lady's vacation during one of the deepest recessions in recent history.

While in Spain, The First Lady stayed in a $2,500.00 per night suite at a 5-Star luxury hotel. The entourage made the journey aboard Air Force 2 and used 47,500 gallons of jet fuel. Carbon emissions were estimated at 1,031 tons of carbon dioxide. As I read about the carbon footprint left by Michelle Obama on this one jaunt alone, I recalled how her husband suggested that the rest of us over-inflate our tires to save gas and reduce the carbon footprint that we leave on our ways to work. One would only have to assume that concerns over "Global Warming" apply only to us "average Americans." Oh, the hypocrisy ...

While some of the numbers are good estimates, one thing is certain: there has never been anyone in the White House *at any time in America's history* that has created such an army of staffers whose sole duties are the facilitation of the First Lady's social life. One wonders why she needs so much help, at taxpayer expense. Hillary Clinton only had three; Jackie Kennedy one; Laura Bush one; and prior to Mamie Eisenhower social help came from the President's own pocket.

When it comes to the Obama's, this scenario is but a symptom of a deeper problem. They govern as though they are above accountability. What, one may ask makes *this* First Lady more deserving than others, especially at a time in America's history when it is overrun by debt and facing an economic collapse? I am reminded of the aloofness of Marie-Antoinette (1755-93), the Queen consort of France's Louis XVI. When she was told that the French populace had no bread to eat she said, "Then, let them eat cake."

From all indications, it appears that the Obama's are equally out-of-touch with what is going on in America. Perhaps, they are just enjoying the "ride" that they believe they deserve—the ride they both may have been "bred and reared" for—regardless of where the country is heading.

I'd say that the extravagant use of servants at the taxpayer's expense is an example of the seductive practice: *Mastering the Art of the Bold Move,* denying reality. Is it any wonder that a growing number of Americans do not believe that Barack and Michelle Obama "get it?" Or, could their actions represent a sense of arrogance and the belief that they are newly-anointed royalty, cast upon the world stage? Whatever the answer, one thing is clear: the Obama's do not understand the economics of running a household on a budget—particularly not "the people's house."

But, the Obama's are not alone. Extravagance and waste have always been synonymous with big government ideologues. This writer was first introduced to this concept through the works of the aforementioned British economist, Dr. Northcote Parkinson. Over the last half century, the meaning of *Parkinson's Law* has given birth to several corollaries: *"Expenditures rise to meet income"* and *"the demand upon a resource tends to expand to match the supply of the resource."* (Wikipedia)

With these observations, it is clear that Parkinson clearly understood the behavior—and insatiable appetite—of government and its self-designated royalty, especially those governments with socialistic and/or dictatorial slants, who live by the rule: *do as we say; not as we do.* According to progressive liberals, wealth redistribution is a noble act ... as long as *their own* wealth is not being distributed. One of my former teachers, James J. Hicks called this form of socialism, "The Kennedy Creed of Social Justice." He grew up during the time that whisky importer and second-tier Illuminist, Joseph Kennedy, (father of John F., Robert, and Teddy Kennedy) was amassing his wealth and power during Prohibition ... when importing or selling any form of alcohol was illegal.

During the period between 2008 and 2010—and in keeping with the policy of "doing what we say ... not what we do"—the U.S. government proved that the demand upon spending and debt will expand to match the supply of money and debt that the American people are willing to swallow. The result of Obama*Change* is that the national debt is at an all-time high ... and still mounting, moving steadily into irreversible territory.

According to *USA Today*, the U.S. debt grows at a rate of $1.4 billion per day or $1.0 million per minute. This means that every legally registered man, woman, and child alive today owes $30,000 to the countries to whom our government owes money—and it's *our* money that our lawmakers have committed toward paying off the debt of retribution—"riot insurance"—to those who keep the lords of the Democrat Party in power.

The *USA Today* article goes on to say, "Despite vows in both parties to restrain federal spending, the national debt as a percentage of the U.S. Gross Domestic Product has grown from about 35% in 1975 to around 65% today. By historical standards, it's not proportionately as high as during World War II—when it briefly rose to 120% of GDP, but it's a big chunk of liability."

The rate at which America's debt is growing is best represented by the following example: Since 2008, the U.S. debt is growing *27 times as fast* as during the rest of our country's history. Metaphorically speaking, if you are driving your car in the right lane of a freeway—and doing 65 miles per hour—and a car rockets past you in the left lane, traveling 27 times faster than your are driving, the other car would be traveling at a speed of 7,555 miles per hour. Clearly, it is time to slow down the rate of government spending and begin to pay down on what is owed. Most economists agree that Washington politicians don't have *revenue* problem. They have a *spending* problem.

Solutions to many of America's problems are already known. The nation climbed back out of a financial hole following WWII, but Americans had a different work ethic in those times. Remember, it was a time in which our "Greatest Generation" was at the wheel. The current one has a lot of measuring-up to do.

As seen in the previous paragraphs, Dr. Northcote Parkinson recorded some of the solutions more than sixty years ago. So, if the natural histories of bureaucracies are known, why don't today's politicians change course? The answer is simple: because politicians tend to behave as politicians; and socialists behave as socialist—*until they obtain power.* Then, they behave as royalty. They—and their allies—embody *another one of* the previously mentioned *Dr. James J. Hicks Principle*: "People who obtain power by undermining the reigning class become that which they claim to have found intolerable on the way *up* the socio-political ladder."

Though not directly, Parkinson also addressed this dilemma. He noted that the greater the number of individuals involved in a decision-making body, the lower the collective IQ of the body, especially when it comes to taking the most prudent course of action. And, while observing the "bold moves" made by the Pelosi/Reed-run 111ᵗʰ Congress, one has to wonder what historians will say about the 111ᵗʰ Congress' collective I.Q. Though Republicans tried to remind Democrats of the principle that one can never spend one's self into prosperity, Democrats in Congress and the White House only heard the Sirens' songs from far across the Atlantic. It was not until Republicans won control of the House of Representatives in the 2010 mid-term elections that President Obama began to listen to the voices of reason. The *big* question is: will the Republicans—sent to Washington to halt the crazymaking taking place in the halls of government—bend ... or hold the ground they promised the American people they would hold? Wisely, President Obama has employed the seductive art: *Effect a Regression ...* or *the appearance* of a regression. Whether his new mask will appease the American electorate remains to be seen.

* * * * * * * * * *

In his book *(Parkinson's Law)*, the economist gives an example of how low the collective I.Q. of a group can be, explaining that a board of directors met to decide upon a corporation's upcoming budget. The first item on the budget called for the purchase of an expenditure of mammoth proportions. Millions of dollars would be needed to retool the company's production line. Only one of several available suppliers was invited to offer a proposal. The discussion was short and sweet. Reminiscent of Obama's healthcare bill, within a few short minutes the board of directors voted to spend millions of dollars (which, today, would amount to *billions* of dollars) on technology that not a single board member understood. For fear of admitting ignorance about the expensive equipment, each board member sat quietly and asked no questions when the opportunity presented itself. The governing body hurriedly voted to acquire a huge debt to purchase something not one member of the board took time to understand. One has to wonder if Parkinson's example was re-embodied by the 111th (Nancy Pelosi/Harry Reid) Congress. Have America's problems become so complex that lawmakers no longer possess the collective I.Q. to solve them? Do they even know the questions to ask? Or do they just sit silent or talk about the things *they can* understand. Just a few short decades ago, there was rarely talk about a trillion dollars. In fact, few Americans could even write the number. Today, the term, trillion, has become part of our everyday language. It is shocking to see the number written: $1,000,000,000,000. That's *twelve* zeros after the digit ... and the U.S. now owes its debtors *$14,300,000,000,000.* The number has become so onerous that it is hard to fathom. And, like the board of directors in Parkinson's scenario, our elected officials in Washington have been quick to add to an already unfathomable number, confirming one of my own observations about human beings and those they elect to lead them: *That which cannot be conceived cannot be expected to be corrected.*

It is well-known fact that a lawmaker's staff provides much of the research on bills and amendments that come to the floor. This being said, a lawmaker is no better than the staff that he, she, or the Illuminati-Islamic Alliance selects on the "lawmaker's" behalf.

As the agenda that Parkinson described in his book moved forward (and toward the end of the meeting) only one item remained on the agenda—the question of whether to provide free coffee in the employee's break room. The discussion was heated, with each member expressing his/her opinions on the matter. After thirty minutes of controversy, the item was tabled to the next meeting.

You see, when it came to providing coffee for employees, everyone at the table felt qualified to render an opinion. The expenditure for doing so amounted to only several hundred dollars a month, whereas tens of millions of dollars had been spent in a matter of minutes for equipment *the same* employees who were denied free coffee were expected to operate.

This story parallels that of the Healthcare Act of 2009 (Obama*Care*). The two-thousand page bill was neither read, nor understood by lawmakers who voted to "change" *forever* the manner in which the machinery of healthcare operates; yet, there was a rush to get it through Congress and signed by the President. Still, experts disagree on precisely how much Obama*Care* will cost the American taxpayer. Why wouldn't they disagree? No one truly understands the nature of the beast or the appetite that will need to be satisfied on the backs of future generations. All agree, however, that it will be expensive and impose onerous restrictions on patients and healthcare providers, alike ... at a time when the United States of America is bleeding red ink.

Perhaps, the most perplexing statement that came out of the healthcare debate in Congress was that of the (now) *former* speaker of the House of Representatives. It deserves repeating ... as often as necessary. Let us never forget! May it be her legacy! Nancy Pelosi said, *"We have to hurry up and pass it (the healthcare bill) so that we can learn what's in it."*

It is this kind of out-of-touch mentality that (in the mid-term elections of 2010) the people rose up to refute. Pelosi's gaff calls to mind and equally as out-of-touch statement voiced by the afore-referenced infamous French matriarch, Marie Antoinette, when she was told that the French people had no bread and were starving. "Then, let them eat cake," she said. Those of us who have looked at the past and present have to wonder how the two "matriarchs" (Nancy Pelosi and Marie Antoinette) would have responded if some fearless mainstream reporter had asked them to explain their equally-as-ridiculous remarks.

The message sent to state capitols as well as to the one in Washington, D.C. is: "We reject your kind of *change*. We reject the way *you* are conducting *our* business. Get smart, get help, or get out."

Hopefully—even facing vilification by the Obama White House and Democrats in Congress—the newly-elected Congress will "do some-thing" that will change the course of American history. Perhaps, the new Congress will take the time to read the bill that was hurriedly rammed through by the previous Congress and determine which portions need to be changed and which need to stand. Hopefully, the new Congress will get a handle on spending, cut waste and discover where unaccounted-for "stimulus money" is. Hopefully, the new Congress will fulfill their oath to "protect and defend" the United States of America and its Constitution against those who would "change" it in ways that would ensure peace, prosperity, and longevity.

Between elections, the American people can only hope that the leaders who conduct our business will act in a responsible manner. And, while Congress is in session, an occasional show of concerned oversight on the steps of the Capitol Building by groups of concerned citizens at the beginning of each fiscal year might serve as necessary reminders that the Lords of Seduction have been exposed for who and what they are.

Perhaps, added to the oaths taken by elected and appointed governmental officials should be a part that affirms that they have read—*and understand*—Parkinson's Law and its corollaries. If they did, lawmakers would see that while promising to be all things to all people might get them elected (or re-elected) their actions have consequences on the long-term survival of the nation they are sworn to "protect and defend against all enemies, foreign and domestic," including those advocating fiscal and social policies that would destroy America's ability to "rally" and do what is right, prudent, and just.

Clearly, many politicians and lawmakers see the world from a different perspective than do their constituents. That they do, is why constituents have to remain vigilant in both understanding what a candidate envisions his or her role in government to be, to be sure that every citizen's vote *is counted* (but no more than once) for the candidate with whom the (legitimate) voter agrees, and in keeping elected officials focused on doing what they said they would do, once in office.

Contrary to what *The Protocols* espouse, politicians must be reminded that—until the people relinquish it—a politician's power comes from—and should remain with—the people. And it important for *the people* to be reminded that unless citizens hand it off, power will always remain with them. When all is said and done, unless the electorate is an *informed electorate,* the masses tend *to follow,* rather than lead. And, that is what the Illuminati-Islamic Alliance is counting on.

Clearly, there are disagreements between nations of the world, between religions of the world, between races of the world and between fiscal, social, religious, and political ideologies. And, unless an electorate comes to understand each of these differences—and deals with them in a direct, yet fair, manner—differences will lead to conflict ... and conflict to war and destruction. But, who is to inform the electorate? As we have seen, *The Protocols* predict—and David Rockefeller confirmed—that the press is controlled by the very group of despots who continue to be veiled from the "lights of publicity."

My reason for writing this book is to encourage people from all walks of life *to think*—to question why some people are out to "change" the world and others are committed to defending the status quo. At times, I hit you, the reader, with disturbing facts and possibilities. This is an *intended* affront. I want you to prove me wrong ... or right. In either respect, if—as former President Ronald Reagan advised—you "trust, but verify" you will come to know the Truth about what you are being fed by the Illuminati-Islamic Alliance's complicit media.

In the precursor to this book (*Before and After*), I re-published the following quote: "Man's mind, once stretched by a new idea, never regains its original dimensions."[67] By bringing some of the issues now facing America—and the reasons why they exist—to the fore, it is my hope that each reader's mind will be "stretched," in a manner that causes it to reach across previously entrenched beliefs ... to stand tall and see what lies over the horizon. For, it is only by venturing beyond one's comfort zone and thinking new thoughts that current attitudes, ambitions and actions are tested. Sometimes exploring the other side of a debate *solidifies* our existing beliefs. On other occasions, experiencing something different makes us question what we've been led to believe. It is what drives humankind ever onward in search for the Truth.

---

[67] *Before and After, McCollough* E.G., Compass Press, Birmingham, AL, 1994.

CHAPTER 10

I n previous chapters, I addressed some of the individuals, groups and policies that could be responsible for America's troubles. I had a reason for doing so.

It was to lay a foundation for what follows. As a young man, I read: once a problem is identified, it is ninety (90) percent solved. Taking this premise as fact, let's look deeper into some of the "change" that has come to America and the problems that the initiators of such "change" have brought about. Beyond considering the nature of each change—ask yourself the all important questions: Who could possibly be behind them ... and why?"

A Global Currency Crisis: The net effect of inflating the value of the U.S. dollar and creating a global economic crisis is to establish a "one-world currency." When the world realizes that the U.S. will neither be able to balance its budget nor pay back the fourteen (plus) trillion dollars ($14,300,000,000,000.00) it owes, the value of the U.S. dollar and America's influence in the world will plummet. This is precisely what the Illuminati want. And, their wishes are consistent with *The Protocols.*

What follows a collapse in the U.S. dollar is a worldwide crisis, with long delays in shipping food and supplies. In effect the world will stand still. More than three million people could perish. Chaos will erupt. Mankind will revert to primal behavior—and according to *The Protocols,* will welcome the One-World Government established *by* and *for* The Illuminati.

When worldwide famine takes place—and, with today's version of "border control"—the U.S. could see a mass invasion of people from Mexico and South America. The American West is likely to become the "Wild West," once again. The difference is that drug lords will rule it (their armies are growing by the day, armed—in part—by the Obama Administration's "Operation Fast and Furious"). There will be an all-out attempt by the U.S. government (led by Obama's successor) to take the West back. Chaos will rule. A lot of blood will be shed. This, too, is spelled out in *The Protocols.*

During this time, the price of commodities will skyrocket. The fortunes of Arab oil magnets will be frozen, and alternative oil reserves in the U.S. will replace OPEC's monopoly, creating new transfer of wealth back to western overlords. Global corruption will reign, and that is when the antichrist will emerge to take control and offer peace. So what will start with a global currency crisis will morph into man's greatest nightmare.

Who is capable of creating such a scenario? And why would anyone or any group want to see it play out? The answer is: *control*—the creation of a One-World Empire, controlled by those who orchestrated it (The Order of the Illuminati).

The above scenario also follows the prophecies laid out in the Revelation of St. John the Divine and the policies of *The Protocols of the Learned Elders of Zion.* So, can humankind prevent such events from occurring? Perhaps, we can *if* we pay attention to what is happening to our world and who is creating the kinds of "change" that would bring America to its knees.

Let us look at some of the other changes that are taking place and ask ourselves: Is the kind of "change" being orchestrated by the Obama Administration making us less *in*dependent or more dependent on a U.S. Government that can take away our freedom and possessions with the flip of a switch or the pressing of a "delete" button on some computer? Are the changes that we are experiencing today moving us closer to One-World (Illuminati-controlled) governance?

The Post Office: Get ready to imagine a world without the post office. This inefficient agency of government is so deeply in financial trouble that there is probably no way to sustain it long term. Fed up with a costly and inefficient system, the people have turned to Email, Fed Ex, and UPS. As a result revenues needed to keep the post office alive have been insufficient. Most of the mail now delivered by the Post Office is junk mail and bills and many of its employees could benefit from a course in "customer service."

The Check: Britain is already laying the groundwork to do away with checks by 2018. It costs the financial system billions of dollars a year to process checks. Plastic cards and online transactions will lead to the eventual demise of the check. Everything is leading to electronic banking and electronic commerce. This plays right into the death of the post office. If you never paid your bills by mail and never received them by mail, the post office would absolutely go out of business.

The Newspaper: The younger generation simply doesn't read the newspaper. They certainly don't subscribe to a daily delivered *print edition*. Newspapers may go the way of the milkman and the laundry man. As for reading the paper online, get ready to pay for it. The rise in mobile Internet devices and e-readers has caused all the newspaper and magazine publishers to form an alliance. They have met with Apple, Amazon, and the major cell phone companies to develop a model for paid subscription services. With all news delivered electronically, it can be more closely monitored by individuals sitting at computers ... and could be intercepted, edited, or deleted with the pressing of a few buttons overriding whatever reporters report. Journalism—as we know it—is facing major changes.

Americans should keep a close eye on new federal regulations that monitor the internet. They are called *"Net Neutrality,"* which allows government bureaucrats to determine what can be transmitted over the internet.

The Book: You say you will never give up the physical book that you hold in your hand and turn the literal pages. Many have said the same thing about downloading music from iTunes. We wanted our hard copy CD. But people around the globe quickly changed their minds when they discovered that they could purchase albums for half the price without ever leaving home. The same thing will happen with books. You can browse a bookstore online and even read a preview chapter before you buy. And the price is less than half that of a hard copy book. And think of the convenience!

The problem is: with all books being offered only in electronic format, it would be easier to delete them from virtual bookshelves and libraries should the "powers that be" consider them a threat.

When all this comes to pass, homes of the future will have no bookshelves. There won't be any reason to have them. Even family photographs can be displayed on electronic devises that roll from photo to photo, also making the hardcopy photo album obsolete.

The Land-Line Telephone: Unless you have a large family and make a lot of local calls, you don't need it anymore. Most people keep it simply because they've always had it. But you are paying double charges for that extra service. All the cell phone companies will let you call family, friends, and customers using the same cell provider for no charge against your minutes.

On the "Big Brother" side of the equation, it is much easier to monitor the calls of a cellular phone than it is to monitor those conducted by land line phones.

Music: This is one of the saddest parts of the change story. The music industry is dying a slow death. Not just because of illegal downloading. It's the lack of innovative new music being given a chance to get to the people who would like to hear it. Greed and corruption is the problem. The record labels and the radio conglomerates are simply self-destructing. Over forty percent of the music purchased today is "catalog items," meaning traditional music that the public is familiar with—older established artists. This is also true on the live concert circuit. It may also explain the growing popularity of satellite radio.

The thoughts and behavior of America's younger generations have always been influenced by music. As is the case with *e*-books, *e*-music can also be more censored—

making only the music that those who control the internet deem "appropriate."

Television: Revenues to the (traditional) networks are down dramatically. Not just because of the economy. People are watching TV and movies streamed from their computers. And they're playing games and doing lots of other things that take up the time that used to be spent watching TV. Prime time shows have degenerated down to lower than the lowest common denominator. Subject matter and content could be part of the problem. Americans are growing tired of being "dumbed down" by a Leftist-leaning entertainment industry.

Cable rates are skyrocketing and commercials run about every 4 minutes and 30 seconds. And, on those channels that are void of commercials, the quality of movies and other forms of "entertainment" continue to deteriorate. Part of this is an act of retaliation against seductive indoctrination practices. Pay attention to whom is being placed in the dumb or subordinate role in commercials—it is the white Anglo-Saxon male. White men are beginning to "get it" and are retaliating with the most effective tool they have—turn away from commercial television.

And, because the traditional networks are feeling the squeeze, some in the Obama Administration have suggested that their nemesis, FOX News, be shut down. This is a hint at what is to come. Remember that *The Protocols* say "we control the press," and David Rockefeller admitted that the press had been a complicit partner in the "supranational sovereignty's" ability to carry out its plan "without being subjected to the lights of publicity."

The "Things" That You Own: Many of the very possessions that we used to own are still in our lives, but we may not actually own them in the future. They may simply reside in "the cloud" (for those of my generation, this is a term used to describe the Internet). Today your computer has a hard drive and you store your pictures, music, movies, and documents. Your software is on a CD or DVD, and you can always re-install it if need be. But all of that is changing. Apple, Microsoft, and Google are all finishing up their latest "cloud services" and creating a "profile" on each user that can be accessed by any computer hacker or government employee wanting to look in on your activities. That means that when you turn on a computer, the Internet will be built into the operating system. So, Windows, Google, and the Mac OS will be tied straight into the Internet. If you click an icon, it will open something in the Internet cloud. If you save something, it will be saved to the cloud. And you may pay a monthly subscription fee to the cloud provider.

In April 2011, it came to light that the locations and travels of Apple's iPod and iPad owners could be tracked and traced through the internet. Big Brother knows every move that the owners of such high-tech devises make. If all this seems far-fetched, consider the hundreds of thousands of "top-secret" documents that were released to the public by WikiLeaks, an internet site ostensibly created by a rouge soldier in the U.S. military.

But, perhaps, the best example of how a computer-controlled world can be manipulated is: a "cyber missile" known as *Stuxnet*, a cyber worm that appears to have been successful in frustrating the Iranian attempt to enrich uranium for the purpose of creating nuclear warheads.

Stuxnet was designed and sent into the area around Iran's Natanz nuclear power plant—just how may never be known—to infect a number of computers on the assumption that someone working in the plant would take work home on a flash drive, acquire the worm and then bring it back to the plant.

Once the worm was inside the plant, the next step was to get the computer system there to trust it and allow it into the system. That was accomplished because the worm contained a "digital certificate" stolen from JMicron, a large company in an industrial park in Taiwan. When the worm was later discovered it quickly replaced the original digital certificate with another certificate, also stolen from another company, Realtek, a few doors down in the same industrial park in Taiwan.

Once allowed entry, the worm contained four "Zero Day" elements in its first target, the Windows 7 operating system that controlled the overall operation of the plant. Zero Day elements are rare and extremely valuable vulnerabilities in a computer system that can be exploited only once. Two of the vulnerabilities were known, but the other two had never been discovered. Experts say no hacker would waste Zero Days in that manner. This was an intelligent form of warfare, developed and launched by intelligent individuals with access to advanced technology— lots of it.

After penetrating the Windows 7 operating system, the code then targeted the "frequency converters" that ran the centrifuges. To do that it used specifications from the manufacturers of the converters. One was Vacon, a Finnish Company, and the other Fararo Paya, an Iranian company. What surprised experts at this step was the fact that the

Iranian company was so secret that not even the IAEA (International Atomic Energy Agency) knew about it.

The worm also knew that the complex control system that ran the centrifuges was built by Siemans, the German manufacturer, and—remarkably—how that system worked as well and how to mask its activities from it.

Masking itself from the plant's security and other systems, the worm then ordered the centrifuges to rotate extremely fast, and then to slow down precipitously. This damaged the converter, the centrifuges and the bearings, and it corrupted the uranium in the tubes. It also left Iranian nuclear engineers wondering what was wrong, as computer checks showed no malfunctions in the operating system.

Estimates are that this went on for more than a year, leaving the Iranian program in chaos. And as it did, the worm grew and adapted throughout the system. As new worms entered the system, they would meet and adapt and become increasingly sophisticated.

During this time the worms reported back to two servers that had to be run by intelligence agencies, one in Denmark and one in Malaysia. The servers monitored the worms and were shut down once the worm had infiltrated Natanz. Efforts to find those servers since then have yielded no results.

This went on until June of 2009, when a Belarusan company working on the Iranian power plant in Beshehr discovered it in one of its machines. It quickly put out a notice on a Web network monitored by computer security experts around the world. Ordinarily these experts would immediately begin tracing the worm and dissecting it, looking for clues about its origin and other details. But that didn't happen because within minutes all the alert sites came under attack and were inoperative for 24 hours.

"Whoever made the worm had a full day to eliminate all traces of the worm that might lead us to them," Eric Byers, a computer security expert who has examined the Stuxnet said. "No hacker could have done that."

Experts, including inspectors from the International Atomic Energy Agency, say that, despite Iran's claims to the contrary, the worm was successful in its goal: causing confusion among Iran's nuclear engineers and disabling their nuclear program.

Because of the secrecy surrounding the Iranian program, no one can be certain of the full extent of the damage. But sources inside Iran and elsewhere say that the Iranian centrifuge program has been operating far below its capacity and that the uranium enrichment program had "stagnated" during the time the worm penetrated the underground facility.

In other words the worm was designed to allow the Iranian program to continue but never succeed, and never to know why.

One additional impact that can be attributed to the worm, according to David Albright of the Center for Strategic and International Studies, is that "the lives of the (Iranian) scientists working in the facility have become a living hell because of counter-intelligence agents brought into the plant" to battle the breach. Ironically, even after its discovery, the worm has succeeded in slowing down Iran's reputed effort to build an atomic weapon. And Langer says that the efforts by the Iranians to cleanse Stuxnet from their system "will probably take another year to complete," and during that time the plant will not be able to function anywhere normally.

But as the extent of the worm's capabilities is being understood, its genius and complexity has created another perplexing question: Who did it?

Much of what the worm "knew" could only have come from a consortium of Western intelligence agencies, experts who have examined the code now believe. The most likely answer ... is that a consortium of intelligence agencies worked together to build the cyber bomb.

I have re-published much of the November 26, 2010 Associated Press article by Ed Barnes for the purpose of making a broader point. While many would agree that—in this instance—Stuxnet may have achieved a noble objective, frustrating the efforts of a nation sworn to the destruction of Israel, the ramifications are more far-reaching. Regardless of who was behind creating the cyber missile, one thing is certain, *The Illuminati has the capacity of gaining—or maintaining—control of it.* Such a weapon in the hands of The Illuminati would make it possible for them—or their emissaries—to use it against any nation, group, or individual for a variety of purposes. And the "changes" mentioned in earlier paragraphs of this chapter make it quite possible for anyone who controls such "worms" to rule a technology-dependent world.

So, has Obama*Change* brought the beginning of a "Big Brother," Orwellian-styled World upon the American people? Recent reports like that of the Stuxnet worm and one that revealed how—for almost twenty (20) minutes— some "computer hijacker" in China took control of *all* internet communications, including those of a "top secret" nature, within the U.S. Government. And, the WikiLeak Crisis certainly suggests that George Orwell saw the future. Is the internet the problem and not the solution? The fact is that Obama*Care* ushers in a mandate for electronic medical records and opens the door for sensitive information about everyone covered by the program to be accessed—and changed—at will, if it were needed to serve the Illuminati's objectives. Is a Siren-in-Chief luring a technology-hungry generation toward the shores of its own destruction, using healthcare as seductive bait?

Privacy: If there ever was a concept that we can look back on nostalgically, it would be privacy. As demonstrated in the previous section, that's gone. It's been gone for a long time anyway. There are cameras on the street, in most of the buildings, and even built into your computer and cell phone. But you can be sure that 24/7, "They" (who chooses to watch) know who you are and where you are, right down to the GPS coordinates, and the Google Street View, particularly if your cell phone is nearby.

If you buy something, your habit is put into a zillion profiles, and the ads you receive on your computer, smart phone, iPad or via snail mail will change to reflect those habits. Big Brother will have access to everything you purchase. They can know where you are and what you are doing at virtually any moment. And "They" will try to get you to buy something else. While the Illuminati smile, George Orwell's "Big Brother" Oceania is becoming more fact than fiction. Are we already "slaves" to the Lords of Technology?

An Increase in Cyber-Theft: As technology advances, more thieves will figure out ways to use technology to take from us what is ours, including our identities. The ability to gain access to critical information and pose as the legitimate holder of that information should give every law-abiding citizen in America reason for pause. It is now possible for identity thieves to confiscate the information that a credit card contains from a remote location. Protecting our identities, assets, homes, families, and nation against those who would seize and destroy all of the above is sure to become one of the great challenges of the emerging techno-generation.

An Increase in Terrorism: Though we don't want to admit it, terrorism has been successful in creating "change" in the way Americans live our lives. Counter-terrorists activities have cost America dearly. We have engaged in war in Iraq, Afghanistan, and Pakistan and we, the people, will never know where else in the world our government is conducting secret operations designed to implement counter-terrorist activities. It is important, here, to reflect the section of *The Protocols* that promise "terror" as a way to usher in their form of a One-World Government. It is easy to see how terrorism helps the Illuminati-Islamic Alliance achieve their mutual goals.

Expensive and disruptive security measures have been installed in public places to try and prevent terrorist activities, changing the way Americans move about in our own land and abroad, effectively making us slaves to the fear of terrorist attacks, all the while relinquishing our rights to privacy. And, because U.S. leaders have chosen *not to play "hard ball"* with countries that support and encourage   terrorism, the monster continues to grow ... and the Illuminati-Islamic Alliance smiles.

An Ever-*decreasing* Presence of Judeo-Christian Values in America's Public Arenas: Leftist, progressive activists doing the Illuminati's bidding have been successful in removing acknowledgment of—and reference to—the

Judeo-Christian God from public arenas—from schools, sporting events, city squares, etc.—as *The Protocols* have promised.

U*n*equal Application of the Law: With the installation of the Illuminati's liberal judges, the U.S. Constitution is under attack. Recently-passed laws have amended the intent of the Constitution's drafters. America's courts provide favored status for law-*breakers* and penalties on law-*abiders*. If a homeowner shoots a criminal who is breaking into the owner's home to commit a crime, it is the homeowner who is put on trial. The Law is upside-down.

Remember what *The Protocols* say about appointing and controlling judges.

An Increasing Push to Install Socialism as a Replacement for Capitalism in America: Before we can engage in a meaningful discussion about the preferences of socialism and capitalism, we must examine the definition of each. *Bing* (Microsoft's version of Google) defines "socialism" as:

1. *A political system of communal ownership:* a political theory or system in which the means of production and distribution are controlled by the people (at the top) and (supposedly) operated according to equity and fairness rather than market principles (though the determinant of "fairness" is unspecified);

2. *A movement based on socialism:* a political movement based on principles of socialism, typically advocating an *end to private*

property;* and to the exploitation of workers;

3. *A stage between capitalism and communism*: in Marxist theory, the stage after the proletarian revolution when a society is changing from capitalism to communism ...

The same source (*Bing*) defines "capitalism" as:

1. *A free-market system*: an economic system based on the private ownership of the means of production and distribution of goods, characterized by a free competitive market and motivation by profit.

So, which is it that Americans would rather have—a "free-market system" based on self-determination *or* one based on "an end to private property, the exploitation of workers" and the transfer of *choice* away from the people and toward government? The answer one gives would depend upon whether one relies upon his or her own skills and ambitions or the government to provide the essentials of life, and is capable of seeing the true character of a One-World Government, *of* ... *by* ... and *for* ... the Lords of Seduction.

With respect to a vibrant democracy, socialism could best be described as "death by a thousand cuts." Do Americans really want to continue down the path that Karl Marx described as "the stage after the proletarian revolution when a society is *changing* from capitalism to communism?" Is this the kind of "change" that President Obama promised during his campaign? It certainly appears to be the kind of "change" that he and his administration have promoted—and imposed—*since* he was sworn in to office.

A New World Order: At the direction of a "supranational sovereignty" that intends to head it up, the world is rapidly moving toward a One-World (totalitarian-styled) Government that was clearly promised in the latest version of the *Protocols of the Learned Elders of Zion* more than a century ago. In order to accomplish this objective the United States of America must, first, be *changed* into a socialistic, secular, entitlement-dependent society, thereby making it easier for intellectuals and world bankers to merge it into a World Government, in which (as *The Protocols* promise) God is surely to be visibly *absent.*

A prime arm of The Illuminati—and enabler of the Rothschild Formula—is the Federal Reserve and its twin sibling, The International Monetary Fund.

The ten member banks of the Federal Reserve are Rothschild allies all: the Bank of London, Warburg Bank of Hamburg, Rothschild Bank of Berlin, Lehman Brothers of New York, Lazard Brothers of Paris, Kuhn Loeb Bank of New York, Israel Moses Seif Banks of Italy, Goldman Sachs of New York, Warburg Bank of Amsterdam, Chase Manhattan Bank of New York. These Rothschild-allied banks are the prime movers not behind a vibrant U.S. economy, but behind the establishment of a One-World Government. More on this later.

The Coming Rebellion against Tyranny: History teaches that human beings will eventually rebel against tyranny. And rebellions can be orchestrated by those who have the power resources, and desire to do so ... as we are about to see.

From The Scriptures, we also know that God will allow mankind to stray ... for a while. Then, He intervenes and makes His presence and expectations known. When both God and Man have had their fill of Evil, both rise up and "change" the course of destiny. *This* is what the Illuminati fear—a "rallying" of Americans behind what we perceive as a threat to national security and the very tenet upon which our nation was founded—the freedom to worship the God of *our* choice—the God of our existence. This is why the Illuminati have to control the press and why they use the ACLU to remove God from the position of prominence that the founders intended. Through the press, they can control what people see, hear, and think (as is overtly described in *The Protocols).*

An examination of the mid-term election of 2010, suggests that a peaceful revolution has begun in the U.S. Will it be successful? Will it be enough? Can the gains made toward righting America's ship of state be sustained? Can the peaceful revolution remain peaceful? Is there another Civil War in America's future? Will (as Ayn Rand proposed in *Atlas Shrugged)* America's "prime movers" go on strike and starve the beast of socialism, driving it into the bottomless pit of despotism? Will God exercise His omnipotent power as he did in the Garden of Eden; with the Great Flood; with the tyrant who orchestrated construction of the Tower of Babel; with Sodom and Gomorrah; with Greece and Rome; and, perhaps, with Germany and the Soviet Union? These are some of the questions that America's *re-founders* must consider.

* * * * * * * * * *

During the "New Age" of Barack Hussein Obama, more progress has been made toward building the great tower of socialism within America's capitol cities than any other time in recent history. Only the terms of Presidents Woodrow Wilson and Lyndon Johnson come close.

The Illuminati-chosen, charismatic, affirmative action *candidate*, Barack Obama, promised "change," and "change" is what America got—the kind of "change" that even a lot of his naïve supporters weren't expecting. You see, the American people are a trusting people. We want to see the oppressed segments of our society rise to unimaginable height. Americans want to believe that their leaders will deliver on campaign promises to do what is best for America. Americans are a fair and generous people. We want individuals from all corners of the U.S. to live the American dream, regardless of color, gender, or religion. America has always pulled for the underdog ... because there was a time when America *was* the underdog.

What we are learning, however, is that outside forces—America's enemies—are using our sense of fairness and Godliness, our election process and our Constitution as Achilles' Heels to seduce us (the U.S.) into submission. One-World architects are in the business of furthering the ambitions of lawmakers who already agree with them, or can be bought. And, as open-minded as Americans are, we don't like the idea of being *had.*

A look at its activities over the past fifty years indicates that The American Civil Liberties Union (ACLU) is anything but what its name implies. The ACLU (an Illuminati operative) is not out to ensure even-handed "liberty." Doing The Illuminati's bidding, the ACLU (as *The Protocols* promise) brings suits against individuals and organizations who are attempting to *preserve* many of the *rights* that the U.S. Constitution ensures. With the assistance of Left-leaning federal judges (who were appointed by Illuminati-supported presidents) the ACLU has truly brought "change" to America—the kind that ensures the death of democracy and the abandonment of God.

Once issues make it to the courts, Constitutional Law is too often being interpreted by progressive, Illuminist Federal and Supreme Court Judges in such a manner that the U.S. Constitution is being re-written by case law—not to empower *the people*—but to empower the people's greatest enemy, big government ... of a totalitarian nature.

Recently, a Federal Judge in California over-ruled the will of the people of California, nullifying the results of an election in which the majority of Californians voted to outlaw same-sex marriage. Chief U.S. District Judge Vaughn Walker (an openly gay jurist appointed by President George H.W. Bush in 1989), has never taken pains to disguise—or advertise—his sexual orientation (SFGate.com).

Judge Walker ruled in favor of a lawsuit brought by two same-sex couples and the city of San Francisco seeking to *invalidate* the will of the people as "unlawful infringement on the civil rights of gay men and lesbians," even though Proposition 8 passed with *fifty-two percent* of the vote in November 2008. When a single judge can "invalidate" *the people's* election, America is no longer a democracy, nor a republic.

Let us hope that when—as many predicted—illegal immigrants and radical Islamists become a majority of the U.S. population, U.S. judges will be equally as committed to upholding the Constitution. The California case and decision affirm the importance of knowing how a candidate for President feels toward upholding *traditional* American values and being assured that he or she will make *lifetime* appointments to Federal and Supreme Courts that uphold the intent of the founding fathers, as the will of the people. The Illuminati understands the importance of the value-systems that are embraced by America's leaders. That's why their policy document (*The Protocols*) contains an entire section outlining how they will choose presidents and judges and the qualifications that their "puppets" must possess. *Their* vision for the U.S.—and the world—depends on it.

Another federal judge (U.S. District Judge, Susan Bolton) overruled the will of the people of Arizona, who had voted measures into law that were intended to secure their state from an invasion by illegal aliens. The law allowed *officers to check a person's immigration status while enforcing other laws.* It is important to note that the law applied to individuals who had *already been detained* for breaking an existing law. However, Judge Bolton ruled: "By enforcing this statute, (the state of) Arizona would impose a 'distinct, unusual and extraordinary' burden on legal resident aliens that only the *federal government* has the authority to impose," (Associated Press) although the federal government (under Barack Obama) has chosen not to exercise its authority to secure the borders. To the contrary, Barrack Obama's Attorney General, Eric Holder, sided *with the illegal's* and filed suit *against* Arizona leaders who were attempting to do what Obama and Holder refused to do. Obama and his agent, Holder, clearly know what they are doing and the effect that their actions have on securing America's borders and increasing the number of future Democrat voters ... and so does Judge Bolton.

What Arizona's law imposed was the enforcement of laws that were already on the books. The "burden" to which Judge Bolton referred is already placed on *legal residents* at either end of the age spectrum. When legal residents approaching senior citizen status request discounts traditionally offered to seniors or when legal residents approaching adulthood are required to show identification when purchasing alcoholic beverages or tobacco products, they must present proof of identification. But, a judge carrying out her duty—knowingly or unknowingly—*to the Illuminati* (not to the American people) ruled that it is too much for an individual who has *already* broken a law to reveal who he or she is and the country of their citizenship. Such a ruling qualifies for the term "crazymaking" that was introduced in a previous chapter.

In Arizona, we have a clear example of state's rights vs. federal rights; the people's will vs. the Illuminati's will; centralized government vs. decentralized government. This is precisely what led to the War Between the States in the 1800s. One hundred and fifty years later, the people of the state of Arizona voted overwhelmingly to act responsibly and defend their state's borders (and state's rights) against all enemies, foreign and domestic. They acted to provide for *their state's* defense—as well as that of the Union to which it belonged. Seems reasonable doesn't it? However, rather than thanking Arizona for doing the federal government's job—and in keeping with Black Liberation Theology—Barack Obama's Attorney General Holder, filed suit against the State of Arizona, ignoring the oath of office to which he was sworn: "protect and defend" the U.S. and its Constitution "against all enemies, foreign and domestic."

To be more specific, Article IV, Section 4 of the U.S. Constitution states, in part: "The United States shall ... protect each of them (each state in the Union) against invasion ..."

Based on the number of *illegal* aliens, drug lords, and the crimes committed by those crossing its border each day, Arizona (like other states along the southern border) is seeing the effects of an "invasion." However, rather than defending Arizona against the invasion, President Obama's Administration decided to side with illegals and criminals. One has to wonder what else is behind the Obama Administration's stance on this issue. Although it is pure speculation, having open borders would allow armies of Islamic radicals to enter the United States and prepare for the Great U.S. Jihad that has been promised. And, while they are preparing for such an act, America's invaders will be cared for by government programs financed by the very target they intend to annihilate—the American law-abiding taxpayer.

To demonstrate how the Constitution is under attack by the Obama Administration, consider its newly-installed policy about searches at airports throughout America. While illegal aliens are given immunity from being searched as they come in through the back door, legitimate citizens are being subjected to both invasive and non-invasive searches when they engage in domestic or international air travel. It's yet another example of how big government is taking from *the people* (citizens) rights that the Constitution guarantees and being *inconsistent* in applying the laws of the land. The question that arises out of these disclosures is: Who benefits most from these anti-American decisions? The answer is: Those who would expedite the completion of Tyler's Cycle of Democracies.

I have gone into some detail about the two rulings of Federal Judges and decisions made by the Obama Administration to emphasize the long-trending agenda *away* from preserving and protecting the America envisioned by the founders of our nation (and its constitution) and *toward* a centralization of power—the kind of power that can be more easily dictated by—and transferred—to a One-World, totalitarian state.

At the time of this writing, the issue of collective bargaining has been taken out of the hands of *the people* and the people's representatives. The Wisconsin Supreme court will decide upon another union-favored decision handed down by two liberal lower court judges.

Clearly, our world is changing right before our eyes. And, many Americans are blinded to the fact that we (the U.S) are the prize that a variety of reformers covet. Our habits, our thoughts, our access to information, "entertainment" and "news," our ability to share information, our security, our courts, our trust in knowing that our vote was counted *as it was actually casted and that the policies and people chosen by our votes would stand*—all of these fundamental American traditions that are summarily being confiscated as we watch.

And, while the "Big Bang" of advanced technology continues to expand into every facet of our lives, modern-day Sirens of Change—implementers of *The Protocols'* policies—continue to beckon us even closer to the "bone heap piles on their beaches."

At the time of this writing, the world is changing at breakneck speed. Demonstrations at home and abroad are but symptoms of a people intentionally being stirred with uncertainty and fear. For us to survive what surely lies ahead, clear heads must prevail. Patriots must be willing to speak out for the dangers that lie in the road ahead.

Perhaps, this book will serve as the kinds of admonitions that Circe gave to Odysseus. If, until they can be driven into the seas of their own excrement, we have to listen to the melodious sounds of today's Sirens—calling us ever closer to the shores of socialism—at least let us use every degree of constraint at our disposal. While we journey through the realms of "in-between," (capitalism and communism) let those of us who love America and still relish the ability to exercise "free will," grab each other's hands, bind ourselves together, and remain focused on a destination of our own choice.

As we continue on the journey to explore the issue of "change," let us be willing to believe that every encounter we experience along the way toward saving America is a lesson learned. Let us remain ever vigilant to the things going on in the world around us—protecting that which should be preserved and changing the things that will surely have the U.S.A. end up in the graveyards of history.

CHAPTER 11

If a group of wealthy and intellectual individuals (The Bilderbergers a/k/a The Illuminati) get together each year to see how they can make the world a better place for each and every inhabitant, I applaud their actions, wish them success in achieving such a noble objective, and retract any and all damning, recriminating references.

If, on the other hand, such a group meets for the purpose of deciding how they are going to breed and rear puppets who can help them take the earth and its bounty from others, let us pray that they soon overstep their inflated levels of self-importance and see their fortunes disappear before their eyes. And, may America be the proverbial straw that broke the camel's back.

In such a scenario, there is a place for every citizen. When one realizes that the Illuminati are no more than disillusioned human beings and one becomes aware of Dr. Laurence J. Peter's work on the hierarchies of "change,"[68] the world will never again look the same. Evidence of the final promotion is rampant—in academics, in businesses, in government ... in despotism. What has become apparent to the perceptive observer is: those who believe themselves to be intellectual elites aren't quite as

---

[68] *The Peter Principle,* Laurence J. Peter, PhD, Bantam Books, New York, NY, 1969.

smart as they think. They may have underestimated us "average" Americans, at least those of us who can recognize a liar and a phony when we see one. We have condoned and rewarded mediocrity for so long that—in many cases—it has, sadly, become the new American standard.

So, going forward, what should be done? America has to realize that it is involved in a war for the hearts and minds of its citizens.

- We have to seek out individuals who understand the reality behind the work of Robert Greene and Machiavelli.
- We have to see that Americans from all walks of life become aware of *The Protocols* that guide the Hidden Hand.
- We have to select leaders who understand the meaning of these works and know how to work both "hard" and "smart."
- We have to hold leaders accountable to the oaths they took upon assuming office.
- We have to turn deaf ears to the liberal agenda of "affirmative action" and "political correctness," roll up our sleeves and put the best people available in every position of responsibility and leadership, regardless of race, creed, and gender.
- We have to continue to lend a helping hand, lift the less-fortunate up, and help them find a "place" or vocation in which they can become productive and proud citizens.
- More importantly, we have to insist that all the troops report for duty—that every

American (regardless of race, religion, creed
or social status) becomes part of the solution
and not part of the problem.

In a previous chapter, I referred to a trusted axiom:
"Insanity is doing the same thing over and over and
expecting a different result." Turning over the destiny of
the world to a group a self-proclaimed "supranational
sovereignty of intellectual elites and world bankers," who
have driven the U.S. to the brink of destruction is a clear
example of "insanity" on the part of those of us who
have allowed it to continue. Unless we become the voice
of reason; call Evil what it is, expose the seductive ways
of America's enemies to the masses, demand
accountability from every person who lives within our
borders, stop the billions of dollars of foreign aid that
buy us nothing—except animosity—from countries that
already despise us, and encourage every American to
become an independent thinker, we can never hope to
expect "a different result" from what failing to do so has
wrought. We'll continue down the road of becoming
owned by the Masters of a One-World Government.
That being the case, people with demonstrated abilities
(obtained within various crucibles of life) must step
forward and let their voices be heard—to identify the best
leaders' available, demand that each elected official hire
the most competent assistants available and encourage
them to assume a leadership role in "changing" the
failed practices of the past. Then, we remain vigilant and
see that the United States of America does not follow
other democracies into the graveyards of history.

Is what I have proposed a *race-based philosophy?*
You bet it is! It is one that has *the human race's* best

interest at heart. It is an *affirmative action* initiative of a reasonable kind, one intended to make people of all colors, religions and ideologies join together, put past differences aside, and march toward a common objective—to save the world's best hope for preserving "human rights," worldwide.

Assuming they will read this far, there will be those on the Left, who will try to twist the meaning of what I have written. It is how they demonize anyone who does not agree with them. However, *let me be clear* (a statement that Americans have heard a lot over the past two years,) **saving America is the only reason that I've invested the time and energy into voicing my thoughts through this venue.** It is the only reason that I have exposed myself to the kind of Rothschildian assaults that are surely to follow the publication of this book.

If you agree that America is worthy of being saved from the boneheaps of history—and will join with me— know that it will be an uphill climb. The mission will only be achieved if a majority of freedom-living patriots become active in the political process ... and move forward ... from a position *of strength*.

* * * * * * * * *

A former Alabama governor once related a conversation he had with U.S. President, Lyndon Johnson. The governor asked the icon of "The Great Society" about the late president's welfare-based programs. Johnson told the governor that he (the president) considered social entitlements "riot insurance." What a threat to hold over a nation. Is it any wonder that America is in trouble? Our government has been dealing with America's problems from a position *of weakness.* Clearly, Johnson's plan is one for the ages. "*Riot insurance* ... how irresponsible, coming from a man, who placed his hand on the Bible and swore an oath to "protect and defend the U.S. against all enemies, foreign and domestic", not surrender to blackmail.

*   *   *   *   *   *   *   *

The man who appears to have been "bred and reared" to sit behind the *Resolute* desk in the Oval office can best be described by one of his Columbia University classmates. His characterization of the sitting U.S President affirms many of the observations previously set out in this book. I only received this "portrait" as I was in the final stages of editing my manuscript, but felt it worthy of inclusion. The recitation that follows has been confirmed by Snopes.[69]

> "Barack Hussein Obama was my college classmate (Columbia University, class of '83). He is a devout Muslim. Do not be fooled. Add up the clues below. Taken individually they're alarming. Taken as a whole, it is a brilliant, Machiavellian game plan to turn the United States into a socialist/Marxist state with a permanent majority that desperately needs government for survival ... and can be counted on to always vote for bigger government.
>
> "Why not? They have no responsibility to pay for it. The *healthcare bill* (that Barack Obama and his Democrat

[69] Note: For emphasis, some words and phrases in this section have been italicized by this author.

colleagues rammed through Congress) had very little to do with healthcare. *It had everything to do with unionizing millions of hospital and health care workers, as well as adding 15,000 to 20,000 new **IRS** agents (who will join government employee unions)*. Obama doesn't care that giving free healthcare to 30 million Americans will add trillions to the national debt. What he does care about is that it cements the dependence of those 30 million voters to Democrats and big government. Who, but a socialist revolutionary (or his puppet masters), would pass this reckless spending bill in the middle of a depression?

Like health care legislation having nothing to do with healthcare, cap and trade has nothing to do with global warming. It has everything to do with redistribution of income, government control of the economy and a criminal payoff to Obama's biggest contributors. Those powerful and wealthy unions and contributors (like **GE**, which owns **NBC**, **MSNBC** and **CNBC**) can then be counted on to support everything Obama wants. They will kickback hundreds of millions of dollars in contributions to Obama and the Democratic Party to keep them (Democrats) in power. The bonus is that all the new taxes on Americans with bigger cars, bigger homes and businesses help Obama "spread the wealth around (While GE continues to pay *NO TAXES!)*."

There is a movement to make Puerto Rico a state. Why? Who's asking for a 51st state? Who's asking for millions of new welfare recipients and government entitlement addicts in the middle of a depression ... certainly not American tax-payers? But this has been Barack Obama's (and his handlers') plan all along. His goal is to add two new Democrat senators, five Democrat congressman and a million loyal Democratic voters who are dependent on big government.

And issuing amnesty to illegal immigrants, gives Barack Obama and his colleagues a boost in political power and in furthering the implementation of the Cloward-Piven Strategy. Just giving these 12 million potential new citizens free health care alone could overwhelm the system and bankrupt America. But it adds 12 million reliable *new Democrat voters* who can be counted on to support big government. Add another few trillion dollars in welfare, aid to dependent children, food stamps, free medical, education, tax credits for the poor, and eventually Social Security.

In the "Stimulus" and "Bailout" packages, where did all that money go? It went to Democrat contributors, organizations (ACORN), and unions—including billions of dollars to save or create jobs of government employees across the country. It went to save GM and Chrysler so that their employees could keep paying union dues. It went to AIG so that Goldman Sachs could be bailed out (after giving Obama almost $1 million in contributions). A staggering $125 billion went to teachers (thereby protecting their union dues).

All those public employees will vote loyally Democrat to protect their bloated salaries and pensions that are bankrupting America.

The country goes broke, future generations face a bleak future, but Obama, the Democrat Party, government, and the unions grow more powerful. The ends justify the means. Raise taxes on small business owners, high-income earners, and job creators. Put the entire burden on only the top 20 percent of taxpayers, redistribute the income, punish success, and reward those who did nothing to deserve it (except vote for Obama). Reagan wanted to dramatically cut taxes in order to starve the government. (Surely, President Reagan had read *Atlas Shrugged).*

"Barack Obama wants to dramatically raise taxes to starve his political opposition. With the acts outlined above, Barack Obama and his regime have created a vast and rapidly expanding constituency of voters dependent on big government; a vast privileged class of public employees who work for big government; and a government dedicated to destroying capitalism and installing themselves as socialist rulers by overwhelming the system. Add it up and you've got the perfect Marxist scheme—all devised by my Columbia University college classmate Barack Hussein Obama using the Cloward and Piven Plan, (a strategy developed by Obama's and his classmate's professors)."

A closer look at President Obama's Columbia University connections provides insight into why he was likely directed to study there. It has to do with two of his professors. The website of ACORN, (Association for Community Organizations for Reform Now) reports:

"Two Columbia University sociologists, Richard Andrew Cloward and Frances Fox Piven were inspired by the riots to develop a new strategy for social change.

In November 1965—barely three months after the fires of Watts had subsided—Cloward and Piven began privately circulating copies of an article they had written called "Mobilizing the Poor: How It Could Be Done." Six months later (on May 2, 1966), it was published in The Nation, under the title, 'The Weight of the Poor: A Strategy to End Poverty.'

The article electrified the Left. Following its May 2, 1966 publication, The Nation sold an unprecedented 30,000 reprints. Activists were abuzz over the so-called 'crisis strategy' or 'Cloward-Piven strategy,' as it came to be called. Many were eager to put it into effect ...

The Cloward-Piven strategy never achieved its goal of system breakdown and a Marxist utopia. But it provided a blueprint for some of the Left's most destructive campaigns of the next three decades.

It will likely haunt America for years to come since *George Soros' Shadow Party* has now adopted the strategy, honing it into a far more efficient weapon than any of its Sixties-era promoters could have foreseen."

The "blueprint for destructive campaigns" seems to have been picked up by the Obama Administration. And, the mention of George Soros and his "Shadow Party" (MoveOn.Org) is—within itself—revealing.

During the 1960s, television talk-show participants promised all-out civil war by 1995 if demands were not met. Apparently, the threats achieved their objective. The cost of Lyndon Johnson's "riot insurance" in the form of entitlements—and the mounting debt that comes with them—continue to eat away at the fabric of a mosaic society that is methodically being torn apart at the seams.

As a concerned patriot, I have agonized over what the future holds. Without intent to patronize, dilemmas facing America in the second decade of the 21st century deserve straight talk and swift action. The challenge we face is not one of pandering to touchy-feely race relations and platitudes, but of improving the manner in which all of the races across America march—hand in hand—toward a common goal: "one nation, under God, indivisible, with liberty and justice for all." Our *individual* role in making America the best it can be is rather simple ... and direct.

Perhaps Martin Luther King, Jr., said it best:

> "If a man is called to be a street sweeper, he should sweep streets even as Michelangelo painted, or Beethoven composed music, or Shakespeare wrote poetry.
> "He should sweep streets so well that all the hosts of heaven and earth will pause to say here lived a great street sweeper who did his job well." [70]

King's less well-known admonition to his faithful followers hits at the heart of red-blooded patriotism. It personifies personal responsibility and the recognition that something greater than ourselves is watching to see which destiny the American people will—as a whole— choose. Our nation is at a turning point; and people like you and me, will decide in which direction the shift will occur.

In the hierarchy of cycles, whether we are doctors, lawyers, teachers, assembly line workers, mechanics, truck drivers, carpenters, housekeepers, presidents or street sweepers—*and are good ones*—we will earn the respect of our fellowman. There is always a job waiting to be done ... somewhere; and taxpaying Americans and the 555 politicians we send to Washington, D.C. have to insist that an entitlement-dependent generation find ways to become part of the solution. When a job doesn't exist,

---

[70] *Motivational Quotes,* Harold V. Melchert, Great Quotations, Inc, Lombard, IL 1984

create one! Don't sit by and wait for "the government" to do so. Offer to do a task for someone that he or she doesn't want to do or doesn't have time to do. Offer to do the job on a *contingency basis*, i.e., accept compensation that the other person deems to be "fair" and be happy for the opportunity to earn that person's respect. It is amazing how often payment might exceed expectations and how often a temporary job will turn into a permanent job.

The above scenario is not hypothetical. I know. It is how I worked my way through medical school.

Some say that the Tea Party Movement is merely a beginning—that conservatives and independents have finally found a home, together—on the right side of Reason.

Conservatives and Independents see a nation in trouble and are doing what any loyal patriot would do—come to the aid of their country. If the Tea Party plays its cards right, it might be able to "broker" future elections. Rather than creating a third party, the Tea Party might be more effective in becoming what is known in political circles as a "bloc vote." This is not a new strategy. The Party of Democrats has several blocs: unions, African-Americans, ACORN, The NEA, the National Organization of Women, Lambda, Hispanics, etc. At this time, Republicans have none.

Tea Party leaders could meet—*in advance*—with potential candidates representing each of the two major parties (at local *and* national levels) to determine which candidate would represent the conservative movement's interest; then, throw its full support to the candidate who shares the Tea Party's ideology and serve as watchdogs at every turn, to ensure that trust is well-placed ... or *replace* the individuals who violated *the people's* trust. Who knows;

it could be the beginning of a whole new era in American politics.

* * * * * * * * * *

Within these pages, we have established that America is in trouble and both of America's major political parties shoulder the blame. Many of the 555 seem more interested in getting re-elected than in doing the heavy lifting. Thankfully, a few are there for all the right reasons.

The next question to address is: Where does an ailing nation turn for advice on healing? It turns to the past. An ancient Chinese sage, (Confucius), advised that the longest journey begins with a single step. When we begin our journey toward prosperity, we may not know exactly where our steps will take us. The important thing, I believe, is to walk toward the future and follow paths traveled by those who have succeed in their own fields of endeavor. As the scenery changes, new obstacles and opportunities will become apparent. Stride confidently. Opportunity involves uncertainty, but the will to overcome, rules ... providing the Lords of Seduction are excluded from the picture.

Someone once wrote, "When we come to the end of all the light we have and step out into the darkness of the unknown, one of two things will happen. We will either step onto a foundation of stepping stones which were laid there for us, or God will teach us to fly."

Numerous examples confirm the conclusions of a 19th century author, James Allen, who advised that the body is the servant of the mind. I have seen the process in action—over and over again, in my own family, in my medical practice, and in my country.

Dr. Allen believed that, "man is the causer of his circumstances, and that while aiming at a good end, he is continually frustrating its accomplishment by encouraging thoughts and desires which cannot possibly harmonize with that end."

If Man is the *"causer"* of his problems, is Man also *the solution* to the problems he caused? Can we realistically blame others for our problems? If the Illuminati have taken control of the U.S. government, can those who allowed it to happen not take it back? If the current 555 politicians working for us are not doing their jobs, isn't it our responsibility to replace them with people who will. I believe that the answer to *this* question lies in a familiar mantra of one of America's two major political parties: "YES ... WE CAN!" Though the meaning may differ from that intended by the Democrats supporting Barack Obama's candidacy, it can be used to indicate that patriots intend to take our nation back from those who seem intent on destroying it.

Orison S. Marden published it a century ago; then, others like Everett Hale and Helen Keller challenged every human being on the planet to adopt the following motto:

> I am only one, but I am one, I cannot do
> everything, but I can do something.
> What I can do, I should do, and with the
> help of God, I will do it![71]

I first published Dr. Marden's admonition, to current and future members of the Godly segment of the *human race,* in 1984 (in *Shoulders of Giants*).

---

[71] *Shoulders of Giants,* McCollough, E. Gaylon, Albright Publishing, Huntsville, AL, p 223.

Because of the profound call to action the words portray, I have republished them in virtually every book I've written since. Perhaps, these words ought to become a personal pledge of allegiance to a cause greater than one's self. Should high-minded people all across America choose to "do something" about the current state of our Union—to work together for one unwavering aim, to "do what we should do" and "with the help of God" save America from the Lords of Seduction, who knows what we could achieve? Who knows what kind of a nation—and world—we could create? Would the result be a World Government whose only rule is *The Golden Rule*? Now, *that's* a One-World Order that I—and millions of like-minded Americans—could enthusiastically support.

CHAPTER 12

As we head down the home stretch, it is necessary to consider *another* revelationary statement made by David Rockefeller, the American Illuminist:

> "This present window of opportunity during which a truly peaceful and interdependent world order might be built, will not be opened for too long. We are on the verge of a global transformation. All we need is the right major crisis and the nations will accept the New World Order."

At first blush, it seems that Rockefeller is advocating a world without war and conflict, seducing the listener into believing that the Illuminati's intentions are noble. Perhaps, Rockefeller envisioned a "truly peaceful world," the people of which had no choice but to do as their new global Lords ordered. The latter part of the statement appears to be right out of *The Protocols*.

To which "major crisis" could Rockefeller been referring? It is important to note that Rockefeller's words were spoken on September 23, 1994. Two months later Mexico experienced a major economical crisis, resulting in

the sudden devaluation of the Mexican peso. The crisis—
likely orchestrated by Rockefeller's fellow Illuminists—is
also known in Mexico as *The December Mistake,* a term
coined by outgoing president Carlos Salinas de Gortari in
reference to newly-elected President Zedillo's sudden
reversal of the former administration's (unpopular to the
Illuminati) "auto-determination" policy of tight currency
controls.

I present Rockefeller's call for a "crisis" and the events
that followed for the purpose of providing a comparison to
what has happened in the U.S. in 2010-2011.

"You never want a serious crisis to go to waste," Rahm
Emanuel, Mr. Obama's former chief of staff, told a Wall
Street Journal conference of top corporate chief executives.
Half way through Barack Obama's term, Emanuel resigned
and became the Mayor of Chicago. The similarity between
Rockefeller's and Emanuel's statements is eerie. Both have
been linked to creating a "New World Order," using a
financial crisis.

According to Wikipedia, the root causes of the 1994
crisis in Mexico are usually attributed to President Salinas
de Gortari's policy decisions while in office, which
ultimately strained the nation's finances. As in prior
election cycles, a pre-election disposition to stimulate the
economy, temporarily and unsustainably, led to post-
election economic instability. (Sound familiar?) There
were concerns about the level and quality of credit
extended by banks during the preceding low-interest rate
period, as well as the standards for extending credit. (Note
the similarity of the Fannie Mae, Freddie Mac, and lending
policies of America's banks during Obama's Administration). Mexico's risk premium was affected by an armed
rebellion in Chiapas, causing investors to be wary of

investing their money in an unstable region. (At the time of this writing, the U.S.' "risk premium" has just been lowered from "stable" to "negative" ... for the first time in the country's history.) The Mexican government's finances and cash availability were further hampered by two decades of increasing spending, a period of hyperinflation from 1985 to 1993, debt loads and a reduction in exports. Mexico's ability to absorb shocks was hampered by its commitments to finance out-of-control spending. (Under Obama's and Emanuel's directorship, the U.S. has spent its way into the largest deficit in history).

Mexico's "December Mistake" seems to have been a "test run" for the Illuminati's U.S. initiative. Devaluation of the Mexican currency, huge debt loads, economic instability ... this is how a "supranational sovereignty of intellectual elites and world bankers" tighten the grip on free and independent nations. And, at their direction, the U.S. has followed its neighbor to the south on the downhill slope of the Cycle of Democracies a "peaceful"—but sure—surrender of auto-determination to the Lords of Seduction.

From the perspective of the Illuminati-Islamic Alliance, an open border allows further mixing of the two nation's woes and an under-policed superhighway for an army of Islamic radicals to enter the U.S.

As previously explained by this author in *The Oath*[72], by promoting and financing the American Civil War, the Illuminati *intended* to have Mexico and the southern states join to become an agricultural nation. Canada and the northern states were to become a separate (industrialized) nation. But President Abraham Lincoln saw through the Illuminati's plan and set out to save the Republic. He did. In retaliation, the Rothschild Formula was invoked,

---

[72] *The Oath*, Ibid.

President Lincoln was assassinated. About a century later, another U.S. president (John F. Kennedy) was assassinated after he bucked a plan for Cuban nationals to overthrow Fidel Castro's communist form of government and return Cuba to its rightful citizens ... and to the U.S. Mafia. In Kennedy's case, it was the American Mafia who felt double-crossed. The Mafia had hoped to regain control of the casinos and horse tracks that the previously American-backed Fidel Castro confiscated when he came to power. With the covert assistance of Russia's Communist Party Castro's rebel army had seduced the U.S. into believing that, once in power, Cuba would be America's ally. Once again, a trusting America—led by former Army General Dwight D. Eisenhower—was 'had" by the despots who—at the time—pulled the world's strings.

With history providing the evidence that a sinister plot to destroy democracies and merge the world into a dictatorial form of governance, why have so many patriots allowed themselves to be seduced into believing that the "change" coming to America is anything but that which came to Mexico, Cuba, Venezuela ... and a host of other countries around the world? Small steps ... small steps, it's a proven way to seize a nation without push back. It's the implementation of several tactics of seduction: *Send Mixed Signals; Create a False Sense of Security—Approach Indirectly; Stir Anxiety and Discontent; Keep Them in Suspense; Mix Pleasure with Pain;* and *Enter Their Spirit.*

The choice you and I must make is to be a victim of these tactics of seduction or a participant in preserving Man's greatest gift—*free will.* We have to decide whether—as a nation—we are satisfied *to be ruled* or prefer *to be a ruler* of our own destiny. But, saving America is more than securing its borders. It may be one of the keys to saving the world from the Illuminati-Islamic Alliance; but the siege is coming on many fronts.

A patriot never knows if—and when—he or she might be called to duty. At some critical moment, the course of destiny might suddenly and deliberately take a turn for the better, but it won't just happen. Someone—or millions of some ones—will have to *make* it happen.

As I wrote the preceding sentence, I was reminded of a lesson instilled into the minds of his players by one of my teachers almost a half a century ago. Coach Paul W. "Bear" Bryant told my teammates and me: "There are three kinds of people in the world: One group is oblivious to what is happening. The second watches what happens, but plays no role in it. The third group makes things happen." The world is made by "makers"—ordinary people like you and me—fearless, prime movers, who step out of our comfort zones, look Evil in the face, call it what it is, and reject its seductive rhapsodies of "change."

* * * * * * * * *

The barriers of upward and downward mobility, are they man-made (as described in *The Protocols*) or a decree from higher and lower realms, depending on which path people and nations choose to take? Is a caste-system inherently inbred into the minds of man? Clearly, pecking orders exist throughout the animal kingdom. Alpha males and females rule herds. Is the human race exempt from natural laws? As *they* were "bred and reared from early childhood" to believe, were members of the thirteen ruling families and their Council of Deputies led to believe that they were the designated alpha males and females of the human race? Can a better way of life be decreed by parliamentary proceedings? Is redistribution of resources and liberties a *necessary* role for government? Is it the fate of nations that a "Robin Hood" (cleverly disguised as a president or preacher) emerges from the ranks of the masses in every generation?

Where does government's role end? Where does that of "citizen" begin? For how long should we remain our brother's and sister's keepers? Where have musical words like "Please" and "Thank You" gone? Is it the responsibility of "organizers" to encourage people to become self-sufficient ... rather than become dependent on *the organizers* and the *seducers* they represent? Is Gratitude dead?

When will environmentalists recognize that cultural "trash" is as threatening to the world as that of a non-biodegradable nature? Perhaps, the people ought to demand a new kind of "waste management system," one that includes the prudent "recycling" of common sense. Is this the long-awaited solution to America's debt crisis? When will we begin the march back to Reason by re-installing the Pledge of Allegiance as part of the day's curriculum ... every day?

These are just a few matters that any individual, organization or nation advocating "change" should be expected to address; for each of the afore-referenced socio-political issues is connected in domino-like fashion. And, in keeping with one of the corollaries of Parkinson's Law, the larger the undertaking and the larger the body of decision makers, *the lower* will be its collective IQ, ensuring that mediocrity will emerge as the new standard.

History affirms that government doesn't *solve* problems. Rather, government tends to make current ones more complex and creates new ones for future generations to solve. *People* solve problems—committed citizens who have a grasp on current circumstances. The resilient American people generally know best what they need and how to acquire them, providing government gets out of the way.

Collectively, *we* are a powerful force. Together, we can move mountains and defend the homeland against "all enemies, foreign and domestic"; including those we've naively put in positions of power.

Here's a question that I've never heard a Left-leaning liberal answer: When the people's wealth has been redistributed so that every person in every nation has an equal amount of assets and income, who will become The Left's scapegoats? When there are no wealthy and prosperous Americans, where will tax revenues come from? Will a "supranational sovereignty" (The Illuminati) redistribute their own massive storehouses of wealth to the masses? Would the New World Order be a "socialist heaven," or would there be a globally-imposed caste system ... with The Illuminati sitting atop the hierarchy? Notice that I eliminated the Islamic partner in the last sentence. The reason is: history shows that the Illuminati use people, nations, and organizations to accomplish their objective; then, the Rothschild Formula is invoked—Islam notwithstanding.

In an Illuminati-ruled environment, will *everyone* be required to work ... or will *no one* be required to work? And, will unions and collective bargaining be allowed? Wouldn't we like to believe that "intellectual elites and world bankers" are accumulating the world's wealth for philanthropic reasons? So far, there has been no evidence that "philanthropy" is a word known to the Illuminati ... or to radical Islam.

With a small group of "intellectual elites and world bankers" running the world, will governments—as we now know them—be abolished? Since local, state, and national governments would no longer be involved in decision-making, their roles would be reduced to policing and regulating the laws generated by the overlords of one "supranational sovereignty." These are not mere speculations. This kind of world is envisioned in *The Protocols.* In a world ruled entirely by a cabal of "despots", human rights, individual freedoms, and entitlements would be dreams of the past. An Orwellian Society would finally exist. And Big Brother would sit on the throne, ruling its subjects with an iron hand.

Is this the kind of "change" that *We, the people* want—a world in which the human being is a subject to totalitarianism? Is it the kind of world that people who voted for Barack Obama enabled? Perhaps good people, who have been seduced by the political left, might want to re-think what they want. Again, one of life's axioms raises its head: "Be careful what you wish for; you might see your wish become reality." If a totalitarian world is not what Americans want, then *the people* have to wake up to the fact that it is just such a future that the "supranational sovereignty" and its "organizers" have in mind.

CHAPTER 13

So, what is to be? Will *we, the people,* be ruled by the Lords of Seduction and their "Council of Deputies;" or, will we be rulers of our own fate? In creative terms, the world shapes us at the same time that we are shaping it. I particularly like the way a 19th century teacher and physician explained it.

> "Every experience in life, everything with which we have come in contact in life is a chisel which has been cutting away at our life statue, molding, modifying, and shaping it. We are part of all we have met. Everything we have seen, heard, felt or thought has its hand in molding us, shaping us ... your whole career will be molded by your surroundings, and the character of the people with whom you come in contact with every day ... A strong successful man (or woman) is not the victim of his (or her) environment. He *creates* favorable conditions. His own inherent force and energy compel things to turn out as he desires."[73]

---

[73] Marden, Orison Swett, *Pushing to the Front,* Thomas Crowell Co., New York, NY, 1909.

Remembering President John F. Kennedy's inaugural address, many Americans ask what they can do for their country. The truth is: It's really not that hard to make a difference. Share a lesson. Speak your mind. Let others know about your concerns. Chances are: they have many of the same thoughts. Talk up the kind of America that we can build ... if we all stick together. Speak openly of the good and bad you see. Join clubs and organizations made up of people like you—patriots who put America first and want to see her endure.

Get to know your elected officials. Hold them accountable. Get involved in the campaign of someone who appears to agree with *most* of your thoughts on the role of government. Insist on fiscal and moral accountability. *Vote!!!* And, take others to the polls with you. Become a pebble in the pond of accountability. Make waves. Build bridges that connect relationships. Be positive. Keep alive the hope that freedom shall reign. And, insist that before "change" is proposed, both short and long range consequences be considered.

Anyone can join America's crusade—one that will hopefully take us once again, to the *uphill* slope of the Cycle of Democracies. If this nation is to return to reason (the lifeblood of independence and prosperity,) an army of patriots will have to take the country back from those who have high-jacked it while we fed and clothed them at what could prove to be the trough of our own destruction.

Mark Twain once wrote, "If you pick up a starving dog and make him prosperous, the dog will not bite you. That is the principal difference between a dog and a man." Based upon the past behavior of some who have been "fed" and cared for by America's prime movers, America should be concerned about the threat that a growing majority of the entitlement generation will one day "bite" the hands that have fed it... so *The Protocols* promise.

* * * * * * * * *

Throughout this book, I have written about the Illuminati in a distrusting manner. But, in the back of my mind, I know that the "supranational sovereignty" are masters of illusion. As in the game of chess, they are highly capable of making their subjects expect one set of moves while another is being crafted. So, let's look at another possible scenario.

As unlikely as it might be, I would like to believe that—rather than driving America into the ground—the Illuminati have a long-range plan to ensure survival of the U.S. ... at least for a while. If keeping America afloat longer would serve the greater purpose, the I-IA would do it. So, here's a theory worth considering:

What if—in shifting the U.S. debt to China—there is a plan to extend the life of a struggling U.S.? It has been said that who controls debt controls the world. China knows this tactic in political warfare, too. It's a game of wits, with one opponent trying to out-maneuver the other. Could having China take the U.S. debt be a masterful use of the Art of Seduction? Think about it. If—after China has been loaded with U.S. Treasuries—a crisis involving North and South Korea were to break out. A state of war would exist. China would no doubt come to the aid of North Korea and the U.S. would come to the aid of South Korea. In effect, the U.S. and China would be at war with each other. With China becoming an overt enemy, the U.S. would be justified in delaying payment on its debt ... or outright default, leaving China holding the bag. And, guess who would come to both superpowers' rescue ... for a few concessions, of course—The Order of the Illuminati.

The scenario is not beyond comprehension. It's how global chess and monopoly are played.

It wouldn't be the first time that war has been used to achieve the Illuminati's goal or that nations have defaulted on loans. A promised default to David Rockefeller's Chase Manhattan Bank is why the Panama Canal (which was initially built *by* the U.S., with U.S. taxpayer dollars under the direction of President Theodore Roosevelt) was "given" to Panama during the Carter Administration. Panama owed David Rockefeller's bank a lot of money and had informed Chase Manhattan Bank that it could not pay off the debt. The $60 million per year that the U.S. government paid Panama to "maintain" the canal was only a pass-through from the American taxpayer to Illuminatist David Rockefeller's bank, satisfying Panama's debt. Who could have predicted that 40 years later, Communist China would "lease" the Panama Canal from Panama, thereby potentially dictating which nations could access it? Imagine the shift of power that this single event created—a shift structured by mighty men powerful enough to broker the deal. The big loser in the transactions is: *the American people.*

If the Korean-China-United States scenario played out as outlined above, the U.S. could erase its debt, clearing the way for more and more socialists programs to take hold. Surely, the Illuminati realizes that by keeping a socialist work force in place to mine the huge cache of America's natural resources (that remained untapped) they could affect the hierarchy of nations sitting at the OPEC table. This kind of global—and subversive—thinking is clearly in keeping with Illuminati tactics.

Let's look at the facts. In 2008, the U. S. Geological Service issued a report that scientists and oil men knew was coming. The average American didn't hear much about it. The U.S. press—in keeping with their promise to allow the Illuminati to work without being exposed to "the lights of publicity"—brushed over the story.

The report revealed just how much oil was beneath the ground in the western two-thirds of North Dakota, western South Dakota, and extreme eastern Montana. The field containing all this oil is known as the Williston Basin or Bakken Oil Formation. It is the largest domestic oil discovery since Alaska's Prudhoe Bay, and *has the potential to eliminate all American dependence on foreign oil.* The Energy Information Administration (EIA) estimates it at 503 billion barrels. Even if just 10% of the oil is recover-able, $107 a barrel, America is looking at a resource base worth more than $5.3 trillion. Imagine the value of recovering 60% of these reserves and how far such a venture could go to solve U.S. dependence on those who don't like us very much.

According to *The Pittsburg Post Gazette,* "This sizable find is not the highest producing oil field found in the past 56 years." The U.S. now has access of up to 500 billion barrels. And because this is light, sweet oil, those billions of barrels will cost Americans just $16 per barrel. That's enough crude to fully fuel the American economy for *2041 years* straight. And, there is more.

An article published two (2) years previously by the Stansberry Report Online revealed *another* field, then considered to be "the "largest reserve in the world." And it is hidden one thousand feet beneath the surface of the Rocky Mountains. It is more than *two trillion barrels.*

Both of the aforementioned discoveries are well-kept secrets. Facts are: the U.S. has more oil inside our borders, than all the other proven reserves **on earth.** Here are the official estimates:

- 8 times as much oil as Saudi Arabia;
- 18 times as much oil as Iraq;
- 21 times as much oil as Kuwait;
- 22 times as much oil as Iran; and
- 500 times as much as Yemen.

And all that oil is *right here* in the Western United States. How can we not be extracting this? The answer is: *because The Illuminati-Islamic Alliance in concert with "puppet" environmentalists and others have effectively blocked all efforts to help America become independent of foreign oil and foreign debt!* Rational Americans are allowing a small group of despot overlords to dictate our lives and our economy. The question is: why?

James Bartis, lead researcher with the study says *we've got more oil in this very compact area of the U.S. than the entire Middle East*—more than 2 trillion barrels untapped. *The Denver Post* says, "That's more than all the proven oil reserves of crude oil in the world today."

How likely is it that OPEC—as a participant in the Illuminati-Islamic Alliance—might be funding the environmentalists in America and contributing heavily to politicians who stand in the way of drilling *here ... now*?

To answer this question, think like an Illuminist. The U.S. oil reserve is one of the greatest assets that exist on the planet. It is a prize that those committed to a One-World

Government must eventually have. And, the Illuminati want it to still be there when *they* gain full control of the U.S. *That's when the reserve will be tapped.* That's when the Illuminati will abandon their Islamic partners and shift the supply of oil *away from* the Middle East and toward their newly acquired U.S., leaving their Muslim Brotherhood allies to drown in their own oil.

And, there is another part of the puzzle. It is also important to remember that the Illuminati are "world bankers." It is in these banks that the oil moguls now keep their fortunes—fortunes that could be frozen in an instant by those who control such banks. In order to get at their money, OPEC oil magnates will be ordered to put pressure on radical Islamic clerics to keep jihadists at bay. The newly founded Arab Union will effectively be placed in "checkmate." The bottom line is: when the Illuminati no longer need Islam, they will find a way to control its followers. *World domination* means just that ... Islam included.

Americans still have time to prevent the Illuminati-Islamic Alliance take-over of America ... if the people will demand of our leaders to do the prudent thing.

With one of the world's largest and most valuable natural assets lying beneath U.S. soil, there is no reason why we should be dependent on any nation for petroleum products and energy. There is no reason why we should be considered a "bad debt risk," as Standard and Poor deemed the U.S. in April, 2011 ... except to weaken the dollar and move toward a one-world currency—the one chosen by the Illuminati.

The only reason that we are sitting on—and doing nothing about—one of the solutions to America's independence from OPEC is that the Lords of Seduction want it that way. And the current administration seems to want what its masters want.

Perhaps, the value of an Illuminati-controlled U.S. is crystallizing. For a lot of reasons, our enemies want what we have ... all of it, including our very souls. Among all the things they covet, it the resolute American spirit that they must have if they are to realize their objective—*world domination.*

The I-IA has successfully seduced a virtual army of environmentalists into making it difficult for America's natural resources to be mined or drilled. Do the Illuminati's past actions indicate that they have a burning desire to save the world's natural parks, beaches, and waterways for the enjoyment of citizens?" The facts are: neither the Illuminati nor its I-IA partner has shown interest in such matters. They are interested in one thing— world domination. They, simply, use naive environ- mentalists to do their bidding and "puppet" politicians to further minimize America's position on the world stage. Hopefully, those who truly do want to save the planet from the evil-intended Invisible Empire will see the errors of their ways ... before it is too late.

* * * * * * * * * *

The U.S. is not the only prize that the I-IA wishes to sack. The other is her traditional ally, the State of Israel.

It is just a matter of time before Iran and Israel will be at war. How could such a war play into the Illuminati's master plan?

Iran has openly stated that it intends to destroy Israel. Israel has stated that it will use all means necessary to survive. Israel already has a nuclear arsenal large enough to remove Iran from the face of the earth. And, Iran is moving as quickly as possible to develop missiles capable of raining nuclear warheads down on Israel. When the exchange of such missiles begins, Israel will prevail—on the nuclear side. But, the declaration of war between Israel and Iran will mobilize Muslims from all around the Middle East, who—being called to the Great Jihad—will gather at Israel's borders and participate in a mass invasion too big to be turned away with conventional warfare. Without divine intervention, Israel will be overrun. Such a scenario was played out in a novel co-authored by Dr. Symm McCord and me. The book is entitled: *The Annunaki Enigma: Armageddon 2012.*[74]

With the fallout of a nuclear war and newly installed instability in the Middle East, America's, Mexico's, and South America's massive oil reserves will finally be tapped. As a result, the axis of *fossil power* will shift from the Middle East to the North American Continent. This is why the Illuminati may take the U.S. to the brink of destruction, but not let her die. They will use a socialist takeover to make it *appear* that the U.S. has survived the crisis ... as described in *The Protocols.*

Regardless of whatever else happens, one has to believe that a Godless, socialist/communist United States of America is part of the Illuminati's master plan for a One-World Government. As far-fetched as all this may seem, it is how the Illuminati has achieved much of their goals down through history—by using crises and pitting people and nations against each other in order to gain an advantage on the world's stage. Why should anyone believe that a "supranational sovereignty" will not continue to

---

[74] *The Annunaki Enigma: Armageddon 2012,* McCollough, E.G. and McCord, S.H., A-Argus Publishing, 2010 *ISBN* 9780984514274

follow an ageless commandeering tactic that has yet to fail
... in the short run—and until *the people* revolt?

With or without the above scenario, clawing our way
back to prosperity will take all the courage that Americans
can muster. And, those who are speaking out are sure to
become victims of the Rothschild Formula, a code name
for eliminating anyone who stands in the Illuminati's way.
When the Rothschild Formula is initiated, campaigns of
distraction are fabricated and propagated. Agents of the
Illuminati attempt to discredit any perceived adversary
through slander and innuendo ... or in the case of IMF
Chief, Strause-Kahn, trumped up criminal charges.

As I write these words, I am reminded of reports by
Fox News host, Glenn Beck, whose exposé of members
and supporters of the Obama Administration resulted in
threats to have him silenced. I've been a spear-catcher, too.
Perhaps, that's why I tend to see things the way I do.

A voice of reason (that of Victor Hugo) cries out from
the past: "*All that is required for evil to prevail is that good
men and women do nothing.*" And, it is this line of
thinking that spawned the Tea Party Movement in
America. The Left eventually pushed too hard and too far.
Grassroots America rose up and declared, "Enough!"

As I have reviewed the stories of history-changers
representing all sexes, races and cultures, I came to realize
that each abhorred complacency and failure. They failed to
be diverted from their *"one unwavering aim"*[5] and rose
above a "do-nothing" lifestyle to create a world of their own
choosing.

For this reason, people who are willing to lead the
Crusade to Save America should be encouraged, by

---

[5] Marden, Orison S, *Rising in the World,* Thomas Y. Crowell Company, New York,
N.Y., 1894.

history's accounting of how repressed peoples—with the help of God—removed despots from their earthly thrones.

If the road to successful outcomes begins with one's state of mind, the following prescription should be appropriate:

> If you think you are beaten, you are
> If you think you dare not, you don't
> If you'd like to win but think you can't
> It's almost a cinch you won't.
> If you think you'll lose, you've lost
> For out in the world you'll find
> Success begins with a person's will;
> It's all in the state of mind.
> If you think you are outclassed, you are
> You've got to think high to rise;
> You've got to be sure of yourself before
> You can ever win the prize.
> Life's battles don't always go
> To the stronger or faster man
> But sooner or later, the one who wins
> Is the one who thinks he can.[76]

Creating a realistic "state of mind" is a central theme that permeates *The Lords of Seduction.*

Comfort often arises from knowing more of the facts, knowing where you are heading and knowing who's in charge—particularly during uncertain times. Consider the following parable:

> "The passengers on the train were
> uneasy as they sped along through the dark,

---

[76] Anonymous

stormy night. The lightning was flashing, black clouds were rolling and the train was traveling fast. The fear and tension among the passengers were evident.

"One little fellow, however, sitting all by himself seemed utterly unaware of the storm of the speed or the train. He was amusing himself with a few toys.

"One of the passengers spoke to him. 'Sonny, I see you are alone on the train. Aren't you afraid to travel alone on such a stormy night?

"The lad looked up with a smile and answered, 'No ma'am I ain't afraid. My daddy's the engineer.'"[77]

The contented young man was confident in the engineer at the wheel. His destiny was guided by trusted hands.

As we embark upon an odyssey to save—and then rebuild—America, we must not let the behavior and opinions of Leftist progressives cause us undue concern. Assuming that we believe we're on the train headed in the right direction and the right engineer, we remain confident.

As we strive to bring the right kind of "change," we must keep in mind that, "In great attempts, it is glorious even to fail."[78]

---

[77] *The Speaker's Sourcebook*, Ibid
[78] Anonymous, *Motivational Quotes*. Great Quotations, Inc. Lombard, IL, 1984

CHAPTER 14

In 1963 Reverend Martin Luther King, Jr. stood before the Lincoln Memorial and delivered his famous "I Have a Dream" speech. The Civil Rights leader stirred the emotions of his followers and helped change the course of American history. The passionate speech affected different segments of America in different ways. In my mind, King's message was not only one of hope, but of mutual responsibility. He dreamed of a day when "a person will be judged not by the color of his skin, but by the content of his character." Many heard; few heeded. Dr. King's "dream" flies in the face of "affirmative action." Perhaps, that is why he was a threat to LBJ's "Great Society" and was gunned down.

As I understand Dr. King's "dream," it called for a colorblind society—one in which no advantage or *dis*advantage would come to a man, woman or child because of the color of his or her skin. It called for a society in which status is earned by building what another of my teachers, Dr. R. Tinsley Harrison, called an "edifice of character," an edifice *that is earned*—not awarded because of the color of one's skin or gender by some federally-imposed mandate. The net effect of "affirmative action" *mandates* discrimination rather than abolishes it.

As an American, I too have a dream. My updated and expanded version is issued not from the Lincoln Memorial, but from the sugar white sands of the Alabama Gulf Coast, where at each day's end multicolored horizons separate Earth from the heavens. Perhaps, patriotic Americans everywhere should come to land's edge and share the vision I have seen here; because here's my dream:

> That one day, men and women, black and white, brown and yellow, can live together as *Americans* (no hyphen needed) in peace and harmony;
>
> That opportunity to improve one's station in life is offered upon the basis of merit, regardless of age, gender, religion or race;
>
> That all citizens have the opportunity to rise up from the ashes of whatever fires they've experienced, muster the drive *to work* for what they receive and the pride to care for it until it can be passed to the next generation;
>
> That all men, women and children will take up the arms of America's religious heritage and launch a "renaissance of Godly values;"
>
> That the Pledge of Allegiance will be put back into schools and public gatherings so that the world will know that we are: "one nation, *under God*, indivisible, with liberty and justice for all";

> That those who swear to "protect and defend the Constitution of the United States against all enemies, foreign and domestic ..." will uphold the oaths to which they have sworn;
>
> That these United States of America shall survive the assault on its *way of life;* and emerge from the ashes of its orchestrated destruction as President Ronald Reagan's "Shining City of the Hill."

If Dr. King's dream becomes reality, so will mine ... and so will those of millions of like-minded Americans. Dreams that we create during waking hours are matters of individual and collective choice. Mine begins with repealing unfairly government-imposed mandates and returning power to local communities, where "the content of one's character" is best built ... and preserved.

In every group, no matter how large or small, difference-makers can be found. They are the ones who rise to the top of the class. Given enough time and with enough stirring, leadership becomes self-evident.

Some people contend that pacesetters are born. However, there is strong evidence that the ability to lead can be learned. And, this is where a teacher's responsibility to teach "character" as well as math, grammar, civics, and science comes into play. The best among America's teachers are able to recognize exceptionalism in students and encourage them to go *beyond* the limits that a student—or the student's environment—may have set on his or her behalf ... by others. Extraordinary teachers know how to make winners out of those who aren't sure that they are. This is the role of a teacher ... unions notwithstanding.

Let's look at a few "ordinary" students who became "extraordinary."

Sir Isaac Newton was next to lowest in his class. Newton failed geometry because he didn't do his problems according to the book. One has to wonder what Newton's teachers thought as they watched him sail into the annals of history.

Albert Einstein failed English but mastered physics. The face of modern science was changed because he was focused on "one unwavering aim"—to discover the unknown dimensions of the universe.

Napoleon was number forty-two (42) in his class and yet conquered the world as it existed in his time. He was bored by long division method of problem solving.

Throughout history trend-setters have often been late bloomers. Abraham Lincoln had great difficulty in becoming elected to the presidency of the United States and getting his fellow countrymen and women to follow his lead in saving The Union.

These examples are brought to the fore in order to demonstrate how seemingly "ordinary" people who dream greater dreams can rise to heights not previously imagined. The whole of humanity profits when "ordinary" becomes "extraordinary" and loses when mediocrity is tolerated or—in the case of "affirmative action," mandated.

* * * * * * * * * *

I have repeatedly emphasized that "change" is a double-edged sword. As caring human beings, our challenge is to make sure that *"different"* will be *"better."* For in many instances, old ways are best. New ideas, especially those manipulated by agenda-setting factions of society can lead to a path of despondency. I think the lyricist explains it better:

> "There was a man who lived by the side of the road and sold hot dogs. He was hard of hearing so he had no radio. He had trouble with his eyes so he read no newspapers. But he sold good hot dogs. He put up signs on the highway telling how good they were.
>
> He stood on the side of the road and cried, 'Buy a hot dog, Mister?'
>
> And people bought his hot dogs. He increased his meat and bun orders. He bought a bigger stove to take care of his trade. He finally got his son home from college to help out.
>
> But then something happened. His son said, 'Father, haven't you been listening to the radio? Haven't you been reading the newspaper? There's a big recession on. The international situation is terrible. The domestic situation is worse.'
>
> Whereupon the father thought, 'Well, my son's been to college, he reads the papers and he listens to the radio, and he ought to know.'
>
> So the father cut down his meat and bun orders, took down his signs, and no longer bothered to stand out on the highway to sell his hot dogs. His sales fell overnight.
>
> "You're right, son," the father said to the boy.

"We certainly are in the middle of a big recession." [79]

The story affirms the importance of getting the facts and questioning a media that—from Illuminist, David Rockefeller's comments—is more in the business of assisting The Illuminati-Islamic Alliance than reporting Truth.

Analysts, criers and tutors aren't necessarily experts. And, even if they are, many insert their *personal* agenda into what they say, write, and teach.

I have confidence in the philosophy that we should lean heavily upon Natural Law, prepare for the test, heed our own instincts and listen loudest to the voice within.

If the old man in the story above had listened to his gut rather than to what others said, he would have continued down the road to prosperity. The lesson to be gleaned from the story is: "If it ain't broke, don't fix it." And, if the Lords of Seduction say it's broke, there's a good chance that it isn't. If, after thoughtful contemplation, we conclude that we are on the side of right, prudence dictates that we stick to our convictions and don't let either the uninformed or misdirected undo what is working well.

Rudyard Kipling tells the self-sufficient individual or nation should deal with adversity. In his poem, *"If,"* he advises, "Keep your head while others about you are losing theirs and blaming it on you ..." The poet's advice spans the ages and transcends vocation.

The misinformed or malcontent social reformist must not cause a patriot to deviate from what he or she knows to be right and honorable. The opinions of most

---

[79] *The Speaker's Sourcebook,* Ibid

"progressives" are merely reflections of the ideology of socialist "organizers" under whose spells they have fallen.

The recurring question for patriots to ponder is, "Why do those who claim to be Americans, support people and programs that are clearly intended to guarantee misery *for Americans?*"

A page from history can provide insight. The Civil War of the 1800s tore at the fabric of America. "... Individuals and families, northerners and southerners, soldiers and civilians, slaves and slave owners, rich and poor, urban and rural (were) caught up on the turbulence of the times." The country almost bled to death, physically and fiscally. Each faction risked everything for an agenda they believed to be in its best interest. That's a tactic upon which overlords convince the populace to engage in all kinds of "*wars.*"

One of the most insightful—yet little-publicized—statements made by President Abraham Lincoln during the War Between the States deserves repeating. He said:

> "If I could save the Union by freeing *all the slaves*, I would do it.
>
> If I could save the Union by freeing *none of the slaves*, I would do it.
>
> If I could save the Union by freeing *some of the slaves and not the others*, I would do it."

The American President's mission was clear. He wanted to preserve the   United States of America. That he could not, tore at his soul. He did not want any single disagreement to rip the seams of a patchwork nation. In the end, he saved a mangled Union that had been torn apart—initially not by slavery—but by the tactics of the

Europe's Illuminati, who instigated the War and, then, financed *both* sides. The same group of despots controlled the slave trade and used it to stir emotions on both sides of the issue. As with every war, the Illuminati were the big winners. The American people—on both sides of the conflict—were the big losers ... and President Lincoln knew it.

Lincoln persevered and initiated the healing process. It is still not complete. Many wounds remain open. And, that they are, tears at the fabric of America ... to the delight of an Illuminati-Islamic Alliance, still intent on unraveling the stars and stripes on Old Glory.

It is important that Americans know the truth about a war-disemboweled nation ... who instigated and financed it. Not until enough of us know who continues to pour salt in old wounds and why they can't allow healing to take place, will the healing truly begin. And, that is the job of a patriot—to rally other Americans around the U.S. flag and to expect a *United* States of America to rise from the rubble of her own seduction.

Awareness of one's responsibility to God and country is established during the highly impressionable years of one's youth. In ancient Greece and Rome, in Nazi Germany and the communist-controlled Soviet Union, secular-based child care centers became the sculptors of a nation's conscience. Failed civilizations cry out to us from the boneheaps' of history. Once again, let us turn to *The Protocols* and see how the Hidden Hand intends to infect the minds of children with anti-American thoughts.

> "The universities must no longer send
> out from their halls milk sops concocting
> plans for a constitution, like a comedy or a

tragedy, busying themselves with questions of policy in which even their own fathers never had any power of thought.

"The ill-guided acquaintance of a large number of persons with questions of polity creates utopian dreamers and bad subjects, as you can see for yourselves from the example of the universal education in this direction ... We must introduce into their (the children's) education all those principles which have so brilliantly broken up their (America's) order. But when we are in power we shall remove every kind of disturbing subject (that conflicts with the Illuminati's mission) from the course of education and shall make out of the youth *obedient children of authority** loving him who rules as the support and hope of peace and quiet (Lucifer's antichrist.")

If someone threatened to plant a deadly bacteria or virus into the body of one of your children or kidnap a member of your family, how would you react—with vigilance and vengeance, right? Well, the people, politicians, judges, professors, and organizations who are bringing *The Protocols* to life have clearly stated that they intend to infest the minds of our children with totalitarian ideas, effectively kidnapping *the minds* of America's youth. And, it doesn't stop there. Every aspect of American culture is being manipulated.

Government has become one colossal collection and re-distribution center. In becoming so, it has assumed the

---

* Emphasis added

role of America's moral compass ... or in some cases, its *immoral* compass. How many times do you hear the phrase, "*The government ought to ...?*" We speak of government as though it is living being—an entity unto itself—rather than the collective conscience of a people, being managed as we *allow it* to be managed. Its judicial branch (in attempts to equalize the field of competition) sometimes causes the pendulum of justice to swing beyond equal opportunity and rationalism—imposing responsibility for past injustices on non-involved parties ... in the name of retribution.

I have previously quoted my Civics teacher at Enterprise High School: "*Your rights end where mine begin; and yours begin where mine end.*" If I owe you respect and opportunity to pursue health, happiness and prosperity, you owe me no less. *That's* "equal opportunity." Transferring shackles from one person (or race) to the other abolishes nothing. It only fosters separatism, feeds a new revolution and ensures various kinds of class warfare ... as *The Protocols* promise and its implementers practice:

> "It is indispensable to trouble in all countries the people's relations ... so as to utterly exhaust humanity with dissension, hatred, struggle, envy and even by the use of torture, by starvation, by the inoculation of diseases, by want, so that the masses see no other issue than to take refuge in our complete sovereignty ..."

In recent years, Left-leaning special interest agendas (driven by the Illuminati's agenda) have seemed to redefine many of the traditional values intended by the United States Constitution's fathers. Today, irresponsibility heads the list in "The Left's Bill of Rights"... and the founding fathers roll over in their graves.

Loss of prominence in global economic circles is a reflection of the domestic trends *away* from high-minded, fiscally-responsible principles. In some circles (and institutions of higher learning) defiance is glorified, perversion is protected, separatism is rewarded, alienation is encouraged and debt is ignored. Students are encouraged by Leftists' instructors to "change" the world, without either fully understanding the consequences of their actions. The I-IA's campaign of seduction is in full swing. And, the children are the prize.

As a result of decisions handed down from hand-picked judges that are addressed in *The Protocols, freedom of speech* has taken on the meaning that "anything goes"—except, that is, the freedom to speak God's name in public gatherings. While founding fathers found free speech necessary for democratic preservation, they also understood treason. What do you think Betsy Ross, Ben Franklin, Thomas Jefferson James Madison, and George Washington could have done with "flag burners" ... or citizens who tried to remove "God" from symbols and institutions representing independence? What would they think if they sat in on sessions of Congress and witnessed some of the votes that summarily "changed" the laws and symbols of the land that they established?

For America, independence and prosperity was won (*with blood*) from a foreign government that was not in touch with its one-time citizens. The pilgrims who settled along the eastern seaboard of the new world made the move to escape the oppressive practices of a monarchial form of government. But the War for Freedom is never over. The enemy simply regroups and comes back another day. Today, the threat comes from a "supranational sovereignty of intellectual elites and world bankers"—the Illuminati and its expanded cabal of conspirators, The Illuminati-Islamic Alliance. Upon reviewing how the Illuminati infiltrated various organizations and used them to do their bidding (i.e. the Freemasons, Catholicism, Hollywood, Universities, the NEA, NAACP, and AARP) it is easy to see how an Islamic alliance could work to the Illuminati's advantage. A Muslim-controlled U.S. could bridge the gap between the U.S. Constitution, Sharia Law, and Global Law (based upon the tyrannical principles of *The Protocols).* Far-fetched, you might think. Put nothing past the Illuminati. They have the power, resources, and commitment to rule the world ... if the people let them.

Perhaps, a closer look at credits and sponsors of the war against standards will demonstrate how the despots work their way into positions of authority. The influence of George Soros (a/k/a György Schwartz) cannot be underestimated. This socialist billionaire is out to "change" America into a nation of his own liking ... or the liking of the despots above him in the hierarchy that he is desperately trying to impress. It's his modus operandi. As previously reported, Soros/Schwartz sold out his fellow Jews to Hitler and the Fuehrer's minions during World War II, revealing the identities of Jews in hiding. Soros' reward was that he shared in the booty confiscated from the Jewish people. It was this "blood money" that helped Soros/Schwartz make his first billion. More on this later ...

I'm not yet convinced that Soros is a member of the Illuminati's Inner Circle. I am convinced, however, that he wishes to be. As I write these words, I am reminded of

Machiavelli's *The Prince.* Machiavelli had a reason for writing his book. He felt that if he could convince Italy's ruling Medici family that he could help them control the people, the Medici's would bring him into their court as an adviser. Keep an eye on George Soros. Unlike the Hidden Hand, Soros is not working totally behind the scenes. Still, he is not to be ignored.

And speaking of scenes, a respected film critic has recognized the Left-leaning *paradigm shift* in the entertainment industry. Michael Medved described what he called the "destructive character" of some modern films, TV, art and music, many of which we are about to review.

Children are the targets of the seductive practices taking place in the "entertainment" industry. Their little hands will one day control tomorrow's switches and mark ballots. The Hidden Hand's plan is working. The children who were targets in the 1990s (when these ideas were presented in my book, *Before and After*) came out in massive numbers and helped elect Barack Obama and a Democrat Congress in the election of 2008.

That's why so much of the Illuminati's energies are spent on young people. In the world of the Illuminati, seduction is a "numbers" game—driven by power, money and greed ... and disguised with Sirenical melodies of "hope" and "change," two mantras that will likely be glaringly *absent* from the Obama Campaign rhetoric in the 2012 election.

Medved also suggests: "In the visual arts, in literature, in music of both popular and classical variety, *ugliness* has been enshrined as a new standard." While the Invisible Empire of the Illuminati is orchestrating this paradigm shift, average Americans like you and I shoulder part of the blame. By *allowing* cultural trash to mount, Medved said,

"We have come to accept the entertainment industry's ability to *shock* an audience as a replacement for the old ability to inspire."

While drafting this book, I decided to study products of the movie industry. Within the past year, I've seen more movies than during the past ten. Both at the theaters and on television, my suspicions have been confirmed—mind pollution rules. Because of the constant battering our minds take, Americans have been desensitized to the kind of cultural trash that many movies throw at audiences. Seduction is a thriving industry!

The Academy Awards program has moved beyond "entertainment" into the arena of special interest promotion. The Oscar too often goes to the movie that portrays *the agenda* agreed to by the majority of the entertainment union—many of whom we wouldn't allow to baby-sit our children for ten minutes, yet by buying tickets to theaters and tuning to the channels that broadcast their agendas, we are allowing them into the heads of our children ... forever.

Hollywood's agenda appears to an extension of *The Protocols*:

> "We have always worked upon the most sensitive chords of the human mind ... directing masses and individuals by means of cleverly manipulated theory and verbiage ... Regulation of life in common ... belongs to the specialists of our administrative brain."

The most recent example of Hollywood's "directing the masses and individuals" away from goodness and toward evil is exemplified in a 2011 Oscar-nominated "Best Picture," entitled: "The Black Swan." The movie is a portrayal of how the goodness of an aspiring ballerina was seen as a detriment by her director and fellow dancers, encouraging her to transform from the pure-in-spirit white swan into the evil black swan *off stage* in order to portray the evil twin sister's character *on stage*.

The dark movie glorified virtually every facet of Godless behavior, ranging from drugs, alcohol, homosexuality, promiscuity, masochism, Satanism, and parent-child discontent ... to mention a few. In the end, the transformed—but lifeless—character (played by 2011 "Best Actress," Natalie Portman) was applauded by the movie's fictitious audience as well as by the Academy of Motion Picture Arts and Science at its annual awards celebration.

The transformed ballerina's dying words affirmed that (by giving her all to the role) she believed that she had achieved perfection. In reality, however, she had merely surrendered her principles to Evil's seductive ways in order to serve as its transformed Siren. And, although Hollywood would not ordinarily like it, the message that I took away from the movie is easily stated: The only reward that awaits those who are seduced by the Wizards of Evil is darkness— the absolute absence of God.

From all that this writer can ascertain, the mainstream media and entertainment industry appear to be functioning quite effectively as an integral part of the Illuminati's "administrative brain." Is it mere coincidence? Does the Hidden Hand control Hollywood, or is it just a conspiracy theory?

Classroom instruction is a sure way to rewrite history ... a stated tactic of *The Protocols:*

"We shall erase from the memory of men all facts of previous centuries which are undesirable to us ..."

There was a time when the media, entertainment industry, and school textbooks gave us heroes bigger than life—icons of patriotism and prosperity. During that era in southern Alabama, my family never locked our doors when we retired for the evening, usually left the keys in the ignitions of our cars, which sat in an open driveway off Main Street. We fearlessly walked the city's streets at any hour of the day or night.

Things weren't perfect. Inequities were far too common. But discipline (self and civil) was the order of the day.

Then, "change" was instituted ... a *"new age"* morality slowly and methodically took hold. In the spring of 1992, I visited my parents who, at that time, lived in the same house. When I drove into the driveway, the impact of The Hidden Hand was profound. Every window and door was covered by burglar bars. Law and order no longer ruled. Chaos had replaced it. Like many Americans, my parents had become prisoners in their own homes. *They*—not the criminals who stalked them—were behind bars.

My wife and her family lived in The Bronx until she was five (5) years old. She happily recalls walking the sidewalks and playing in the streets with her older brother, without fear of danger. Susan recently took our children to her old neighborhood. Even though they were behind locked doors in a taxi, she feared for their lives. The Bronx has become a war zone. Crime runs rampant. "Change" has clearly come to this part of America, too.

White flight from America's inner cities is not based on the color of the skin of one's neighbors. It is based on what Martin Luther King, Jr. called "the content of the character" of those who have chosen to defy King's admonitions and live as they do, defying the laws of the land.

Security has become a top priority in neighborhoods around the nation. The freedom to walk in the woods or stroll down the streets has been stripped because the criminal elements of our society intimidate ... and rule. The mere thought of an unattended child walking to school is beyond comprehension. Child predators no longer fear getting caught. The Law, as it is currently administered by Illuminati-chosen or supported judges, is too easy on them. The rights of criminals overshadow the rights of law-abiding citizens ... and innocent children.

The "*war against standards*" naturally leads to hostility. Religion is a prime target. *The Protocols say so.* From our religions and beliefs, Americans develop standards of right and wrong and the concept of accountability because "God is watching," a position still honored by "mainstream America," but one that is regularly ridiculed in America's "mainstream" media and among growing armies of street gangs. Of greater concern is that the reckless attack on religion is increasingly tolerated by a nation whose founders had imprinted on its currency, "*In God We Trust.*" Is this just another coincidence or the elimination of God part of the Illuminati's plan? Let's review what *The Protocols* have to say about this:

> "It is indispensable for us to undermine
> all faith, to tear out of the mind (of our
> subjects) the very principle of god-head and

the spirit, and to put in its place arithmetical calculations and material needs."

If nothing else in *The Protocols* stirs your emotions, this should. No matter what your religion affiliation or into which religious family you were born, the idea that a concerted effort to destroy *"the very principle of god-head and the spirit"* should be reason enough for concern.

Is there a concerted attempt on the part of a variety of news, entertainment, and political "puppets" to destroy God from the mind of Man? Consider the facts: the words "under God" in the Pledge of Allegiance is the main reason why the Left wants the Pledge removed from schools and why prayer is no longer a part of the daily curriculum.

In a recent speech in Indonesia, Barack Obama participated in a bit of history re-writing. He said that America's motto was *e pluribus unum,* when in fact it is "In God We Trust." Did the president intentionally eliminate God for fear that it might insight Allah-worshiping Muslims in his former homeland, Indonesia?

Christmas is often written as "Xmas," eliminating the name of The Christ, whose birthday the season is intended to honor. And "Thanksgiving Day" is often referred to as "Turkey Day." The day was not set aside by the founders of this nation to honor *a turkey,* but to pause and thank God for the blessings he bestowed on the early settlers. What are we thinking? Why are we letting the imple-menters of *The Protocols* take our religious-based holidays away?

The intent of one of America's most visible clergymen raised eyebrows during a 1990s address to a political convention. The Reverend Jesse Jackson's reference to

Mary (the mother of Jesus) as an "unwed mother" certainly created confusion in the minds of a generation engaged in value definition.

* * * * * * * * *

Some might question whether the fact that negativism is displayed through "art" and "entertainment" really has a detrimental impact on behavior. The data and thoughts expressed by the afore-mentioned Michael Medved suggest that it does.

It seems that the *war on standards* corresponds with increasingly destructive behavior on the part of the young people who are the most devoted observers of these media.

Teenage suicide is at an all-time high. It is the second most common cause of death among this age group— second only to accidents, which far too often are influenced by mood-modifying chemicals and drugs that are supplied by an underground society comprised of Illuminati subgroups that the current U.S. Government seems impotent in curtailing ... or unwilling to try.

Guardians would be wise to take the time to analyze what the children are being exposed to. But, when you do, prepare to be shocked. The "*new age*" music industry gives us songs that appear to glorify and encourage suicide and murder, while the extremes of perversion play between the refrains. Parents who allow young people to purchase and experience this kind of "music," or video games even unknowingly, contribute to self-destructive behavior (and the increasing wealth of those who produce them).

Some forms of cable television and movie videos glorify abuse and defiance of the law. Outlaws like Bonnie and Clyde, Thelma and Louise, and a host of others make fools of law enforcement officials on the big and small screen. The focus seems to be on the law-breaking segment of society. American children will have watched an average of 15,000 murders on television and at the theater by the time they've reached the age of 18. What value can anyone realistically expect them to place on life?

One must question the connection between the entertainment industry's obsession with—and glorification of—crime and violence and the fact that the number of teenagers arrested in 1990 (when the paradigm moved from shifting toward an avalanche) was 30 times what it was in 1950 (when the media and entertainment industry exercised discretion and prudence). In 2006, almost half of violent crimes were committed by perpetrators under the age of 25.

Respect for authority and discipline is at an all-time low. If you doubt me, ask the teachers who work in public and inner-city schools or even-handed law enforcement officers who risk their lives on a daily basis for Americans, like you and me.

I know of which I speak. Between college and medical school, I worked in the criminal justice system. Perhaps that's one reason I view some of the things going on around us today from the perspective set forth throughout this book. As an assistant probation officer in the juvenile court of Tuscaloosa County, I witnessed—up close and personal—the kind of reasoning going on in the minds of both the "*haves*" and the "*have not's*." Child offenders shared with me some of the anti-establishment and retribution indoctrination to which they were being subjected as far back as the 1960's, under the guise of "civil rights."

In an earlier chapter, I restated a conversation that the architect of *"The Great Society"* of the 1960s (Lyndon Johnson) had with a southern governor. President Johnson said that his welfare and entitlement initiatives should be thought of as *riot insurance*. The idea of paying Americans not to riot qualifies as blackmail. The appetite of a beast created with *riot insurance* is never satisfied. A half century and 14.3 trillion tax dollars later, the deficit is still growing; the appetite is increasing; the "beast" is feasting; and inner city crime is at an all-time high, with no signs of being curtailed.

During the height of the Iraqi War, I was astounded to learn that more Americans were murdered in the city of Chicago *each month* than the number of soldiers who died in the line of duty, while defending the rights of criminals, at home. Criminals no longer fear the law. Led by the likes of The Reverend Jesse Jackson and Reverend Al Sharpton, whiners and wailers have been allowed to have their way. Tax-exempt pulpits are being used to encourage class warfare against Americans who foot the bill for the entitlement programs that "minorities" have been taught to demand. Intimidation forestalls reprisal. Law-breakers have been indoctrinated to use aggressive behavior against law enforcement, especially if a camera is around.

Following Japan's 2011 devastating earthquake the host of a nationally broadcast radio show noted the Japanese people did not loot stores and homes. Even though there was a shortage of food and water, respect for person and property was demonstrated. If a similar disaster occurred in the U.S. could we expect the same behavior from the people who live here? If your answer is: "No," then why ...? Is it because law enforcement officers, local officials, judges, governors and lawmakers haven't been allowed by federal judges and The Obama Admin-istration's Attorney General (Eric Holder,) to make public safety a priority?

As a result of the Illuminati's efforts in appointing judges, the ability of police officers to uphold the law and bring criminals to justice has been hampered. Is what I have just stated a myth? Let's see what *The Protocols* say:

> "In general, *our judges* will be elected by us only from among those who thoroughly understand the part they have to play ... The young generation of judges will be trained in certain views regarding *the inadmissibility of any abuses that might disturb the established order of our subjects ...*"

The phrase: "... established order of our subjects," is telling. It affirms that the Illuminati have long been creating an "order" of "subjects" who are loyal to them and their cause, including judges.

As a result of inadmissibility of evidence, arresting law enforcement officers are forced to defend an arrest, even when constitutional laws are defiantly broken. Today, criminals know that they have the upper hand. Many a criminal has gone free because his "rights" were not read or damning evidence was considered by judges to be "inadmissible." The expanding rights of criminals are no coincidence. *The Protocols* address this issue as well. The authors write:

> "In the most important and fund-amental affairs and questions, *judges decide*

as we dictate to them ... Even senators and the higher administration accept our counsels ... (They) see matters in the light wherewith we enfold them."

The long and short of it is that the Lords of Seduction seem to have a hand in every institution established by America's founding fathers "dictating" that their agenda of chaos and despotism is carried out. And—as *The Protocols* and American Illuminist, David Rockefeller, admitted—the press is a complicit partner. As a result, America is being torn apart at the seams. Many neighborhoods resemble combat zones. Defiant graffiti, outright threats and trash messages don posters, buildings, fences and public structures; and yet federal dollars continue to flow to the ungrateful perpetrators of these acts.

Who is underwriting the programs of "*The Great Society,* the "riot insurance" that President Johnson set into motion, and the Obama-driven "Experiment in Social Change?" Law-abiding, working Americans are—those who pay taxes into the giant American distribution center we know as "government," the same government that is held hostage by those who defy its laws...and continue to demand more.

If the phenomenon of double standards is allowed to continue, the scales of justice will only be tilted farther Left. And, once again, "change" and prosperity will become estranged companions.

CHAPTER 15

I have, heretofore, alluded to a conversation I had with a physician from a communist bloc country, who told me that what America's enemies feared most was its ability to "rally" when its backs were against the wall. That's how the "*cold war*" was won and the Berlin Wall came down. It all happened under the able-bodied, patriotic leadership of former President Ronald Reagan. Strength—not weakness—deters. But, in 2011, America is now under a new kind of leadership—one that seems to pander to America's professed enemies.

As previously stated, a concern that many Americans have is that the current President of the U.S. is an unmistakable socialist with Muslim loyalties. He must have been indoctrinated into believing some of the same feelings about western civilization and Israel, as have been expressed by Muslim leaders. The question that deserves an answer is: When Barack Obama converted to the Black Liberation Theology kind of Christianity; did he denounce his previous Muslim beliefs and vows? If he *did not*, he has seduced the American public into believing that he no longer thinks like a Muslim. If he *did (convert to Christianity),* Barack Obama violated Sharia Law in leaving the Islamic religion and is a candidate for Sharia Law's severest form of reprisal—death. Either way, President

Obama should have a hoard of people questioning his truthfulness and motives.

The best evidence that Barack Obama *has not* denounced Islam lies in a statement from his book: *Audacity of Hope* in which he pledged: "I will stand with the Muslims should the political winds begin to blow in an ugly direction." This pledge was not uttered in an off the cuff comment to a reporter or a statement prepared by a staff of writers and read off a Teleprompter, it was premeditated and deliberately written in his book for Muslims (worldwide) to see. Now this is the epitome of audacity, especially for a man who aspires to be president of the United States of America. He must have known that he was being "groomed" by "the Elders" to be a future Commander-in-Chief. *The Protocols* address how the process works:

> "We shall arrange elections in favor of such presidents as have in their past some dark, undiscovered stain ... then *they will be trustworthy agents for the accomplishment of our plans* out of fear of revelations and from the natural desire of everyone who has attained power, namely, the retention of the privileges, advantages and honor connected with the office of president. The chamber of deputies will provide cover for, will protect, will elect presidents, but we shall take from it (the chamber of deputies) the right to propose new, or make changes in existing laws, for this right will be given by us to the responsible president, *a puppet in our hands*."

It is utterly dumbfounding that all major networks and news outlets haven't hammered Mr. Obama about his promise to "stand with Muslims ..." but they haven't. The best explanation that I can give as to the mainstream media's complicit behavior is that they are a party to the charade being played out at the direction of the Lords of Seduction. In fact *The Protocols* provide insight as to why the press has been mute on the President's declaration:

> "Not a single announcement will reach the public without our control."

There is no doubt that enemies of time-tested American values live among us and are pulling the strings of America's "puppet" officials and lawmakers. The Hidden Hand and its unlikely allies are successfully high-jacking the minds of our children, deciding what we need to know, telling us what to think, and dividing us to the point that unification of purpose will become increasingly more difficult.

As I was concluding the preparation of this manuscript, I could sense a new kind of "change" coming to America. I'd like to think that Americans of all races, creeds and vocations are regrouping, armed with the digital missile (the finger) that controls electronic switches and those in the voting booths. Opportunity knocks—to take back a great and beautiful mosaic society from highjackers who prey upon the minds of innocents (and the tolerance of well-meaning citizens).

It is not too late to dream of a new American Camelot—one in which respect for person and property is embraced from "round tables" in every kitchen and dining room—where people of all races, creeds and religions will take up their arms to drive back each and every enemy of the U.S. and its Constitution. This is the kind of "change" in which losers would be anyone out to divide, weaken, or mislead the American people.

* * * * * * * * *

Once again, we turn to simple lessons to solve big problems.

The story is told about a clever youngster who devised what he perceived to be the perfect scheme to test his older teacher.

Concealing a butterfly in his hands, he confronted the man (who had been tested in the crucibles of life) and asked: "If you're as smart as everyone claims, you should be able to tell me if this butterfly is alive or dead."

The teacher knew full well that the youth controlled the butterfly's destiny. If the teacher said it was dead, the student intended to open his hands and allow the butterfly to fly away. If the teacher said "alive," the cunning youngster intended to crush life from the butterfly's helpless body.

The teacher said to his student, "My son, the butterfly can be whatever you choose it to be."

And that is the message I have tried to convey throughout this book. Like the lad in the story, regardless of who chooses to be our enemy, we hold the keys to our own—and America's—future in our hands.

The American electorate are masters of our fate—one nation, with a common origin and a common destiny. **Our America is what we have allowed it to become; but our children's America is whatever we now choose it to be ... beginning on the next Election Day.**

The challenge each of us must now answer is this: Will we, as a responsible people, be willing to do whatever is necessary to see that an ailing "Uncle Sam" is revitalized and his "children" allowed to pursue the American dream—to be the best they can be, no matter what the cost in time or energy?

When you have given thought to the foregoing question, then gaze into the mirror of self-reflection and pray the prayer that has been adopted by individuals who temporarily lost their battle with addictive behavior and poor choices. It is a fitting prayer for a society that has done so:

> "God grant us the serenity to accept the things we cannot change ... the courage to change the things we can ... and the wisdom to know the difference."

Americans of all ages, races and socio-economic strata have been confused. The Lords of Seduction have done a masterful job at indoctrinating us into believing that we are helpless. But a new day is dawning. The good-hearted, giant American golem—one who walks softly and carries a big stick—is about to be awakened. When an army of patriots speak the true name of God and ask for his help, the golem will be transformed and make its presence known.

People from communities throughout America are joining the crusade to save their beloved country. If this noble objective is to be realized, generations of Americans must come to grips with the fact that many of the things being marketed as rights and entitlements are not "rights" at all, but privileges available to every legal citizen of the United States of America that contributes to protecting and defending his or her nation from the Lords of Seduction.

So that the collective force will come to know history—as it actually occurred—universities, as well as government institutions, have to be subjected to the lights of scrutiny. They can no longer be allowed to coerce America's youth into following in the ways that its enemies dictate. For, "to effect the destruction of the collective force" (which is America) the Illuminati-Islamic Alliance has to achieve a stated goal of *The Protocols:* seize—and maintain—control of both university faculties and those who turn the wheels of government:

> "In order to effect the destruction of all collective forces *except ours* we shall emasculate the first stage of collectivism— **the universities** by re-educating them in a new direction. Their officials and professors will be prepared for their business by *detailed secret programs of action* from which they will not with immunity diverge, not by one iota. They will be appointed with especial precaution, and will be so placed as to be wholly dependent upon the

government (whose strings the Illuminati pull)."[80]

Such blatant acts of seduction are difficult to imagine, so much so that it is hard for a trusting people to believe that a group of self-designated "despots" would have the audacity to reduce to writing their intent to destroy a way of life that stands in the way of their greed-driven, One-World Government.

I hope that I have presented enough evidence for you—the reader—to see through the veil of seduction that has been crafted by a group of Luciferian overlords. If ever there was need for a citizenry to look deeper into the character and actions of its leaders, it is now.

---

[80] As noted in other excerpts from *The Protocols*, italicized words and phrased are the author's way of drawing special emphasis to them.

CHAPTER 16

From this writer's perspective, the Odyssey to revive the resilient American spirit has been both instructive and humbling.

While reviewing the pages that you have just read, I realized that I haven't even come close to considering all the questions, but as I attempted to get inside the heads of America's unwavering patriots—her prime movers—I have had the opportunity (for a brief moment in history) to sit "upon the shoulders of giants." Having been temporarily lifted by the accomplishments of America's heroes, I have seen part of what lies *behind us* as well as that which waits over the horizons ahead.

At times, I've been guilty of pontification, a practice known where I come from as "soap-boxing." I'll be the first to admit that my blood pressure rises and my heart races when I sense that someone is doing harm to those—and that—I love. And, after linking *The Protocols* with the actual events taking place in the world, I became convinced that there are those who would take America down if it would serve their own agenda. The best term that I can come up with to describe legally-registered citizens of the U.S. who are directly—or indirectly—involved in such activities is *"traitor."* The best term I can use to describe those who *are not dutiful U.S. citizens*—or aspire to be— is:

"enemy." And, the best term that I can come up with to describe anyone who would stand tall against either a "traitor" or an "enemy" is *"patriot."*

Most Americans agree that Abraham Lincoln was a visionary, a good man and an exceptional leader during some of The Union's darkest days. In a letter that President Lincoln wrote to newspaperman, Horace Greely, the president voiced a truism that few Americans attribute to him—the revered emancipator of slaves. He said that his only objective during those dark days was to "save the Union," and that he would do whatever it took to do so.

As history notes, President Lincoln did, indeed, save the Union, albeit one that was battered and worn. As he addressed a newly-reconstituted nation the president delivered a message for the ages. It deserves repetition.

> "You cannot help the poor by destroying the rich. You cannot strengthen the weak by weakening the strong. You cannot bring about prosperity by discouraging thrift. You cannot lift the wage earner up by pulling the wage payer down. You cannot further the brotherhood of man by inciting class hatred. You cannot build character and courage by taking away people's initiative and independence. You cannot help people permanently by doing for them, what they could and should do for themselves."

And, if this once great nation is to turn back the Lords of Seduction, its people must rise up and heed Lincoln's admonition. The people must demand from our leaders the kinds of responsible government that can direct us back to a time when the words: "one nation, under God, indivisible, with liberty and justice for all" were unashamedly uttered by every true-blooded American ... daring anyone to question the acknowledgment of—and expressed gratitude to--the Sources of our being, *wherever* and *whenever* we chose to do so.

* * * * * * * * * *

In a couple of years, I'll be seventy years old. That's not forever, but one can, clearly, see the collective history of humankind from there. With all I've seen—and from the research that I've conducted—I am concerned about the "change" taking place in my country. The evidence shows that there are real and present dangers which deserve to be addressed frankly and boldly by the only people capable of saving the United States of America—*the unabashed American patriot.*

As we come to the end of this mind-stretching odyssey into—and back from—the catacombs of Hell, I'd like to reach back, once more, to the turn of the last century and to the timeless wisdom of Dr. James Allen. In *As a Man Thinketh*, Dr. Allen wrote,

> "Good thoughts and actions can never produce bad results. Bad thoughts and actions can never produce good results. This is but saying that nothing can come from corn but corn, nothing from nettles but nettles..."[81]

---

[81] Allen, James, *As A Man Thinketh,* Brownlow Publishing Company, Ft. Worth, TX, reprinted, 1985

I plead guilty to thinking bad thoughts and making harsh statements about the people who are out to destroy my country. It would have been much easier to compose a manuscript that paints a pretty picture of my beloved United States of America; however, if I had done so I, too, would have been guilty of seducing you, the reader, into believing that everything is alright; and the spirits of my father's generation would forever, haunt me for missing an opportunity to be their voice. Truth is: if all *we, the people* know is what we see or read from the mainstream American media, we don't know what we don't know. And, that fact alone should be enough to awaken the curiosity of every red-blooded American.

I'd like to believe that those who consider themselves to be progeny of the "mighty men" addressed in Genesis 6:4 suffer from delusions of grandeur. I'd like to believe that the documents describing how a group of those same "mighty men" plan to guide America toward a chartered shore heaped with the carcasses of others who fell prey to the Sirens calls, doesn't exist ... except in my own mind. I'd also like to believe that *The Protocols of the Learned Elders of Zion* are—as some claim—pure fiction ... a hoax of the highest order. However, as I have repeatedly pointed out, world events seem to follow both the spirit and agenda that *The Protocols* set forth. And, because they do, some of those whose job it is to shield the *false flag* Wizards from the lights of publicity would like for you to believe that by attaching the words "... Elders *of Zion*" to the title of the document and the pejorative term "goyim" within the text, directs the finger of blame at the Jewish people, or Christians who trust the theocracy of God. Nothing could be farther from the truth. While some of the documents' drafters may have been born into traditionally Jewish families, the men who penned *The Protocols* summarily turned away from the faith of their birth and became *secularist*, which is a 21ˢᵗ century and "politically correct" way to say "atheist."

Though Elders of the Invisible Empire denounce God, they embrace God's eternal adversary—His once-favored angel, The Illuminated One, Lucifer, Angel of Light. And, it is from the fallen angel's title—the one he held in the Hierarchy of Angels—that the Illuminati derived the moniker by which they are identified. This group of Satanic worshipers—the devout disciples of a Luciferian "Revolutionary Faith"—are the professed enemies of God's creations, preying on the one made in God's own image. *The Protocols* tell us so.

In the 21ˢᵗ century, two additional "Revolutionary Faiths" (Black Liberation Theology and radical Islam) have emerged as threats to peace and prosperity ... for all, but the two revolutionary religion's faithful. Is the sitting President of the United States of America among them?

* * * * * * * * * *

So, now that we know who America's enemy is—now that we know their objective and have a copy of their plan—what are we to do? I like the way that an anonymous sage said it:

> "We punish and reward ourselves—make our own heaven or our own hell ... The universe God has created is governed by [non-amendable] laws, and whoever breaks any of these laws suffers the consequences ... Every act of love and service, every grand

and noble deed, every kind and loving thought, every bit of help to our earthly brothers and sisters, every step forward ... is an expression of man's ultimate purpose."

The hour is late; but Americans still have the ability to "make our own heaven or our own hell." Until we relinquish our right to make our voices heard in the town square, at PTA/PTO meetings, at check-our and ticket counters, on order forms, in coffee shops, department stores, hair salons, places of worship and in ballot boxes, we remain a powerful force. We are the last bastion standing between a world that worships God or one that worships His enemy. It's an onerous responsibility, but one that we must shoulder ... for humanity's sake.

So, as we head toward what could prove to be a Great American Revival, let us turn deaf ears to the Sirens of Change. Let us join hands and stick together; follow the Golden Rule; set expectations high; and stand our ground against the "Grand Wizard of Evil" and his disciples. Let us—conservative, God-trusting Americans—adopt the *same* mantra that vaulted Barack Obama into the Oval Office. Let us demand "CHANGE" in every seat of government that runs counter to America's sovereignty—and not the sovereignty established *by* and *for* a handful of self-designated "despots" and their hand-picked "puppets."

If enough *patriots* methodically and passionately commit to saving America, the enemy cannot win! For, they are few ... and we are many. And, if America's enemies realize that they cannot have America, perhaps— like the Sirens in Homer's, *The Odyssey*—they will throw themselves into their autocratic seas of despair and drown in an abyss of their own greed and arrogance.

In other sections of this book, I referred to what Dr. Orison Swett Marden called "one wavering aim." The doctor dedicated an entire chapter of his book, *Rising in the World,* to the subject. While there are many, one inspiring admonition seems fitting for this, the final chapter of *Lords of Seduction:*

> "To fix a wandering life (or nation) and give it direction is not an easy task, but a life (or nation) which has no definite aim is sure to be frittered away in empty and purposeless dreams ... A healthy, definite purpose is a remedy for a thousand ills ... Discontent and dissatisfaction flee before a definite purpose ..."[82]

More than a century ago, Dr. Marden provided future generations of Americans with a prescription for continued success; a remedy for a thousand ills that so desperately needs to be taken as directed ... sooner rather than later!

Let us hope that what you have read to this point is theory and that the Illuminati-Islamic Alliance is no more than a figment of my imagination. Let us hope that *The Protocols* are purely fictional. Let us hope that there is no concerted effort to create a One-World Government that intends to bring all the peoples of the world under a totalitarian form of governance. Let us hope that intelligence reports of President Obama's reluctance to approve the raid on the Pakistani compound that resulted in Osama Bin Laden's alleged death turns out to be false and that what the world has been told about the planning

---

[82] *Rising in the World (Architects of Fate),* Orison Swett Marden, Thomas Y. Crowell Company Publishers, New York, NY, 1894

and execution of the mission is the truth. Let us hope that the motive behind consolidating power into the hands of a few "intellectual elites and world bankers" that pull the President's strings is for a just and noble cause. Let us pray that *The Lords of Seduction* represents no more than far-fetched ruminations of, yet, another conspiracy theorist.

On the other hand, if I am right, the hour is at hand. The time has come for America's caretakers to band together and cure the ills of our nation—to watch "discontent and dissatisfaction flee before a definite purpose ..." As we move toward that aim, let us never lose sight of the fact that while one person can make a difference, millions of "ones" make a grass-roots revolution—a Second American Revolution, an exorcism of geo-political demons, boldly designed and executed to regain the liberties that we allowed to be taken away ... while we were distracted by—and trusted—a line-up of false prophets, who promised "change" that *we thought* we could believe in.

* * * * * * * * * *

Earlier, I said that I view my role as a catalyst. In that role I have presented to you, the reader, a tall challenge: Re-examine everything you think you know about the world of politics, education, communications, and world banking. Pay close attention to who is teaching and 'entertaining' your children. And, while I truly pray that what I have offered up is theory, there is one part of *The Protocols* that suggests otherwise.

It is the section that describes its drafters' plan to establish a "supranational sovereignty" or One-World Government. The document fast-forwards to a time when—

at the hands of the I-IA—Hell is in session and the fate of the whole world hangs in trial. The final seduction is about to unfold.

> "When we have accomplished our coup d'etat we shall say then to the various peoples: 'everything has gone terribly badly, all have been worn out with suffering. We are destroying (going to destroy) the causes of your torment, nationalities, frontiers, differences of coinages. You are at liberty, of course, to pronounce sentence upon us (for being the causers of your plight,) but can it possibly be a just one (sentence) if it is confirmed by you before you make any trial of what we are offering you ...'
>
> "Then will the mob (masses) exalt us and bear us up in their hands in a unanimous triumph of hopes and expectations."

The last sentence is eerily reminiscent of the 2008 Obama Campaign. "Hope" and the expectations of "change" moved the masses enough to vault Barack Obama into the Oval Office, ushering in a time when "everything has gone terribly badly ..." Was it coincidence, or premeditated "suffering" that the American people were handed in return for trusting a man they knew little about?

For centuries a shroud of secrecy has protected *"The Protocols"* and their drafters from the "bright lights of publicity." Now that you have seen portions of the documents, you should better understand why I felt a responsibility to share my findings. *The Protocols* provide the best evidence yet that the "supranational sovereignty of world bankers and intellectual elites" are who—and what—they claim to be; how a conspiracy of "despots" intend to "rule the affairs of the whole world;" why an alliance with the radical arm of Islam is advantageous at this juncture in history; and how it is conceivable that an Illuminati-Islamic Alliance could have inserted a "puppet," who was "bred and reared from early childhood," in the White House.

But, have the Lords of Seduction underestimated the resilient American spirit and its passion for truth, freedom, and independence? Is the Judeo-Christian God—the one that has historically helped those willing to help themselves—waiting for this generation of Americans to make a move back in His direction before He decides whether to intercede?

A clue to the mystery could have been provided by Daniel Webster, one of America's most prolific orators and socio-political conservatives. It serves as a fitting climax to this treatise and emboldens the message that I have attempted to deliver.

> "If we work upon marble, it will perish;
> if we work upon brass, time will efface
> it; if we rear buildings, they will crumble
> into dust; but if we work upon mortal
> souls, if we imbue them with immortal
> principles, with the just fear of God and
> love of   fellowman, we engrave on
> those tablets something that will
> brighten all eternity."[83]

---

[83] Quotation Book, Daniel Webster, in a speech to the City Council, Boston, Massachusetts, May 22, 1852.

Something that will "brighten all eternity" and give humanity a chance to redeem itself in the eyes of the only Sovereign that matters is a strong, free and independent United States of America. Will the U.S.A. emerge as the first prodigal democracy in history to return to its religious and Constitutional roots, defying Tyler's Law?

Can you imagine a world without a free and independent United States of America? Can you see yourself, your children and grandchildren in such a world? Unquestionably, there are individuals, political parties, and organizations that loathe America and thirst for her extinction. Only one thing stands in their way—the people they intend to rule. Never forget the lesson that saved Odysseus from the Sirens. The instant that the masses refuse to be seduced, the overlords that rely upon the dark art of seduction to rule them are rendered powerless.

Inescapably, history will be written. While the ending of America's chapter is yet to be determined, it will most assuredly begin:

> "Once upon a time, in the land of the free, there was a shining city on a hill. And, the people who lived there held the future of the whole world in their hands. Theirs was the 'chance of a lifetime in a lifetime of chance ...'"[84]

* * * * * * * * *

Annuit Coeptis!

END

---

[84] "Run for the Roses," a song by Dan Fogelberg

Epilogue

A book like *The Lords of Seduction* presents an extraordinary challenge to an author and publisher. The world is a more complex place than most people realize ... and getting more so by the minute.

Confidence in America's government is approaching an all-time low. According to polls, less than 50% of Americans believe that the president is doing a good job.

Even less—in the 20% range—of the American populace believes that congress is doing a good job.

In any other businesses—or organization—the kinds of job performance ratings that America's president and lawmakers have earned would call for immediate dismissal.

The American people have finally come to realize that our government is broken, and in need of repair. Too many of the 555 politicians we rely upon to conduct the country's business have turned deaf ears to us—the segment of the citizenry that represents the backbone of this nation, the unapologetic American patriot.

America's internal problems have reached a crisis level. For too long, we have allowed government to get away with run-a-way spending. As a result, cities, counties and states have joined the federal government in a race toward bankruptcy. And, the most perplexing part of it all is that it appears that America's plight is part of an ingeniously orchestrated plan, devised and conducted by an unlikely coalition of enemies.

The current state of The Union makes the upcoming 2012 elections one of the most important in American history. Only an informed and motivated electorate can make the kinds of choices that determine who—among the potential candidates—should be included in the 555 men and women who will hold our nation's destiny (and perhaps that of the world) in their hands.

If you found *The Lords of Seduction* worthy of sharing with family, friends, and neighbors I urge you to do so ... before they cast their votes in the next election.

About the Author

E. Gaylon McCollough, M.D., F.A.C.S.

Since entering practice, Dr. E. Gaylon McCollough has obtained international recognition as a surgeon and teacher. Dr. McCollough was an Academic All-American center on Alabama Coach Paul "Bear" Bryant's 1964 National Championship Team. Dr. McCollough was honored by the March of Dimes as Alabama Citizen of the Year for 1994-1995, and is listed in the National Registry of *Who's Who in Medicine.* Dr. McCollough has been included in *The Best Doctors in America,* since 1994 and listed among *America's Top Plastic Surgeons.* On September 19, 2008, Dr. McCollough received the *2008 John Dickinson Teacher Award* from the American Academy of Facial Plastic and Reconstructive Surgery.

Dr. McCollough is the co-author of several major textbooks on facial and nasal plastic surgery. He completed an approved program of specialized training in facial plastic surgery in Beverly Hills, California; New Orleans, Louisiana; and Boston, Massachusetts ... and is "board-certified" by The American Board of Facial Plastic and Reconstructive Surgery and has served as the Board's President. Dr. McCollough is founder of the American College of Rejuvenology and serves as the college's president. He was also elected President of the International Council of Integrative Medicine. He is also certified by the American Board of Otolaryngology, ("representing the specialty of Otolaryngology- Head and Neck Surgery").

Dr. McCollough was inducted into the American Board of Cosmetic Surgery as an honorary member and served as president of the American Association of Cosmetic Surgeons and the American Academy of Facial Plastic and Reconstructive Surgery. He is *Clinical Professor of Surgery* (Facial Plastic and Reconstructive Surgery) in the Department of Surgery at the University of South Alabama, College of Medicine. In 2007, Dr. McCollough was honored for the international release of his book, **Let Us Make Man** at the Waldorf Astoria in New York City, New York.

Since that time, Dr. McCollough has also written **Shoulders of Giants** (Albright Publishing, 1986), **Before and After** (Compress Press, 1994), **The Long Shadow of Coach Paul "Bear" Bryant,** (Compress Press, 2008) a profile of the late, great Alabama football Coach, **The Appearance Factor** (Compress Press, 2009), a consumer's guide to plastic surgery as a method of appearance and health enhancement, **The Oath** (A-Argus Better Book Publishers, LLC), his first novel, **TAE: Armageddon 2012** (Co-Authored, A-Argus Better Book Publishers, LLC) and his latest release, **The Lords of Seduction** (A-Argus Better Book Publishers, LLC).

Dr. McCollough has traveled to India, Columbia, Germany, England, Canada, Italy, Mexico, Australia, South Africa and Spain to teach seminars and techniques of head and neck plastic surgery to surgeons from around the world. After 25 successful years in Birmingham, one of *The Best Doctors in America*, Nasal and Facial Plastic Surgeon, E. Gaylon McCollough, M.D., F.A.C.S., and the internationally acclaimed McCollough Plastic Surgery Clinic moved to Gulf Shores, Alabama, where he founded the 35,000 square foot McCollough Institute For Appearance & Health, an interdisciplinary professional complex dedicated to helping people from all walks of life look, feel, and perform better ... longer. The McCollough Institute was honored by the Alabama Gulf Coast Chamber of Commerce as "Business of the Year" 2002.

Dr. McCollough and his wife, Susan, have two children and four grandchildren.

Other books by Dr. E. Gaylon McCollough

The Long Shadow of Coach Paul "Bear" Bryant:
An up close and personal look at the patriarch of the Alabama Football Family, his decision to relinquish power, the turbulent years he predicted for Alabama football, and his bridge-building plan designed to create the Crimson Tide's next "larger than life" coach.

Let Us Make Man:
A new paradigm (arising from the reexamination of Genesis and the creation, evolution and responsibilities of a god-like species) erases the division between Science and Theology.

The Appearance Factor:
Secrets to enhancing your appearance and how they could lift your spirits, improve your health, and tilt the scales of opportunity in your favor.

The Oath: an unlikely president sacrifices everything to save his beloved nation from an Evil Empire.

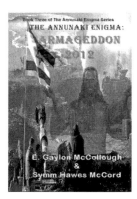

The Annunaki Enigma: Armageddon 2012: Current events and the actions of today's leaders fulfill the prognostications of the early writers of the Bible.

To obtain your copy of other books by
E. Gaylon McCollough, M.D.,
visit your local bookstore,
or, order online
www.a-argusbooks.com
www.mccolloughplasticsurgery.com

Watch for more from this dynamic author
and
A-Argus Better Book Pubishers.

Made in the USA
Charleston, SC
17 October 2014